Shakespeare in Tongues

Shakespeare in Tongues interrogates the popular conflation of "the language of Shakespeare" with English by examining the role Shakespeare's works have played in overlapping histories of colonialism, slavery, and migration that continue to shape the linguistic cultures of the United States.

Opening up urgent and overdue conversations about linguistic oppression, racism, and resistance within the settler colonial nation-state, Kathryn Vomero Santos draws our attention to artists, activists, and educators who have conjured, embraced, remade, and rejected Shakespeare in service of multilingual counternarratives that push back against dominant perspectives, refuse assimilation, and strive for more polyglot and polyvocal futures. As they shine a bright light on the legacies of the federal Indian boarding school system, Indigenous language revitalization efforts, the militarization of the U.S.–Mexico border, and battles over ethnic studies in classrooms, these critical and creative engagements with Shakespeare offer powerful examples of how his works might be used to facilitate a more truthful understanding of the past and to identify restorative paths forward.

Shakespeare in Tongues issues an imperative to redirect the material and intellectual resources that have been devoted to Shakespeare and his language toward truth, justice, and healing. This is essential reading for anyone studying or researching Shakespeare, race, translation, adaptation, and comparative literatures.

Kathryn Vomero Santos is Associate Professor of English at Trinity University, USA. She is a co-founder of the award-winning Borderlands Shakespeare Colectiva and the co-editor of several books, including *The Bard in the Borderlands: An Anthology of Shakespeare Appropriations en La Frontera* (with Katherine Gillen and Adrianna M. Santos).

Spotlight on Shakespeare
Series Editors: John Garrison and Kyle Pivetti

Spotlight on Shakespeare offers a series of concise, lucid books that explore the vital purchase of the modern world on Shakespeare's work. Authors in the series embrace the notion that emergent theories, contemporary events, and movements can help us shed new light on Shakespeare's work and, in turn, his work can help us better make sense of the contemporary world. The aim of each volume is two-fold: to show how Shakespeare speaks to questions in our world and to illuminate his work by looking at it through new forms of human expression. *Spotlight on Shakespeare* will adopt fresh scholarly trends as contemporary issues emerge, and it will continually prompt its readers to ask, "What can Shakespeare help us see? What can he help us do?"

Spotlight on Shakespeare invites scholars to write non-exhaustive, pithy studies of very focused topics—with the goal of creating books that engage scholars, students, and general readers alike.

Available in this series:

Shakespeare in the Age of Mass Incarceration
Edited by Liz Fox and Gina Hausknecht

Shakespeare in Tongues
Kathryn Vomero Santos

For more information about this series, please visit: www.routledge.com/Spotlight-on-Shakespeare/book-series/SOSHAX

KATHRYN VOMERO SANTOS

Shakespeare in Tongues

Routledge
Taylor & Francis Group

LONDON AND NEW YORK

Designed cover image: *Highlights of the Flawed and Imperfect* by Fausto Fernandez
(Collage, acrylic, spray paint and gold leaf on canvas, 36 x 28, 2020)

First published 2025
by Routledge
4 Park Square, Milton Park, Abingdon, Oxon OX14 4RN

and by Routledge
605 Third Avenue, New York, NY 10158

Routledge is an imprint of the Taylor & Francis Group, an informa business

© 2025 Kathryn Vomero Santos

The right of Kathryn Vomero Santos to be identified as author of this work has been asserted in accordance with sections 77 and 78 of the Copyright, Designs and Patents Act 1988.

All rights reserved. No part of this book may be reprinted or reproduced or utilised in any form or by any electronic, mechanical, or other means, now known or hereafter invented, including photocopying and recording, or in any information storage or retrieval system, without permission in writing from the publishers.

Trademark notice: Product or corporate names may be trademarks or registered trademarks, and are used only for identification and explanation without intent to infringe.

British Library Cataloguing-in-Publication Data
A catalogue record for this book is available from the British Library

ISBN: 978-1-032-27450-8 (hbk)
ISBN: 978-1-032-27449-2 (pbk)
ISBN: 978-1-003-29283-8 (ebk)

DOI: 10.4324/9781003292838

Typeset in Joanna MT
by codeMantra

For everyone who has taught me

Contents

Acknowledgments   x

Introduction: The Languages of Shakespeare   1

Breathing Native Breath   **One**   40

Being Now Awake   **Two**   92

The Oppressor's Wrong   **Three**   119

What's Past Is Prologue   **Four**   161

Further Reading and Resources   206

Index   217

Acknowledgments

When John Garrison and Kyle Pivetti described the *Spotlight on Shakespeare* series to me upon its inception, they encouraged me to keep it in mind as an option for a possible second book. As everything about my life as a scholar and teacher was upended by the onset of the COVID-19 pandemic, I realized that the book I thought would be my first could wait. *Shakespeare in Tongues* was the book I needed to write *now*. One of the myriad reasons why this project felt so vital during a period of isolation and uncertainty is that it gave me an opportunity to forge and deepen relationships with many truly wonderful people. Though insufficient at best, these acknowledgments are an attempt to express my profound thanks to John and Kyle for giving me the prompt to start this journey and to the community who sustained me with their generosity along the way.

It is a common convention of this genre to save gratitude for one's partner until the very end, but this book would quite literally not exist without the support of my husband Marc. As we traveled together by plane, car, or foot during various research trips, he helped me to bear witness and process our shared experiences in real time. He listened to me read countless paragraphs aloud and asked thoughtful questions that sharpened my thinking and kept me grounded in reality. His unending love and belief in me not only made this work possible but also continue to make my life richer every single day.

I have been fortunate to learn from many brilliant scholars over the years, but the intellectual and personal care I receive from those who have become my dear friends is the greatest gift of this profession. Katherine Gillen read every chapter in draft form and offered honest suggestions that made the work unquestionably stronger. I am enormously grateful for our collaborative partnerships, and I know I am a better writer and thinker because I have had the privilege of working in dialogue with someone as brilliant and ethical as Kate. Ruben Espinosa has championed my work on language, migration, and identity since I was a graduate student just entering the field, and his bold scholarship continuously inspires me to find my voice and to do work that matters. The ethos of this book was also deeply influenced by the formation of the Borderlands Shakespeare Colectiva, and I thank Adrianna M. Santos, Jesus Montaño, Jazmine Janay Cuevas, and Matthew Harrison in particular for their incisive feedback, encouragement, and solidarity at critical stages.

Early conversations with the amazing Vanessa Corredera were crucial as I was developing this project, and she has remained a steadfast thought partner and weekly writing companion along with Dennis Britton, whose warmth and good cheer make the difficult work of academia seem more possible. Before she was my coach, Nedda Mehdizadeh was my friend, and I have learned so much from her about how to develop the clarity to be able to say yes to the projects that mean the most to me. I am lucky to have known Lehua Yim for many years and cannot even begin to express what a gift it was to have her as my daily virtual work partner and interlocutor during the summer of 2023. In the nearly fifteen years since Debapriya Sarkar and I first met in the Folger Dissertation Seminar, she has been an honest friend and writing accountability partner whose sharp feedback, witty humor, and genuine kindness have buoyed me and helped me to grow. It is an honor to share space in the *Spotlight on Shakespeare* series with Ambereen Dadabhoy, who supported me in manifold ways during the writing of this book and repeatedly shows me what it means to be intellectually fierce and unapologetically committed to justice.

As readers will no doubt see in the following pages, *Shakespeare in Tongues* is deeply indebted to the ShakeRace and RaceB4Race communities, whose transformative intellectual frameworks have made the study of race indispensable to the study of Shakespeare and premodernity. I feel enormously fortunate to have participated in the RaceB4Race First and Second Book Institutes while I was working on this project and developing the next. The feedback I received from colleagues in those spaces was equal parts challenging and affirming, and the experience of reading their scholarship-in-progress was invigorating. I am especially grateful to Patricia Akhimie, Dennis Britton, and Jean Howard for their thoughtful facilitation of those institutes. I thank Ayanna Thompson for her visionary leadership of the RaceB4Race initiatives and for giving me a platform to share my work as an early career scholar. Kim F. Hall and Margo Hendricks have long inspired me, not just with their field-defining scholarship, but with the care they show to the next generation of premodern critical race studies scholars. Farah Karim-Cooper has likewise offered me both personal support and a model for working toward institutional transformation.

Conversation and communion with a long list of friends and colleagues over the years have nourished this project in both direct and indirect ways. Liza Blake not only pushed me intellectually throughout our time together in graduate school at NYU and well beyond but also taught me the value of collaboration in a profession that can often feel individualistic. I am endlessly grateful to Jason Farr, Jenny Sorenson, and Sandrine Sanos for their companionship at Texas A&M University–Corpus Christi, where I started my career in 2014, and for their continued friendship in the years since. I will always cherish the conversation I had with my longtime friend Katherine Schaap Williams on my front porch right after we had each received our first round of COVID vaccines in early 2021. At the time, I was just starting to conceive of this book, and Kat gave me the confidence I needed to lean into what felt urgent and meaningful about it. Pete Kirwan has been an extraordinary mentor and model for how to nurture the field and encourage others to do their best work. Carla Mazzio, whose own scholarship on language was an inspiration to me as a young graduate student, has championed this project since its earliest stages. I feel very fortunate to have had many opportunities over the past several years to be in dialogue with Scott Manning Stevens and to learn from his work on the intersections and gaps between Shakespeare studies and critical Indigenous studies. Mira 'Assaf and Nora Williams have both shown me what bravery and radical care can look like in this profession, and it is a privilege to be able to do this work in dialogue with thoughtful, creative, and genuinely kind scholars such as Brandi K. Adams, Ariane Balizet, Lisa Barksdale-Shaw, Hanh Bui, Patricia Cahill, Urvashi Chakravarty, Hillary Eklund, Mariam Galarrita, Louise Geddes, Marissa Greenberg, Miles Grier, Musa Gurnis, Sujata Iyengar, Arthur Little, Jr., Joyce Green MacDonald, Jenn Park, L. Monique Pittman, Marjorie Rubright, Madeline Sayet, Stephen Spiess, Laura Turchi, and Geoff Way.

My thinking and writing benefitted enormously from the opportunity to share work in progress with several generous audiences. I thank Sara Barker and John Gallagher for inviting me to present to the Interdisciplinary Renaissance and Early Modern Seminar at Leeds University. It was a true honor to present early work on this project at "Shakespeare and the Poetics and Politics of Relevance," a conference at the Huntington Library organized by my beloved undergraduate mentor, Dympna Callaghan, who later welcomed me back to speak at my alma mater, Syracuse University. Many thanks to Barbara Bono and Maria Horne for inviting me to present parts of this book during their Folger Institute program in Buffalo, New York. The Shakespeare Association of America has long played an essential role in the development of my scholarship, and I am grateful for the feedback I received from colleagues at several annual meetings. I also had the great fortune of discussing parts of this project with student audiences at the University of California, Riverside, Texas A&M University–San Antonio, Texas Lutheran University, and the University of Houston–Downtown. I thank Carla Mazzio, Katherine Gillen, Adrianna M. Santos, Lauren Shook, Anita Raychawdhuri, and Lisa Jennings for the invitations to do so.

While research funding and an academic leave from Trinity University have both been essential to the development of this project, I could not have written *Shakespeare in Tongues* without the support of my colleagues at my current institutional home. I thank the staff at Coates Library for fielding my many and sometimes obscure requests for books, articles, and films. I am also grateful to my colleagues in the English Department, especially Jenny Browne, Kelly Carlisle, Michael Fischer, Shaj Mathew, Andrew Porter, David Rando, Claudia Stokes, and Betsy Tontiplaphol. Our conversations over the years have undoubtedly made me a more curious and creative writer. This work has benefitted from various forms of support and friendship from my colleagues across campus, including Greg Clines, Rubén Dupertuis, Sarah Erickson, Kyle Gillette, Sajida Jalalzai, David Ribble, Nathan Stith, Gina Tam, and Katherine Troyer. Mil gracias to Dania Abreu-Torres, Elseke Membreño-Zenteno, and Rita Urquijo-Ruiz for welcoming me into the MAS/Global Latinx Studies community and to the inimitable Norma Elia Cantú for encouraging me to slow down and embrace the spiritual aspects of research and writing.

My Trinity students, some of whom I only met through a screen during the height of COVID, have been a true inspiration over the past several years. Their willingness to have vulnerable conversations in the classroom pushed my thinking in new directions and affirmed the importance of using Shakespeare to open up difficult dialogues. I am especially grateful to Xavier Alva for engaging deeply with me on the topic of Chapter 4 during our independent study on *The Tempest* and its educational afterlives. I admire his passion for educating young people in ways that are culturally sustaining and socially just.

The process of working on this book brought me into contact with one of the most inspiring groups of people I have ever had the privilege of knowing: the Friends of Friendship Park, a coalition of activists working to create a truly international park on Kumeyaay/Kumiai land at the border between San Diego and Tijuana. The situation at Friendship Park changed rapidly and in devastating ways in the short time since I first visited in March 2022, but I continue to be moved by the fact that people on both sides of the border work tirelessly to forge friendship and connection in the face of increasingly high walls and hostile militarization. I am particularly grateful to John Fanestil, María Teresa Fernández, Diane Keeling, Mona Kuczenski, Tania Mendoza, Nanzi Muro, Pedro Rios, Natalia Ventura, and Dan Watman for sharing their insight into the history of the park and for welcoming me into their ongoing efforts to promote truthful counternarratives about the border that celebrate the humanity and dignity of fronterizos.

I would like to express my sincere gratitude to Randy Reinholz for sharing materials about Off the Rails and Native Voices at the Autry with me and for making vital connections to support my research for this book's first chapter. I thank Liza Posas, Christina Lehua Hummel-Colla, and Alejandra Gaeta for facilitating my visit to the Native Voices archives at the Autry Museum and Ted DeLong of the Oregon Shakespeare Festival for granting me access to the archival recording of the 2017 production of Off the Rails. I will never forget the kindness with which Nancy Carlson and Claire Urugutia welcomed me and my husband to the Genoa Indian School Museum in Nebraska, where they and other volunteers have created deeply meaningful opportunities for survivors and their descendants to reunite, remember, and heal from the traumas of the federal Indian boarding school system. I also wish to thank Jim Gerencser at the Carlisle Indian School Digital Resource Center for fielding my requests for image reproduction and the National Native American Boarding School Healing Coalition for the incredible work they do in service of truth, justice, and healing.

It was a wonderful coincidence and privilege to be able to meet Guillermo Gómez-Peña and Balitrónica Gómez during their visit to Trinity in 2022 while I was learning and writing about Gómez-Peña's poem "El Hamlet Fronterizo," which is the subject of this book's third chapter. I thank them both for their enthusiasm for my work and for their permission to reproduce archival materials here. I likewise thank Iris De Anda for permission to include her poem "To be a Pocha or not to be" and Peter Goin and Eugenio Castro for allowing me to feature their important photography here. José Cruz González and Mark Booher showed me such warmth in sharing materials related to José's play *Invierno*. I give thanks to Nakia Zavalla and Richard Applegate for contributing their knowledge of Samala to *Invierno* and for documenting their efforts to revitalize the language of the Santa Ynez Band of Chumash Indians. It has been a great honor to get to know El Librotraficante Tony Diaz, whose unwavering commitment to protecting and promoting Latinx literature is awesome in the truest sense of the word. I am grateful to Lorna Dee Cervantes for allowing me to reproduce "A Chicano Poem" and for sharing her Shakespeare story with me.

The enormously talented artist Fausto Fernandez generously granted me permission to use his stunning collage titled *Highlights of the Flawed and Imperfect* (2020) on the cover of this book. When I first saw it, I was struck by its multilayered cartographic quality and by the inky black paint splatters amid vibrant colors. Inspired by the Japanese Kintsugi practice of using gold to mend broken pottery, the collage is part of a series that reimagines damaged Navajo rugs similarly repaired with gold to highlight imperfections rather than rendering them invisible. This image seemed fitting for a book about efforts to redress the linguistic and cultural harms caused by settler colonial violence in the lands known today as the United States. The title of Fernandez's work also reminds me to embrace what is flawed and imperfect about the act of writing—a profoundly human and often messy attempt to make sense of the world as it was, as it is, and as it could be.

Many people at Routledge are responsible for shepherding *Shakespeare in Tongues* from the proposal stage through the many steps of the publication process. I give my sincere thanks to Polly Dodson, Karen Raith, Chris Ratcliffe, Helen Strain, Uma Maheswari, and the entire production and marketing teams working behind the scenes.

The Vomero and Santos families have been a consistent source of love and support in my life. My parents, Lisa and John, fostered my love of reading and writing from an early age and never once questioned my decision to study literature. I can always count on my dad to send me every Shakespeare *Jeopardy* clue and to text "Beware" on the Ides of March. Special thanks go to my siblings-in-law, Michael and Chelsea Santos, for their hospitality during my research trips to San Diego.

Because this profession so rarely allows us to live near the people with whom we grew up, I am also grateful to the community I have found here in the beautiful city of San Antonio (Yanaguana). My Tuesday night run club in particular consistently helped me to get out of the house, move my body, and find light in a dark world.

Finally, I would be remiss if I did not acknowledge my more-than-human companions, Lexington and Una, who brought me great comfort and joy while I wrote, especially during periods of pandemic-induced isolation. My beloved cat Hudson left this world just as I was starting this project, but I remain inspired by the lessons he taught me about how to overcome fear, how to build trust, and how to love fiercely.

***

An earlier iteration of Chapter 2 appeared in *Shakespeare and the Poetics and Politics of Resonance*, edited by Dympna Callaghan and Sophie Chiari (Palgrave, 2024). Parts of this chapter also served as the foundation for the introduction to José Cruz González's *Invierno* in the second volume of *The Bard in the Borderlands: An Anthology of Shakespeare Appropriations en La Frontera*, edited by Katherine Gillen, Adrianna M. Santos, and Kathryn Vomero Santos (ACMRS Press, 2024). A version of Chapter 3 was published in *Latino Studies* in 2024.

Guillermo Gómez-Peña's "El Hamlet Fronterizo" is reprinted with permission from Routledge. Iris De Anda's "To be a Pocha or not to be" and Lorna Dee Cervantes's "A Chicano Poem" are both reprinted with permission from the authors.

Introduction

The Languages of Shakespeare

Late in the first season of the hit television series *The West Wing* (1999–2006), key members of the Republican-led Senate threaten to introduce controversial legislation that would make English the official language of the United States. As the President's Deputy Chief of Staff Josh Lyman attempts to educate himself about the issue, he turns to political consultant and pollster Joey Lucas in search of a possible counterargument against such a law. Although Joey remains unconvinced that Republicans would actually introduce a bill that is opposed by "seventy-five percent of Hispanics," who comprise "the second largest ethnic block of voters in the country," she proceeds to illuminate the flawed logic of an official English policy: "Aside from it being bigoted and unconstitutional," Joey contends, "it's ludicrous to think that laws need to be created to help protect the language of Shakespeare."[1]

The linguistic irony of this moment is that Joey—played by Deaf actress Marlee Matlin—uses American Sign Language to deliver her counterargument, which is subsequently translated into "the language of Shakespeare" by her interpreter Kenny. And while we could simply chalk her clever retort up to show creator Aaron Sorkin's penchant for writing snappy dialogue, similar words were in fact spoken on the floor of the U.S. House of Representatives about four years before this episode first aired in 2000. In response to the

DOI: 10.4324/9781003292838-1

Bill Emerson English Language Empowerment Act of 1996, a measure that would make it to the Senate but never become law, Democratic Congressman Frank Pallone of New Jersey proclaimed:

> I consider this legislation basically an insult to the English language and also un-American because basically it violates free speech and also discourages diversity, which I think is a hallmark of our American tradition. The legislation has nothing to do with protecting the English language. English is a wonderful language that has survived for years in various places. To think that the language of Shakespeare has to have government help to survive.[2]

Much like that of the fictional Joey Lucas, Pallone's argument is two-fold: to declare English the national language—and thereby threaten advancements in language access services and bilingual education—is to make a law that is antithetical to constitutional rights (free speech) and "our American tradition" (diversity). But it is also, Pallone claims, "an insult to the English language," a tongue which has evidently endured by virtue of its own merits. We're talking about the language of *Shakespeare*, after all, right?

The painful truth, of course, is that the English language has not merely "survived for years in various places" without powerful government assistance. In the lands that became the United States of America, English was first imposed upon enslaved Africans and Indigenous Peoples by British settlers. The dominance of English grew by similarly violent colonial means as the U.S. empire expanded across North America in the name of Manifest Destiny and began to claim or intervene in places beyond the continent, such as Puerto Rico, Guam,

Hawaiʻi, Alaska, and the Philippines. Although Congressman Pallone was speaking out against discriminatory language legislation in the late twentieth century, his remarks and their echoes on *The West Wing* nevertheless failed to acknowledge that the survival and spread of English has largely depended on the attempted eradication of Indigenous or otherwise preexisting languages, on the enslavement and forced labor of Black people, on the colonial and military occupation of territories around the globe, and on the institutionalized pressures of assimilation that have defined the experiences of so many immigrants who often come to this country seeking refuge from what Jay Caspian Kang describes as "the collateral damage of American imperialism."[3]

But what exactly does Shakespeare have to do with debates about declaring a national language or implementing English-only policies throughout the country? It would be easy enough to argue that his name is being used in the above examples as a metonym or synonym for the English language. It would also be compelling to observe that Shakespeare and his works are often held up reflexively as the pinnacle of what is possible in English, serving as a testament—a monument, we might even say—to the apparent greatness and endurance of the language itself. In much the same way that Pallone's argument does not account for the "government help" that English has had in surviving, however, such an observation overlooks a far more complicated relationship between Shakespeare and language in the United States.

Shakespeare in Tongues seeks to explore that relationship in its ongoing complexity by studying the ways in which Shakespeare has been both wielded as a weapon of linguistic oppression and reclaimed to counteract the harms of such violence. For many people whose lives have been shaped by intersecting histories of colonization, slavery, migration, and assimilation, Shakespeare represents the hegemony of the English language and of white Western culture more broadly. Mohegan playwright, director, and scholar Madeline Sayet describes it most concisely when she distinguishes between Shakespeare's written works and "the Shakespeare system," or "the complex and oppressive role his work, legacy, and positionality hold in our contemporary society."[4] Indeed, the policies and practices responsible for enshrining Shakespeare's works and making them synonymous with English are bound up with longstanding attempts to dispossess peoples of their lands and languages and to maintain a hierarchy that privileges whiteness above all else. Because Shakespeare's works have occupied an outsized presence in U.S. school curricula, theater programming, and social and political discourse, however, it is no small coincidence that they have also become a means by which to call attention to experiences that are all too frequently obscured by forces of linguistic and cultural domination. When read and reimagined from marginalized perspectives, in other words, Shakespeare's works can be deployed to testify to multilingual, multifaceted, and often uncomfortable truths.

Although the title of the series in which this book appears is *Spotlight on Shakespeare*, my aim in *Shakespeare in Tongues* is not so much to turn the spotlight on Shakespeare as it is to use Shakespeare—an author who adapted foreign sources, wrote at the edges of English, and routinely dramatized contact and conflict between languages—as a spotlight to illuminate lesser-known histories of linguistic oppression and resistance within the settler colonial nation-state. In so doing, I follow the lead of the artists and activists I study throughout this project, who are far less interested in reproducing

Shakespeare in new contexts than they are in redirecting the attention and resources that have accrued to his works toward a more truthful understanding of the past and of themselves. *Shakespeare in Tongues* therefore invites readers to see Shakespeare not as a static symbol for English but as a writer who created a set of dynamic texts and performance traditions that continue to be alive to the multiplicities of tongues, to the fluid and embodied borders of language, and to the resilience of those who refuse assimilation. What if we started reading, teaching, and engaging with "the language of Shakespeare"—or rather, the *languages* of Shakespeare—to explore the many dimensions of linguistic identity and to grapple with the ongoing effects of linguistic imperialism and racism? How might we use Shakespeare and his legacies to challenge the hegemony of English and to collectively strive for more polyglot and polyvocal futures?

SHAKESPEARE AND THE IDEA OF AN AMERICAN LANGUAGE

Before we can begin to take these questions up, however, we must first attempt to understand how Shakespeare and English became so powerfully aligned in discourses about the linguistic identity of the United States. In an address delivered at the 1932 dedication of the Folger Shakespeare Library in Washington, DC, scholar and inaugural director Joseph Quincy Adams reflected on the enduring presence of Shakespeare in American culture across three periods of the nation's history:

> first, the period of the British settlement of the colonies, when the foundations of our racial stock and of our American culture were laid; secondly, the period of territorial expansion, when frontier conditions came to

> modify the characters of our nation as a whole; and thirdly, the period of foreign immigration, when the ethnic texture of our population was seriously altered.[5]

Much of the scholarly commentary on this address has focused on Adams's description of the third period, where his expression of American nativism is most evident as he celebrates Shakespeare's role in helping to preserve the homogeneity of English culture amid the increasing "flood" of European immigrants, who "swarmed into the land like the locust in Egypt" and became "a menace to the preservation of our long-established English civilization."[6] Just when "America seemed destined to become a babel of tongues and cultures," he recounts with relief, the country established "a system of free and compulsory education of youth."[7] In Adams's view, this was a decidedly good thing, as it not only gave all children "the stamp of a common schooling" but also helped to assimilate immigrant communities into mainstream U.S. culture and accelerate their learning of English.[8] Included in the curriculum for such schools were, of course, the works of Shakespeare. In the opinion of Theodore D. Weld, who advocated for the "advantages of Shakespeare as a study" in 1886, Shakespeare's works offered "our best model of idiomatic English, the staunchest bulwark of our grand old Saxon, beating back the floods that threaten it. Nothing would so withstand the rush into our language of vapid, foreign dilutions, as a baptism into Shakespeare's terse, crisp, sinewy Saxon."[9] Like Adams, Weld regarded exposure to Shakespeare as a powerful line of defense against the perceived threat of linguistic and cultural heterogeneity.

In addition to its blatant nativism, Adams's triumphalist account of Shakespeare as a homogenizing hero in American history whitewashes a far more complex reality. As Elisabeth H. Kinsley has demonstrated in her work on nineteenth-century European immigrants who routinely adapted and translated his plays into languages such as German, Yiddish, and Italian, Shakespeare and English were not as aligned as Adams seemed to suggest.[10] Jason M. Demeter has astutely observed, moreover, that Adams's presentation of an America unified through Shakespeare makes no mention of Black Americans or the entanglements of Shakespeare with the legacies of slavery, the Civil War, and Reconstruction.[11] Adams likewise does not acknowledge Asian immigrants, who came in large numbers to the United States in the mid-nineteenth century to work in mines and build railroads but faced intense hostility that eventually led to the Page Act of 1875 and the Chinese Exclusion Act of 1882, the first federal immigration policies to target a specific nationality or race.[12] Demeter surmises that such omissions were perhaps intentional, suggesting that "the speech is illustrative of the gradual reconsolidation of whiteness that occurred following the enactment of immigration restrictions in the 1920s," namely, the Johnson–Reed Act of 1924, which established quotas limiting immigrants from Eastern and Southern Europe and barred Asian immigrants altogether.[13]

Among the most striking acts of erasure in Adams's speech and in scholarly engagements with it, however, are those related to the peoples living and working on the lands that the British and Americans settled during the first two periods of history that he describes. The British settlement of the colonies was, in his words, a challenging period of "driving back hostile savages," "felling primeval forests," "building homes," farming the land, and creating infrastructure in order to eventually "establish in the New World something like the social order of their native land."[14] Shakespeare, he explains, was part of that social order, but it was only after the British had carried out the difficult work of settlement that they could embrace their "love for the literature of the imagination, a love inherited from the golden age of Elizabeth."[15] Here, the Indigenous Peoples of North America are framed not just as uncivilized themselves but also as the enemies to civilization who needed to be driven from their lands in much the same way that the "primeval forests" needed to be cleared. There is, perhaps unsurprisingly, no mention of the enslaved African and Indigenous people who were forced to carry out the hard physical labor of settlement for the British colonists.

This erasure of Indigenous and Black communities continues in Adams's account of Shakespeare's role during "the period of territorial expansion." According to his narrative, the American West was a "constantly retreating frontier" where the "task of creating a civilization" was an arduous process for the "pioneers" and "restless spirits [who] marched toward the setting sun."[16] With nary a reference to those who were displaced, removed, massacred, or coerced to labor in service of U.S. imperial agendas, Adams presents Shakespeare as a companion and source of cohesion for white settlers during a time "when our territory was being rapidly expanded."[17] His language is conveniently passive and possessive here, eliding the violent means by which such expansion happened, including the 1846 U.S. invasion of Mexico, which was motivated in part by the desire to extend the reach of slavery.

Shakespeare was there, too. Not long after the official annexation of Texas in December 1845, U.S. Army soldiers who had been deployed to defend the disputed southern border in Corpus Christi mounted a production of *Othello* with a young Ulysses S. Grant cast in the role of Desdemona. We can only speculate as to why they chose to stage this particular tragedy with an interracial marriage at its center, but, as Charlotte M. Canning suggests, it hardly seems coincidental given the white supremacist ideologies of expansion that brought troops to the Texas–Mexico border. Although details about it are scant, Canning contends that this 1846 staging of *Othello* in the Army Theatre on the eve of war does less to affirm a common love of Shakespeare among white settlers than it does to demonstrate that Shakespeare and theater more broadly were "integrated into the infrastructure that allowed the United States to seize what it so firmly believed was its Manifest Destiny."[18]

At the end of the two-year military conflict that ensued, Mexico was forced to cede more than half of its territory to the United States through the 1848 Treaty of Guadalupe Hidalgo, thus dramatically redrawing the border between the two nations. It was only a matter of decades before Spanish, a language that had been imposed on Indigenous communities through the Spanish colonial mission and Mexican rancho systems, was replaced by English as the official language of the law. Spanish soon became increasingly racialized as foreign, inferior, and decidedly not white. While educational policies and practices were by no means uniform throughout the region, and some settlers spoke other European languages such as German and Czech, schools in the U.S. Southwest promoted Americanization through English-language instruction, and many ethnic Mexican children were segregated from their white peers and placed in substandard "Mexican schools," where teachers used corporal punishment and humiliation tactics to prevent them from speaking Spanish.[19]

As I will discuss in more detail in Chapter 1, it was also during the nineteenth-century period of territorial expansion and dispossession that the United States began to develop a federally funded boarding school system that removed Native American children from their communities and subjected them to a strict acculturation program designed to strip them of their languages, cultures, and beliefs. Although the United States government began to systematically fund Christian missionary schools with assimilationist objectives in 1819 through the Civilization Fund Act, the model for federally operated schools was established in 1879, when Captain Richard Henry Pratt, a veteran of the Indian Wars, opened the Carlisle Indian School on the site of a former army barracks in Carlisle, Pennsylvania. Believing that education was a benevolent alternative to extermination, Pratt advocated instead to "kill the Indian in him, and save the man."[20] For Pratt, the path to salvation involved Christian conversion, English-language instruction, and industrial training that would prepare Native boys to work in trades and Native girls to work in domestic roles. Pratt believed so strongly in this approach that, in an 1892 address on "The Advantages of Mingling Indians with Whites," he invoked the institution of slavery as evidence that being "forced into association with English-speaking and civilized people" is what saved Africans from being "surrounded by their fellow-savages" and made them industrious people who would eventually be on the path to citizenship.[21] "Horrible as were the experiences of its introduction, and of slavery itself," he reasoned, "there was concealed in them the greatest blessing that ever came to the Negro race."[22] Native children, in his view, would likewise benefit from such a "blessing." And in their case, the benefits would be far easier to come by since they would be granted the privilege of going to school, whereas enslaved Black people had been prohibited from learning how to read and write and had no access to formal education.

Testimonials, student newspapers, and administrative records indicate that Shakespeare's works played a key role in this harsh assimilationist agenda, which was carried out in over 400 locations across the country. Students enrolled in various Indian boarding schools not only read Shakespeare but also performed his plays and recited speeches and poems aloud. Their exams featured questions about Shakespearean characters such as Portia, Brutus, and Shylock. At Carlisle, where one Arapaho boy called Red Turtle took the moniker William Shakespeare when he was forced to replace his Native name with an English one, a visiting professor once proclaimed that "Shakespeare's works came next to the Bible."[23] "The desire," explains Akwesasne Mohawk scholar Scott Manning Stevens, "was both to imprint the importance and superiority of Shakespeare on the children and to provide showpieces for public declamation by which the children could prove to the settler public the effectiveness of their education."[24]

In her solo play *Where We Belong*, Madeline Sayet paints a vivid picture of the devastating realities of this system:

> Imagine you are a child, stolen from your home from everything you know, taken somewhere far away with terrible living conditions, and when you try to speak your language, the one way you have of expressing yourself – you are beaten for it. You try again and you're beaten harder – because they don't want you to express yourself. They want you to become like them. So you learn to speak English to survive. The government thought it was so important that our cultures be removed and be replaced, they didn't care how many thousands of Native children died at the schools. That's a part of the legacy of how we came to speak Shakespeare ...[25]

Shakespeare, in other words, was implicated in the abuse of hundreds of thousands of children and the attempted eradication of Native languages, the effects of which are still being felt across generations today. Although reforms introduced in 1934 restored some tribal control over the education of Native children and provided funding for students to attend local public schools or day schools on their reservations, the federal boarding school system continued to operate through the 1970s. It was not until 1975, after years of Native activism, that the Indian Self-Determination and Education Assistance Act was signed into law. Only in 1990, with the Native American Languages Act, did it become U.S. policy to "preserve, protect, and promote the rights and freedom of Native Americans to use, practice, and develop Native American languages" and to "encourage and support the use of such languages as a medium of instruction" in schools at all levels.[26] As we will see in Chapter 2, however, centuries of colonial suppression have left many Indigenous languages in a dormant or endangered state, making the work of revitalizing and stabilizing them enormously challenging but all the more essential to Native futures.

By the time Adams delivered his address at the opening of the Folger Shakespeare Library in 1932, Shakespeare had become firmly entrenched in the American mass education system and the American consciousness more broadly. As Denise Albanese explains in her book *Extramural Shakespeare*, "Shakespeare and what he represented were enlisted, sometimes overtly, to serve the cause of a eugenicist 'race knowledge,'" leading to a form of "all-but-compulsory exposure" to his works for students enrolled in American schools, even as those schools were, and sometimes continue to be, segregated in many parts of the country.[27] Educational practices in the

United States continue to be governed by what Michael Bristol calls "the tyranny of Shakespeare's goodness," as Shakespeare is currently the only author required by name in the Common Core State Standards for English Language Arts. Students who pursue educations and careers in theater, moreover, are often expected to study and be able to perform Shakespeare, in large part because his works have been produced in American theaters more frequently than those of any other playwright.[28] What this means both structurally and culturally is that Shakespeare is bound up with the forms of assimilation and conformity that are demanded—both explicitly and implicitly—of those who are not white and those who speak languages other than standard white American English.

RITES/RIOTS OF ASSIMILATION

Given the prominence of Shakespeare in educational spaces, cultural institutions, and political discourses about the primacy of English in the United States, it is perhaps unsurprising that his works have become a shared touchstone for many writers and artists of color who have felt the social pressures to express themselves using someone else's linguistic tools and to see themselves in someone else's stories. In his 1964 essay "Why I Stopped Hating Shakespeare," for instance, James Baldwin recalls his resentment that he should have to read the works of the white English author most closely associated with the language that had been imposed upon his ancestors: "because I felt it so bitterly anomalous that a black man should be forced to deal with the English language at all—should be forced to assault the English language in order to be able to speak—I condemned him as one of the authors and architects of my oppression."[29] As the title of his essay suggests, however, Baldwin's relationship to the language of Shakespeare shifted over the course of his life as he realized that English "might be made to bear the burden of [his] experience if [he] could find the stamina to challenge it, and [himself], to such a test."[30] Indeed, it was when he was living in Paris and speaking French that he came to appreciate the fact that the language he grew up speaking was not the "King's English" but rather an English that had been "forged" by the "immense experience" of Black Americans, becoming "one of the tools of a people's survival."[31] "My relationship, then, to the language of Shakespeare," Baldwin explains, "revealed itself as nothing less than my relationship to myself and my past."[32] It was not that he needed to search for himself within Shakespeare's words but that he, like Shakespeare, and like his Black ancestors, could use and even refashion the language to reflect his lived experience and what he saw in the world around him.

Shakespeare provokes a similar sense of ambivalence for Minal Hajratwala, a U.S.-born author of Indian descent who has spent much of her life navigating the dynamics of assimilation, which she defines as "the internalized engine of colonization: the act of submission to another's narrative."[33] In her 2016 essay "On Shakespeare and the Quest for Belonging," Hajratwala describes Shakespeare as a "rite/riot of assimilation." Because he speaks "from the center of a language that became, with him and in his aftermath, hegemonic," Shakespeare is a "necessary grappling" that many people on the margins of English feel they must undertake on their quest for belonging. However, as Baldwin's essay testifies, grappling with Shakespeare and the language he has come to represent, can also provide the tools for disrupting the very system that determined the conditions of that quest in the first place.[34]

We see this tension between rites and riots of assimilation early on in Chang-rae Lee's 1995 debut novel *Native Speaker*, where the protagonist Henry Park recounts a memory from his childhood when a group of white women customers entered his Korean immigrant father's produce store on the Upper East Side of Manhattan: "My father, thinking that it might be good for business, urged me to show them how well I spoke English, to make a display of it, to casually recite 'some Shakespeare words.'"[35] For Henry's father, "Shakespeare words" clearly represent the height of fluency in English, promising to serve as the perfect medium through which to demonstrate his family's successful absorption into American culture. Just as he has created a careful display of fruits and vegetables to be consumed by his wealthy white clientele, Mr. Park hopes "to make a display of" his son's ability to speak English and thereby increase his own earning potential in the American capitalist marketplace.

Henry, on the other hand, resentfully understands himself as his father's "princely Hal" in this moment and refuses to perform for the benefit of a white American audience, choosing to "grunt [his] best Korean" to the other employees in the store instead.[36] Like Shakespeare's Prince Hal in *Henry IV, Part 1*, Henry resists his father's demands to speak and behave in a manner that is legible to and deemed respectable by the center of power. Henry's choice to align himself with the store's immigrant workers echoes Hal's preference to consort with the denizens of London's underworld, where he boasts of his ability to "drink with every tinker in his own language" (2.4.17–18).[37] But the fact that Henry has to "grunt [his] best Korean" in this scene indicates that he is not totally comfortable in his father's language either, leaving him uneasily suspended between his ancestral and adopted linguistic identities. Lamenting the reality that he "will always make bad errors of speech," Henry explains later in the novel that he often hears himself "displacing the two languages, conflating them—maybe conflagrating them—for there is so much rubbing and friction, a fire always threatens to blow up between the tongues."[38]

At first glance, Henry Park's allusion to Prince Hal may seem like a passing reference in a childhood memory of a father-son conflict in which "Shakespeare words" stand in for the English language itself, but Shakespeare's youthful heir to the throne serves as a kind of foil for Henry Park throughout Lee's depiction of a man who suffers the pain of a fractured identity as the child of immigrants. Whereas Shakespeare's Hal goes on to be the center of a nationalist narrative about absorbing linguistic and cultural difference in the name of an emerging English empire, Lee's Henry is treated, like so many Asian Americans, as a perpetual outsider, unable to fully assimilate into white American society.[39] At the conclusion of the war between the English and French at the end of Shakespeare's *Henry V*, the former prince turned king marries the French princess Katherine, who speaks English "brokenly." Conversely, the main character of *Native Speaker* is estranged from his white American wife, who works as a speech therapist for immigrant children learning English. Whereas King Henry V has to disguise himself as Henri Le Roi in order to hear what his soldiers really think of him, Henry Park is successful in his career as an industrial spy precisely because he is invisible in a society that refuses to see him. As the novel progresses and we learn that Henry is often hired to spy on wealthy and powerful immigrants, he becomes a literal manifestation of the Earl of Warwick's description of Prince Hal in *Henry IV, Part 2* as someone who "studies his companions / Like a strange tongue, wherein, to gain the language" (4.3.68–9).⁴⁰ But for Henry Park, the connection between learning a "strange tongue" and being a strategic observer of people's behavior is not metaphorical. It is the reality of his life as an outsider in American culture. As he says at the end of the novel:

> But I and my kind possess another dimension. We will learn every lesson of accent and idiom, we will dismantle every last pretense and practice you hold, noble as well as ruinous. You can keep nothing safe from our eyes and ears. This is your own history. We are your most perilous and dutiful brethren, the song of our hearts at once furious and sad. For only you could grant me these lyrical modes. I call them back to you. Here is the sole talent I ever dared nurture. Here is all of my American education.⁴¹

What Henry has learned growing up as the child of immigrants in the United States is that the promise of assimilation is ultimately a one-sided and often unfulfilled agreement that demands intensive learning of American culture and forgetting of one's heritage. To be his father's "princely Hal" in this context is to inherit a profound sense of ambivalence about language and identity and to learn the truth of what Julissa Arce calls "the lie of assimilation."⁴²

While Shakespeare's Hal offers a compelling counterpoint for Lee's Henry as he experiences alienation in the United States, it is Caliban's rebellion against linguistic domination in *The Tempest* that has served as a potent symbol of resistance for a wide range of marginalized writers as they reflect on their educational and professional journeys. Recalling how her speech was shaped by the accented, ungrammatical, misused, mistranslated, borrowed, or "bad" English of her Korean immigrant community in Los Angeles, Korean American poet Cathy Park Hong turns Caliban's name into a verb as she explains how she moved beyond embarrassment and developed a sense of pride about her ability to expose and control the language of empire:

> It was once a source of shame, but now I say it proudly: bad English is my heritage. I share a literary lineage with writers who make the unmastering of English their rallying cry—who queer it, twerk it, hack it, Calibanize it, *other* it by hijacking English and warping it to a fugitive tongue. To *other* English is to make audible the imperial power sewn into the language, to slit English open so its dark histories slide out.[43]

Like Baldwin, Hong wants to make the dominant language bear the burden of her experience, but as she celebrates the vibrant tradition of "unmastering of English," Hong demonstrates her mastery of the Western canon by invoking the Shakespearean character who seizes control over the language imposed upon him by his colonizers after they assume that he does not "know [his] own meaning" and that he merely "gabble[s] like / A thing most brutish" (1.2.57–8).[44] "You taught me language," Caliban retorts, "and my profit on't / Is I know how to curse" (1.2.364–5). As she embraces this rebellious spirit in her own writing, Hong also leans into the longstanding associations between Caliban's name and cannibalism by actively refusing to be incorporated and thereby erased by English: "My own method of othering English is to eat English before it eats me."[45] It is through this method of both Calibanizing and cannibalizing English that she has found "a form—a way of speech—that decentered whiteness" instead of merely imitating it or responding to it on its own terms.⁴⁶

This resistance against the homogenizing dominance of standard white American English infuses the work of Jamaican-born poet Safiya Sinclair, whose 2017 debut collection of poems *Cannibal* reclaims the colonial discourses of monstrosity in and around *The Tempest*. As she details in an essay titled "Gabble Like a Thing Most Brutish," Sinclair moved from Jamaica to the United States to attend Bennington College in "the bright white bubble of Vermont," where she all too often encountered the anti-Black, anti-immigrant racism of her teachers and classmates.⁴⁷ After one student repeatedly crossed out instances of Jamaican Patois in one of Sinclair's drafts and scrawled "Can you say this in English?" again and again in the margins, Sinclair began to understand why she was writing: "In the face of prejudice, something indestructible had flourished. What had been only a hardening seed finally devoured all the air in my lungs and all by itself grew roots, became cannibal."⁴⁸ She soon returned to the creative writing workshop with a literary manifesto in which she compared herself to Caliban:

> Many people in this workshop have sought to subdue the work with the colonial marks of their pens—questioning the flora, fauna, and dialect of my native land, questions that have offended and plagued me as I contemplated who I was writing for. ... Like Caliban, I have to question my identity as an Other, as defined by the colonist, while I am expected to express myself in the language of the colonist. But I want to define my identity and writing on my own terms, *if me haffi bruk it dung inna patois*, or iron it out in the Queen's English—while *always* keeping the "u" in colour.⁴⁹

When Sinclair's white peer asked her to translate her Jamaican Patois—a creole language that reflects the resilience and creativity of the African diaspora—into a narrowly defined version of English, what she was actually asking was to be accommodated, to be catered to for her own comfort, without considering the fact that Sinclair had made a deliberate artistic and personal choice about how to tell the story she needed to tell. Her classmate was engaging in what Gloria E. Anzaldúa refers to as "linguistic terrorism," an act of delegitimizing hybrid or "wild" tongues born out of colonialism and survival.[50] "If you really want to hurt me," writes Anzaldúa, "talk badly about my language. Ethnic identity is twin skin to linguistic identity. I am my language."[51] But like Anzaldúa, and indeed like Caliban, Sinclair refuses to allow her wild tongue to be tamed.

The histories of colonization, slavery, and displacement that *The Tempest* only begins to glimpse live in the bodies and tongues of many writers who experience the kind of racism and hostility that Sinclair faced in the Bennington workshop. As Vietnamese American scholar and Pulitzer Prize–winning writer Viet Thanh Nguyen lamented in a 2017 piece for the *New York Times*, the ideologies that shape these workshops in the United States are often rooted in white, male, Anglocentric values masquerading as universal—the same set of values that are perpetuated by persistent claims about Shakespeare's universality. When Indigenous people, Black people, people of color, immigrants, and refugees come into these spaces, they discover that their lives, languages, and stories are often not welcome:

> We, the barbarians at the gate, the descendants of Caliban, the ones who have no choice but to speak in the language

we have—we come bearing the experiences and ideas
the workshop suppresses. We come from the Communist
countries America bombed during the Cold War, or where it
sponsored counter-Communist efforts. We come from the
lands America occupied, invaded or colonized. We come as
refugees and immigrants, documented and undocumented.
We come from the ghettos, barrios, reservations and
borders of America where there are no workshops. We come
from the bedrooms and the kitchens of the American home,
where we were supposed to stay, and stay silent. We come
speaking languages other than English. We come from the
margins, where English is broken. We come with financial
aid and loans and families that do not understand what
"creative writing" is. We come from communities we do
not wish to renounce in the name of our individualism. We
come wanting to do more than just sell our stories to white
audiences. And we come with the desire not just to show,
but to tell.[52]

I quote this passage at length, not just to honor the diversity of voices that Nguyen seeks to highlight but also to call attention to the scope of the genealogy he traces back to Caliban, an emblem of linguistic defiance for those who have been dispossessed of their tongues, displaced from their lands, and left little choice but to speak the language of the colonizer. Nguyen is, of course, speaking figuratively here, but, as the works explored in Chapters 3 and 4 will show, Caliban continues to resonate because colonialism is not a thing of the past. American imperialism is not a thing of the past. It is pervasive and ongoing. It has taken on new forms, and it affects generations of people in lasting and compounding ways.

And yet, it is for this same reason that there are serious limits to what Shakespeare's plays can offer. "We are so much more than the fucking *Tempest*," Madeline Sayet reminds us in *Where We Belong*.[53] Although Caliban may have been Shakespeare's projection of an Indigenous person, and although many people have seen themselves in this character's responses to colonial oppression and enslavement, the language of Shakespeare was, and is, simply not enough to encompass the diverse peoples, tongues, and traditions of the so-called New World. To suggest that his sixteenth- and seventeenth-century English plays are universal requires us not only to overlook what is troublesome, stereotypical, and historically situated about the texts he wrote but also to close ourselves off to the other stories, other voices, and other worldviews that can show us what we need to begin the process of healing from the traumas of empire and settler colonialism. Toward the end of her play, Sayet puts the problem of overvaluing Shakespeare's words into sharp relief:

> Yes, I could *try* to show you with Shakespeare
> Bend the words of a four-hundred-year-old English poet
> Who never saw outside his Christian monarchy
> To pretend he understood more than he did
> That's what you want, isn't it?
> For me to show you how his words are *universal*
> Those few words written at a time
> When we still had ours
> Our Words
> We still had all *our words*
> But every single one of his
> Even the ones he made up
> Even the ones that meant nothing
> You gave value

You saved
Treasured
Cared for
But ours
You tore from our throats and you threw them away
Because you did not understand them.⁵⁴

While Shakespeare was writing at a time when British imperial expansion was still in its nascent stages, the subsequent preservation, elevation, and canonization of his works were aligned with the explicitly colonial project of asserting English hegemony around the world.⁵⁵ They were also, as Joseph Quincy Adams celebrated in his 1932 dedication to the Folger Shakespeare Library, aligned with the consolidation of an Anglo-American identity as the United States continued to expand at the expense of those who were displaced, massacred, enslaved, and forcibly assimilated. From Sayet's perspective as a member of a community whose entire language was all but destroyed while the words of one single man have been tirelessly protected and repeatedly given new life, it is devastating to contemplate the disproportionate attention Shakespeare has been afforded. As Sayet concludes, this is not just a tragedy for the Mohegans or for Indigenous Peoples more broadly: "It's a waste / For all of us / For humanity not to have the words it needs right now to survive."⁵⁶

What, then, are the possible paths forward? As Sayet so powerfully demonstrates in *Where We Belong*, those paths have little to do with Shakespeare. Her play and its production history in prominent institutions such as the Folger Shakespeare Library, the Public Theater in New York City, and the Oregon Shakespeare Festival, however, also show us how the material and intellectual resources we have collectively devoted to Shakespeare can be redirected through what Vanessa I. Corredera and Louise Geddes define as "acts of redistribution."[57] We should not need to find a connection to Shakespeare to understand the importance of Indigenous language revitalization, to recognize why we should support the work of marginalized artists, or to develop culturally sustaining pedagogy that affirms the diverse heritages of our students. But, for now, Shakespeare is a tool that we have at hand. *Shakespeare in Tongues* seeks to use it to pry open urgent and overdue conversations about the political, social, and deeply personal dimensions of one of the most essential parts of our humanity: language.

TONGUES UNTAMED

The chapters that follow draw our attention to several places in the present-day American West and Southwest where Shakespeare has been conjured, embraced, remade, and rejected in service of counternarratives that resist dominant colonial perspectives and challenge longstanding attempts to whitewash history. *Shakespeare in Tongues* builds on my collaborative efforts with Katherine Gillen and Adrianna M. Santos to theorize the ways in which Chicanx, Indigenous, and Latinx theatermakers have radically reimagined Shakespeare's texts to reflect the lived realities of the U.S.–Mexico Borderlands and to affirm the languages, cultures, and lifeways of a region that continues to be affected by ongoing structures of coloniality.[58] Such appropriations of Shakespeare, we argue, strive to open up what Chicana historian Emma Pérez terms "the decolonial imaginary"—"a rupturing space, the alternative to that which is written in history."[59] As they refract Shakespeare's canonical works through the prism of their language practices, their histories, and their visions for social and political justice, Borderlands artists show audiences and readers how "to retool, to shift meanings and read against the grain, to negotiate Eurocentricity."[60] The artists, activists, and educators I highlight in this book likewise mobilize Shakespeare toward a deeper engagement with the past as they invite us to imagine futures in which repair, revitalization, and liberation become possible.

This multidirectional orientation to time and place reveals the power of taking up Gloria Anzaldúa's charge to embrace "a tolerance for ambiguity" in the interest of exploring what Ruben Espinosa terms "the temporal borderlands of Shakespeare."[61] When we allow multiple temporalities, epistemologies, and languages to resonate together and sometimes sit in tension with one another, Espinosa suggests, Shakespeare and his own historical contexts cease to be "the incontestable focal point" and instead become "an element to which we, on the temporal and physical borderlands, can add nuance and layer with manifold meanings."[62] Throughout *Shakespeare in Tongues*, we will see how unsettling Shakespeare in these ways can transform his body of work into a vehicle and arena for working out questions about the ongoing impacts of linguistic and epistemic violence and for identifying restorative paths forward.

Situated at different intersections among land, language, and identity, each of the chapters in this book follows Shakespeare to a specific place or set of places that have been shaped by overlapping imperial histories and by the endurance of Indigenous knowledges. Whether I am engaging with plays written for professional theater companies, performance poems, pedagogical methods, or protest movements, I follow performance studies scholar Diana Taylor in recognizing "embodied practice as an episteme and a praxis, a way of knowing as well as a way of storing and transmitting cultural knowledge and identity."⁶³ The practices, epistemologies, and geographies I examine here are also deeply informed by archival records maintained by community organizations, museums, libraries, theaters, and government agencies. The archives themselves, moreover, contain the voices of people who endured the traumas of colonial violence and demonstrated incredible resilience as they resisted domination and worked to preserve their languages and cultures in both large and small ways. Because colonialism and racism have been perpetuated through legal measures and continue to be reinforced through state and federal legislation, this book also engages with various laws and political battles over language, sovereignty, migration, and education in the United States.

Attending to such histories and present realities is not only urgent but, in many cases, long overdue. As Scott Manning Stevens writes in a recent essay published in *The Oxford Handbook of Shakespeare and Race*, "We have come to the point where ignoring the legacies of genocide, dispossession, and forced assimilation is no longer tenable—especially for Native Americans living in the United States."⁶⁴ Chapter 1 of this book therefore looks at those legacies head-on by studying Choctaw playwright Randy Reinholz's 2015 play *Off the Rails*, an adaptation of *Measure for Measure* set in the town of Genoa, Nebraska, when it became the site of the fourth federally operated off-reservation Indian boarding school in the late nineteenth century. By situating Shakespeare's notorious "problem comedy" within the unjust systems that stripped Native Americans of their lands, languages, and lifeways, Reinholz's play explores the complexities and horrors of the federal Indian boarding school era while holding space for a range of Native responses to the realities of living under the genocidal regime of Manifest Destiny and westward expansion. As it uses, and in some cases refashions, the legal, moral, and social frameworks of Shakespeare's troubling play to shine a bright light on this largely obscured history, *Off the Rails* invites us to consider what it means to seek truth and work toward justice. Ultimately, however, this chapter contends that true restitution requires thinking well beyond Shakespeare and taking action that supports the revitalization of Indigenous languages and cultures, facilitates the return of land, and provides resources for healing.

Maintaining our focus on the importance of Indigenous language revitalization and reclamation movements, Chapter 2 moves to the Central Coast of California to tell the story about how Samala, the long-dormant but newly awakened language of the Santa Ynez Band of Chumash Indians, came to be incorporated into Chicano playwright José Cruz González's 2010 play *Invierno*. I show how González's reimagining of *The Winter's Tale*, which toggles between the nineteenth century and the present day, amplifies the tragicomic structure and multitemporal features of Shakespeare's late romance to explore the dynamic relationship between past and present and to activate the land-based knowledges that were suppressed by successive colonial forces but not forgotten. Like *The Winter's Tale*, *Invierno* and the revitalization of Samala remind us that reconciliation and healing can only begin to happen when that which was thought to be lost is found again.

While the nineteenth-century plotline of González's *Invierno* depicts the immediate aftermath of the rupture that occurred when Mexico was forced to cede more than half of its land to the United States following the two-year war that ended in 1848, the poetic texts I consider in Chapter 3 explore the reverberating legacies of the colonial land grab that established the U.S.–Mexican border as we know it today. Described by Anzaldúa as "una herida abierta," or an open wound, this "unnatural boundary" runs right through Native lands, dividing peoples, families, and communities from each other.[65] As I analyze Guillermo Gómez-Peña's "El Hamlet Fronterizo" alongside Iris De Anda's "To be a Pocha or not to be," I show how these two artists use the languages, geographies, and ontological concerns of the Borderlands to reframe the Danish prince's famously introspective speech as a performance text that can express what Anzaldúa terms "a consciousness of the Borderlands."[66] For both Gómez-Peña and De Anda, Hamlet's soliloquy becomes a means through which to reject Western colonial worldviews, to refuse assimilation, and to center Borderlands ways of knowing, being, and doing. The most urgent question is not whether or not to be but rather what it means to be someone whose existence is made vulnerable precisely because it exceeds the increasingly policed boundaries of nation, language, race, and gender.

The merging of Borderlands epistemologies and politics with Shakespeare's body of work continues in Chapter 4, where I focus on a critical moment when *The Tempest* was embroiled in the controversy surrounding Tucson Unified School District's exemplary Mexican American Studies (MAS) program. As Republican lawmakers set their sights on destroying an enormously successful curriculum that empowered Latinx students and increased their graduation rates, mainstream media coverage quickly zeroed in on the absurdity of banning Shakespeare without considering precisely why *The Tempest* would have been included on a reading list of texts written primarily by Black, Indigenous, and Latinx authors in the first place. This chapter reveals that the MAS program's inclusion of *The Tempest* is, in fact, part of the long tradition of claiming Caliban as an emblem of the dispossessed who use the tools of their education to speak back in the language of the oppressor and to counteract the weaponization of books as a means of political, social, and colonial control. Indeed, Shakespeare's play about linguistic and epistemic domination resonated in uncanny ways with efforts to stifle the impacts of a program designed to affirm and sustain youth of color. Sadly, the relatively recent events I explore in this final chapter are not relegated to the past, and the forms of resistance, solidarity, and hope I highlight here are increasingly necessary amid rising book bans and efforts to suppress socially just pedagogies and honest engagements with history.

Shakespeare in Tongues will be published in 2025, the year that Kim F. Hall and Peter Erickson identified as "a landmark by which to measure subsequent progress toward establishing the field of early modern race studies" in the introduction to their 2016 special issue of *Shakespeare Quarterly*.[67] Their hope for the ensuing decade was that the already robust field, which they each helped to build, would develop "a stronger foundation through a wide spectrum of social issues, a broader scholarly framework, a larger academic audience, and deeper public engagement."[68] This book is the product of a deliberate shift I made in my own scholarly commitments as a white woman living and teaching in South Texas for the last decade. Although I had been writing about issues of language, migration, empire, and otherness in Shakespeare's own time, Erickson and Hall's galvanizing call—echoed by the bold and innovative articles in that groundbreaking special issue—was the push I needed during an especially fraught political moment to be, as Ruben Espinosa writes, "unafraid to employ a cross-historical approach that engages contemporary understandings of ethnic, racial, and cultural politics."[69]

In taking this more transtemporal, interdisciplinary approach to Shakespeare and his legacies, I am influenced by the work of several scholars who have shaped the dynamic and growing field of premodern critical race studies. Ayanna Thompson's 2011 book *Passing Strange* modeled the importance of being "willing to engage in cultural studies in the broadest sense" and of considering a wide range of sources and media to "gauge the American cultural engagement, assessment, and employment of Shakespeare and race."[70] Shakespeare, Thompson reminds us, "was/is always defined through the recreation of his identity, image, texts and performances."[71] *Shakespeare in Tongues* seeks to show that the instability and contingency of Shakespeare can be an asset for those who wish to enter into what Joyce Green MacDonald identifies as "recreative dialogue" with his works or to repurpose them to shed light on issues that have not typically been the purview of mainstream discourses.[72] Indeed, as Kānaka Maoli scholar L. Lehua Yim astutely observes, "cultural colonialism works both ways, especially when colonized peoples appropriate colonizers' texts of high cultural capital into their own languages, put towards their own uses."[73] Such acts of appropriation, or what Vanessa I. Corredera terms "adaptive re-vision," have the potential to disrupt myths about Shakespeare's universality and to resist the dominance of white Eurocentric perspectives.[74]

Shakespeare in Tongues is animated by the conviction that studying antiracist and decolonial engagements with Shakespeare is not just an academic exercise for its own sake. As Margo Hendricks contends, asking questions about how European texts from the premodern past continue to shape ideas about race, language, identity, and sovereignty in the present "can effect a transformation of the academy and its relationship to our world."[75] Such a transformation requires disrupting disciplinary divides, thinking across languages, elevating Indigenous knowledges, combating erasure, sustaining dialogues with communities beyond universities, and ultimately decentering Shakespeare in our inquiries. It requires a willingness to shift what we value and how we know. The social, political, and linguistic issues I explore in what follows will undoubtedly resonate with much broader histories of colonial domination, imperial expansion, migration, and assimilation. But what I hope resonates most of all is the spirit of resistance and resilience that runs throughout the following pages. In contrast to the disciplinary forms of education that have demanded conformity or used Shakespeare to perpetuate ideas about white, Anglo-American supremacy, this book seeks to amplify modes of teaching and learning that are oriented toward collective liberation. The language of Shakespeare does not need to be excluded from such conversations, but it should be just one among many distinct, hybrid, wild, and beautiful tongues.

NOTES

1 *The West Wing*, season 1, episode 21, "Lies, Damn Lies and Statistics," directed by Don Scardino, written by Aaron Sorkin, aired May 10, 2000, on NBC.
2 Congressman Pallone, speaking on HR 131, on August 1, 1996, 104th Cong., 2nd sess., *Congressional Record* 142, pt. 15: 21189.
3 Jay Caspian Kang, *The Loneliest Americans* (Crown, 2022), 59.
4 Madeline Sayet, "Interrogating the Shakespeare System," *HowlRound*, August 31, 2020, https://howlround.com/interrogating-shakespeare-system.
5 Joseph Quincy Adams, "Shakespeare and American Culture," in *Shakespeare in America: An Anthology from the Revolution to Now*, ed. James Shapiro (Library of America, 2014), 421.

6 Adams, "Shakespeare and American Culture," 431.
7 Adams, "Shakespeare and American Culture," 431.
8 Adams, "Shakespeare and American Culture," 432.
9 Theodore Dwight Weld, "Shakespeare in the Class-Room," *Shakespeariana* 3 (1886): 437–8.
10 Elisabeth H. Kinsley, *Here in This Island We Arrived: Shakespeare and Belonging in Immigrant New York* (The Pennsylvania State University Press, 2019), 57–94.
11 Jason M. Demeter, "'The Soul of a Great White Poet': Shakespearean Educations and the Civil Rights Era," in *White People in Shakespeare: Essays on Race, Culture and the Elite*, ed. Arthur L. Little, Jr. (Bloomsbury, 2023), 239.
12 For more on this legislation and the racial violence of exclusion, see Beth Lew-Williams, *The Chinese Must Go: Violence, Exclusion, and the Making of the Alien in America* (Harvard University Press, 2018).
13 Demeter, "'The Soul of a Great White Poet,'" 239.
14 Adams, "Shakespeare and American Culture," 421
15 Adams, "Shakespeare and American Culture," 422.
16 Adams, "Shakespeare and American Culture," 427.
17 Adams, "Shakespeare and American Culture," 430–1.
18 Charlotte M. Canning, "'Put Money in Thy Purse. Follow Thou the Wars': *Othello*, the Mexican–American War, and Manifest Destiny," *Theatre Survey* 65, no. 2 (2024): 94–112, esp. 96. For more on this episode, see James Shapiro, *Shakespeare in a Divided America: What His Plays Tell Us About Our Past and Future* (Penguin Random House, 2020), 23–31. According to contemporary accounts, Grant was not especially well suited to the role and was soon replaced by a professional actress named Mrs. Hart. See also Katherine Gillen and Adrianna M. Santos, "Borderlands Shakespeare: The Decolonial Visions of James Lujan's *Kino and Teresa* and Seres Jaime Magaña's *The Tragic Corrido of Romeo and Lupe*," *Shakespeare Bulletin* 38, no. 4 (2020): 553–4.
19 For a more detailed history of Spanish and education in the Southwest, see Rosina Lozano, *An American Language: The History of Spanish in the United States* (University of California Press, 2018). On the continued racialization of Spanish, see Jonathan Rosa, *Looking Like a Language, Sounding Like a Race: Raciolinguistic Ideologies and the Learning of Latinidad* (Oxford University Press, 2019).
20 Richard Henry Pratt, "The Advantages of Mingling Indians with Whites," in *Proceedings of the National Conference of Charities and Correction*, ed. Isabel C. Barrows (Boston: George H. Ellis, 1892), 46.

21 Pratt, "The Advantages of Mingling Indians with Whites," 51.
22 Pratt, "The Advantages of Mingling Indians with Whites," 50–1.
23 "General School News," *The Carlisle Arrow* 11, no. 7, October 16, 1914, 3.
24 Scott Manning Stevens, "Shakespeare Studies and the Indigenous Turn," in *Histories of the Future: On Shakespeare and Thinking Ahead*, ed. Carla Mazzio (University of Pennsylvania Press, 2024), 109.
25 Madeline Sayet, *Where We Belong* (Methuen, 2022), 38.
26 Native American Languages Act, Public Law 101–477, 105 Stat. 1152, October 30, 1990. The act was amended in 1992 to provide grant funding for the development of Native American language nests and language survival schools.
27 Denise Albanese, *Extramural Shakespeare* (Palgrave, 2010), 68–9. See also Coppélia Kahn, Heather S. Nathans, and Mimi Godfrey, eds., *Shakespearean Educations: Power, Citizenship, and Performance* (University of Delaware Press, 2011).
28 Michael Bristol, *Shakespeare's America, America's Shakespeare* (Routledge, 1990), 5. For other studies of Shakespeare in U.S. culture, see Kim C. Sturgess, *Shakespeare and the American Nation* (Cambridge University Press, 2006); Ayanna Thompson, *Passing Strange: Shakespeare, Race, and Contemporary America* (Oxford University Press, 2011); Alden T. Vaughan and Virginia Mason Vaughan, *Shakespeare in America* (Oxford University Press, 2012); and Shapiro, *Shakespeare in a Divided America*.
29 James Baldwin, "Why I Stopped Hating Shakespeare," in *The Cross of Redemption: Uncollected Writings*, ed. Randall Kenan (Vintage Books, 2010), 65.
30 Baldwin, "Why I Stopped Hating Shakespeare," 67.
31 Baldwin, "Why I Stopped Hating Shakespeare," 68.
32 Baldwin, "Why I Stopped Hating Shakespeare," 68.
33 Minal Hajratwala, "On Shakespeare and the Quest for Belonging," *Granta*, April 22, 2016, https://granta.com/shakespeare-quest-belonging/.
34 Hajratwala, "On Shakespeare and the Quest for Belonging."
35 Chang-rae Lee, *Native Speaker* (Penguin, 1995), 49.
36 Lee, *Native Speaker*, 49.
37 William Shakespeare, *King Henry IV, Part 1*, ed. David Scott Kastan, The Arden Shakespeare Third Series (Bloomsbury, 2002).
38 Lee, *Native Speaker*, 218.
39 On the Asian American literary tradition of writing about assimilation, see Patricia P. Chu, *Assimilating Asians: Gendered Strategies of Authorship in Asian America* (Duke University Press, 2000). See also Viet Thanh Nguyen,

  Race and Resistance: Literature and Politics in Asian America (Oxford University Press, 2002).

40 William Shakespeare, *King Henry IV, Part 2*, ed. James C. Bulman, The Arden Shakespeare Third Series (Bloomsbury, 2016).

41 Lee, *Native Speaker*, 297.

42 Julissa Arce, *You Sound Like a White Girl: The Case for Rejecting Assimilation* (Flatiron Books, 2022), 6.

43 Cathy Park Hong, "Bad English," in *Minor Feelings: An Asian American Reckoning* (Oneworld, 2020), 97.

44 William Shakespeare, *The Tempest*, ed. Virginia Mason Vaughan and Alden T. Vaughan, The Arden Shakespeare Third Series (Bloomsbury, 2011).

45 Hong, "Bad English," 98. On the theory that Caliban's name is an anagram of "cannibal," see Alden T. Vaughan and Virginia Mason Vaughan, *Shakespeare's Caliban: A Cultural History* (Cambridge University Press, 1991), 26–32.

46 Hong, "Bad English," 104.

47 Safiya Sinclair, "Gabble Like a Thing Most Brutish," *Poetry Foundation*, September 20, 2016, https://www.poetryfoundation.org/articles/90781/gabble-like-a-thing-most-brutish.

48 Sinclair, "Gabble Like a Thing Most Brutish."

49 Sinclair, "Gabble Like a Thing Most Brutish."

50 Gloria E. Anzaldúa, *Borderlands/La Frontera: The New Mestiza*. 5th ed. (Aunt Lute Books, 2022), 65–7.

51 Anzaldúa, *Borderlands/La Frontera*, 65.

52 Viet Thanh Nguyen, "Viet Thanh Nguyen Reveals How Writers' Workshops Can Be Hostile," *New York Times*, April 26, 2017, https://www.nytimes.com/2017/04/26/books/review/viet-thanh-nguyen-writers-workshops.html.

53 Sayet, *Where We Belong*, 36.

54 Sayet, *Where We Belong*, 51.

55 On the colonial contexts that shaped the preservation, editing, and dissemination of Shakespeare, see Leah S. Marcus, *How Shakespeare Became Colonial: Editorial Tradition and the British Empire* (Routledge, 2017).

56 Sayet, *Where We Belong*, 52.

57 Vanessa I. Corredera and Louise Geddes, "'A Fair House Built on Another Man's Ground': Public Shakespeare at Seneca Village," *Shakespeare Bulletin* 41, no. 4 (2023): 587.

58 Katherine Gillen, Adrianna M. Santos, and Kathryn Vomero Santos, "Tracing the Traditions of Borderlands Shakespeare," in *The Bard in the Borderlands: An Anthology of Shakespeare Appropriations en La Frontera*, vol. 1, ed. Katherine Gillen, Adrianna M. Santos, and Kathryn Vomero Santos (ACMRS Press, 2023), xv–xxxii. For an insightful study of Latinx appropriations of Shakespeare's works for young adult readers, see Jesus Montaño, *Young Latinx Shakespeares: Race, Justice, and Literary Appropriation* (Palgrave, 2024).

59 Emma Pérez, *The Decolonial Imaginary: Writing Chicanas into History* (Indiana University Press, 1999), 6.

60 Pérez, *The Decolonial Imaginary*, xvii.

61 Anzaldúa, *Borderlands/La Frontera*, 85–86. Ruben Espinosa, "Traversing the Temporal Borderlands of Shakespeare," *New Literary History* 52, no. 3/4 (2021): 606.

62 Espinosa, "Traversing the Temporal Borderlands of Shakespeare," 606.

63 Diana Taylor, *The Archive and the Repertoire: Performing Cultural Memory in the Americas* (Duke University Press, 2003), 278.

64 Scott Manning Stevens, "Monstrous Indigeneity and the Discourse of Race in Shakespeare's England," in *The Oxford Handbook of Shakespeare and Race*, ed. Patricia Akhimie (Oxford University Press, 2024), 131.

65 Anzaldúa, *Borderlands/La Frontera*, 17.

66 Anzaldúa, *Borderlands/La Frontera*, 85–6.

67 Peter Erickson and Kim F. Hall, "A New Scholarly Song: Rereading Early Modern Race," *Shakespeare Quarterly* 67, no. 1 (2016): 3.

68 Erickson and Hall, "A New Scholarly Song," 3.

69 Ruben Espinosa, "Stranger Shakespeare," *Shakespeare Quarterly* 67, no. 1 (2016): 61.

70 Thompson, *Passing Strange*, 43, 14.

71 Thompson, *Passing Strange*, 17.

72 Joyce Green MacDonald, *Shakespearean Adaptation, Race and Memory in the New World* (Palgrave, 2020), 6

73 Laura Lehua Yim, "Reading Hawaiian Shakespeare: Indigenous Residue Haunting Settler Colonial Racism," *Journal of American Studies* 54 (2020): 39.

74 Vanessa I. Corredera, *Reanimating Shakespeare's Othello in Post-Racial America* (Edinburgh University Press, 2022), 22. Corredera has rightfully cautioned in this study and elsewhere that "appropriation as a mode

does not ensure an antiracist approach." See Corredera, "Shakespeare, Race, and Appropriation," in *The Oxford Handbook of Shakespeare and Race*, 499.

75 Margo Hendricks, "Coloring the Past, Rewriting Our Future: RaceB4Race," Race and Periodization Symposium, Folger Shakespeare Library, September 5, 2019, transcript and audio, 23:31, https://www.folger.edu/research/featured-research-projects-and-initiatives/race-and-periodization.

REFERENCES

Adams, Joseph Quincy. "Shakespeare and American Culture." In *Shakespeare in America: An Anthology from the Revolution to Now*, edited by James Shapiro. Library of America, 2014.

Albanese, Denise. *Extramural Shakespeare*. Palgrave, 2010.

Anzaldúa, Gloria E. *Borderlands/La Frontera: The New Mestiza*. 5th ed. Aunt Lute Books, 2022.

Arce, Julissa. *You Sound Like a White Girl: The Case for Rejecting Assimilation*. Flatiron Books, 2022.

Baldwin, James. "Why I Stopped Hating Shakespeare." In *The Cross of Redemption: Uncollected Writings*, edited by Randall Kenan. Vintage Books, 2010.

Bristol, Michael. *Shakespeare's America, America's Shakespeare*. Routledge, 1990.

Canning, Charlotte M. "'Put Money in Thy Purse. Follow Thou the Wars': Othello, the Mexican–American War, and Manifest Destiny." *Theatre Survey* 65, no. 2 (2024): 94–112.

Chu, Patricia P. *Assimilating Asians: Gendered Strategies of Authorship in Asian America*. Duke University Press, 2000.

Corredera, Vanessa. I. *Reanimating Shakespeare's Othello in Post-Racial America*. Edinburgh University Press, 2022.

Corredera, Vanessa I. "Shakespeare, Race, and Appropriation." In *The Oxford Handbook of Shakespeare and Race*, edited by Patricia Akhimie. Oxford University Press, 2024.

Corredera, Vanessa I., and Louise Geddes, "'A Fair House Built on Another Man's Ground': Public Shakespeare at Seneca Village." *Shakespeare Bulletin* 41, no. 4 (2023): 579–600.

Demeter, Jason M. "'The Soul of a Great White Poet': Shakespearean Educations and the Civil Rights Era." In *White People in Shakespeare: Essays on Race, Culture and the Elite*, edited by Arthur L. Little, Jr. Bloomsbury, 2023.

Erickson, Peter, and Kim F. Hall. "A New Scholarly Song: Rereading Early Modern Race." *Shakespeare Quarterly* 67, no. 1 (2016): 1–13.

Espinosa, Ruben. "Stranger Shakespeare." *Shakespeare Quarterly* 67, no. 1 (2016): 51–67.

Espinosa, Ruben. "Traversing the Temporal Borderlands of Shakespeare." *New Literary History* 52, no. 3/4 (2021): 605–23.

"General School News." *The Carlisle Arrow* 11, no. 7. October 16, 1914.

Gillen, Katherine, and Adrianna M. Santos. "Borderlands Shakespeare: The Decolonial Visions of James Lujan's *Kino and Teresa* and Seres Jaime Magaña's *The Tragic Corrido of Romeo and Lupe*." *Shakespeare Bulletin* 38, no. 4 (2020): 549–71.

Gillen, Katherine, Adrianna M. Santos and Kathryn Vomero Santos, "Tracing the Traditions of Borderlands Shakespeare." In *The Bard in the Borderlands: An Anthology of Shakespeare Appropriations en La Frontera*, vol. 1, edited by Katherine Gillen, Adrianna M. Santos and Kathryn Vomero Santos. ACMRS Press, 2023.

Hajratwala, Minal. "On Shakespeare and the Quest for Belonging." *Granta*, April 22, 2016. https://granta.com/shakespeare-quest-belonging/.

Hendricks, Margo. "Coloring the Past, Rewriting Our Future: RaceB4Race." Race and Periodization Symposium. Folger Shakespeare Library, September 5, 2019. Transcript and audio, 23:31. https://www.folger.edu/institute/scholarly-programs/race-periodization/margo-hendricks.

Hong, Cathy Park. "Bad English." In *Minor Feelings: An Asian American Reckoning*. Oneworld, 2020.

Kahn, Coppélia, Heather S. Nathans, and Mimi Godfrey, eds. *Shakespearean Educations: Power, Citizenship, and Performance*. University of Delaware Press, 2011.

Kang, Jay Caspian. *The Loneliest Americans*. Crown, 2022.

Kinsley, Elisabeth H. *Here in This Island We Arrived: Shakespeare and Belonging in Immigrant New York*. The Pennsylvania State University Press, 2019.

Lee, Chang-rae. *Native Speaker*. Penguin, 1995.

Lew-Williams, Beth. *The Chinese Must Go: Violence, Exclusion, and the Making of the Alien in America*. Harvard University Press, 2018.

Lozano, Rosina. *An American Language: The History of Spanish in the United States*. University of California Press, 2018.

MacDonald, Joyce Green. *Shakespearean Adaptation, Race and Memory in the New World*. Palgrave, 2020.

Marcus, Leah S. *How Shakespeare Became Colonial: Editorial Tradition and the British Empire*. Routledge, 2017.

Montaño, Jesus. *Young Latinx Shakespeares: Race, Justice, and Literary Appropriation*. Palgrave, 2024.

Native American Languages Act. Public Law 101–477. 105 Stat. 1152. October 30, 1990.

Nguyen, Viet Thanh. *Race and Resistance: Literature and Politics in Asian America*. Oxford University Press, 2002.

Nguyen, Viet Thanh. "Viet Thanh Nguyen Reveals How Writers' Workshops Can Be Hostile." *New York Times*, April 26, 2017. https://www.nytimes.com/2017/04/26/books/review/viet-thanh-nguyen-writers-workshops.html.

Pérez, Emma. *The Decolonial Imaginary: Writing Chicanas into History*. Indiana University Press, 1999.

Pratt, Richard Henry. "The Advantages of Mingling Indians with Whites." In *Proceedings of the National Conference of Charities and Correction*, edited by Isabel C. Barrows. Boston: George H. Ellis, 1892.

Rosa, Jonathan. *Looking Like a Language, Sounding Like a Race: Raciolinguistic Ideologies and the Learning of Latinidad*. Oxford University Press, 2019.

Sayet, Madeline. "Interrogating the Shakespeare System." *HowlRound*, August 31, 2020. https://howlround.com/interrogating-shakespeare-system.

Sayet, Madeline. *Where We Belong*. Methuen, 2022.

Scardino, Don, dir., *The West Wing*. Season 1, episode 21, "Lies, Damn Lies and Statistics." Written by Aaron Sorkin. Aired May 10, 2000, on NBC.

Shakespeare, William. *King Henry IV, Part 1*. Edited by David Scott Kastan. The Arden Shakespeare Third Series. Bloomsbury, 2002.

Shakespeare, William. *King Henry IV, Part 2*. Edited by James C. Bulman. The Arden Shakespeare Third Series. Bloomsbury, 2016.

Shakespeare, William. *The Tempest*. Edited by Virginia Mason Vaughan and Alden T. Vaughan. The Arden Shakespeare Third Series. Bloomsbury, 2011.

Shapiro, James. *Shakespeare in a Divided America: What His Plays Tell Us About Our Past and Future*. Penguin Random House, 2020.

Sinclair, Safiya. "Gabble Like a Thing Most Brutish." *Poetry Foundation*, September 20, 2016. https://www.poetryfoundation.org/articles/90781/gabble-like-a-thing-most-brutish.

Stevens, Scott Manning. "Monstrous Indigeneity and the Discourse of Race in Shakespeare's England." In *The Oxford Handbook of Shakespeare and Race*, edited by Patricia Akhimie. Oxford University Press, 2024.

Stevens, Scott Manning. "Shakespeare Studies and the Indigenous Turn." In *Histories of the Future: On Shakespeare and Thinking Ahead*, edited by Carla Mazzio. University of Pennsylvania Press, 2024.

Sturgess, Kim C. *Shakespeare and the American Nation*. Cambridge University Press, 2006.

Taylor, Diana. *The Archive and the Repertoire: Performing Cultural Memory in the Americas*. Duke University Press, 2003.

Thompson, Ayanna. *Passing Strange: Shakespeare, Race, and Contemporary America*. Oxford University Press, 2011.

United States Congress. *Congressional Record*. 104th Cong., 2nd sess., vol. 142, pt. 15, 1996. https://www.govinfo.gov/app/details/GPO-CRECB-1996-pt15.

United States Indian Peace Commission. "Report to the President by the Indian Peace Commission, January 7, 1868." In *Annual Report of the Secretary of the Interior*. United States Department of the Interior, 1868.

Vaughan, Alden T., and Virginia Mason Vaughan. *Shakespeare's Caliban: A Cultural History*. Cambridge University Press, 1991.

Vaughan, Alden T., and Virginia Mason Vaughan. *Shakespeare in America*. Oxford University Press, 2012.

Weld, Theodore Dwight. "Shakespeare in the Class-room." *Shakesperiana* 3 (1886): 437–50.

Yim, Laura Lehua. "Reading Hawaiian Shakespeare: Indigenous Residue Haunting Settler Colonial Racism." *Journal of American Studies* 54 (2020): 36–43.

Breathing Native Breath
One

Recalling his time as a student at the U.S. Indian Industrial School in Genoa, Nebraska, Flandreau Santee Sioux tribal elder Sidney H. Byrd characterized the school's prohibition on returning home to his reservation as a form of banishment: "It was like being exiled from home, loved ones, and familiar surroundings. It was almost as if I had been given a sentence of death!"[1] When he arrived to Genoa by train in 1926, Byrd was among the youngest children to be removed from their families and sent to one of more than 400 boarding schools that were operated or financially supported by the federal government from 1819 through the 1970s. During this more than 150-year period, the United States undertook a sustained, systematic effort to strip tens of thousands of Indigenous children of their languages and cultural identities, weaken ties to their tribal communities and lands, and prepare them to assimilate into white settler capitalist society as trained laborers and domestic workers. Children who attended these schools often suffered physical and sexual abuse at the hands of the teachers and religious leaders charged with their care. Many died of malnourishment and disease. Others perished while trying to escape and make the journey back home to their reservations. For those who survived, the process of reckoning with and healing from the traumas they endured has been an enormously difficult one with ongoing intergenerational impacts.

DOI: 10.4324/9781003292838-2

While efforts to educate and convert the Indigenous Peoples of the Americas have roots in the early Spanish and English colonial periods, the U.S. federal government began to lay the groundwork for its devastating boarding school system with the Civilization Fund Act of 1819, which Congress put in place "for the purpose of providing against the further decline and final extinction of the Indian tribes, adjoining the frontier settlements of the United States, and for introducing among them the habits and arts of civilization."[2] In practice, this fund was used primarily to pay white Christian organizations to run missionary day schools on reservations and to create boarding schools designed to separate children from the linguistic and cultural influences of their tribal communities. As representatives of the federal government persuaded, coerced, or threatened tribes into signing dozens of treaties over the next several decades, many of their agreements explicitly included provisions for "civilizing" and educating Native youth in exchange for control of vast amounts of land. The attempted eradication of Indigenous languages and cultures, in other words, often went hand in hand with forced removal, displacement, and dispossession.

Assimilationist education continued to be a federal priority under President Ulysses S. Grant's 1869 Peace Policy, which was shaped in large part by the recommendations of the Indian Peace Commission, created by Congress to establish peaceful relations with the Great Plains Indians amid westward expansion, white settlement, and railroad development. In their 1868 report, this group of military leaders and civilians attributed much of the "trouble" between settlers and Native Americans to linguistic difference. Claiming that "sameness of language" would produce "sameness of sentiment and thought," the commissioners recommended that "schools should be established, which children should be required to attend," and that "their barbarous dialect should be blotted out and the English language substituted."[3] As Congress allocated more funding for such schools, U.S. federal policies actively eroded Indigenous sovereignty, thus making it possible to accelerate the theft of both children and land. With the Indian Appropriations Act of 1871, the United States stopped recognizing Indigenous Peoples as sovereign nations, deeming all Native persons wards of the state instead. In 1883, Native religious and cultural practices were outlawed under the Code of Indian Offenses that was established and enforced by the Department of the Interior's Bureau of Indian Affairs. Soon after passing the General Allotment or Dawes Act of 1887, which led to the breakup of communally held tribal lands, Congress passed a compulsory attendance law that empowered federal boarding school agents to forcibly take Native children away from their families or to withhold rations and other necessities if they did not cooperate. While many parents complied out of fear, desperation for resources, or hope for survival under colonial occupation, others actively resisted by hiding or refusing to relinquish their children, a form of defiance that in one case led to the military imprisonment of nineteen Hopi men at Alcatraz in 1895.[4]

During the time when the U.S. government was ramping up its efforts to acculturate Native children, many settler Americans regarded assimilationist education to be a benevolent alternative to decades of mistreatment, forced removal, and extermination. Captain Richard Henry Pratt—a veteran of the Indian Wars who established the first federally operated boarding school in 1879 by converting old Army barracks in Carlisle, Pennsylvania, into the Carlisle Indian Industrial School—infamously advocated to "kill the Indian in him, and save the man."⁵ The Friends of the Indian, a group of white social reformers, clergymen, and politicians who declared themselves allies to Native Americans, enthusiastically supported boarding school education as a form of restitution for past wrongs and a pathway to future self-sufficiency and citizenship.⁶ In effect, though, the cultural genocide enacted through this system was an extension of the violent eliminatory tactics that settlers had carried out against Indigenous Peoples for centuries. As Australian scholar Patrick Wolfe contends, "assimilation is one of a range of strategies of elimination" employed by settler colonial powers precisely because it is intended to destroy the lifeways, social cohesion, and kinship ties that sustain Native communities.⁷

The horrors of the boarding school experience began the moment children were separated from their families and taken to locations that were often deliberately far away. Upon arrival, their hair was cut short; they were bathed in harsh chemicals such as kerosene or DDT; and their traditional clothing was replaced with military-style uniforms. Students were also forced to adopt "Christian" names and forbidden from speaking their native tongues under threat of corporal punishment, a reality that bewildered and terrified young Sidney Byrd in Genoa:

> The most shocking experience for me was a strict rule that required all students not to speak in their tribal languages while on campus. Only the English language was allowed. Woe be to the student who did not speak in the authorized version! If caught violating that rule we were severely beaten and assigned to extra duty. How in the world was I going to communicate? I didn't know how to speak English. Perhaps by sign language?⁸

The cruelty of a system designed to suppress Native children's familial and ancestral languages became even more profoundly apparent when Byrd was finally allowed to return home to see his grandparents: "Grandmother with tears of joy running down her cheeks, embraced me like she would never let me go. She began speaking words of endearment. That's when I discovered that I could not speak Lakota! It had been beaten out of me. I wept bitterly."[9] It was then that Byrd vowed to relearn Lakota—a vow he kept as he worked throughout his life to preserve and even strengthen his cultural identity in spite of the boarding school program's aims to destroy it. Perhaps most notably, Byrd would use his renewed knowledge of Lakota to write down the accounts of tribal elders who survived the 1890 Wounded Knee Massacre and to compile them in an essay titled "The Betrayal at Wounded Knee Creek," which was published annually on the anniversary of the massacre in *Indian Country Today* for many years.[10] Byrd thus embodied what K. Tsianina Lomawaima describes as "Indian students' stubborn refusal to jettison their Indian identity" as he actively worked against the erasure of his community's language, history, and cultural memory until he passed away at the age of ninety-seven in 2016.[11] He was the last living survivor of the Genoa Indian School.

The resilience of Indian boarding school survivors and their descendants has shaped a rich and diverse Indigenous literary tradition that grapples with the legacies of these and similar institutions in settler nations such as Canada, Australia, and New Zealand.[12] Through autobiographical accounts, memoirs, poems, plays, and fictional stories, survivors and their descendants have drawn on the linguistic and rhetorical tools of their assimilationist education to process the complexities of a system that at once inflicted very real wounds and provided economic opportunities and intertribal connections that were otherwise not available to them.[13] In 2015, the boarding school that Byrd attended became the setting of one such story: Choctaw playwright Randy Reinholz's play *Off the Rails*, an "irreverent, subversive adaptation" of Shakespeare's *Measure for Measure* that takes place in 1880s Genoa, Nebraska, when the school was first established.[14] Originally written for Native Voices at the Autry, the Equity theater company that Reinholz founded with his wife Jean Bruce Scott in 1994 to support the development of Native playwrights, actors, and directors, *Off the Rails* went on to have its world premiere at the Oregon Shakespeare Festival (OSF) under the direction of Bill Rauch in 2017. It was the first play by a Native American writer to be produced in the festival's eighty-two-year history. For Reinholz and his collaborators, reimagining Shakespeare's *Measure for Measure* in Genoa became a way to "shine a light right on" the history of Indian boarding schools instead of looking away or pretending that it never happened.[15] With its treatment of legal (in)justice, sexual coercion, and reproduction, Shakespeare's notorious "problem comedy" offered a compelling framework within which to grapple with the abuses of power and the arbitrariness of the laws that shaped the boarding school system and federal Indian policy more broadly. The play's repeated emphasis on words and tongues, moreover, allowed for a deep exploration of the power of language to persuade, to pray, to punish, to coerce, to harm, to erase, to testify, to remember, to atone, and to forgive.

Perhaps even more crucially, though, the lack of resolution at the end of *Measure for Measure* allowed Reinholz to emphasize the present urgency of seeking truth, justice, and reconciliation in the ongoing aftermath of such harms, not just on the part of Native Americans but on the part of all Americans. While

Native communities have been all too aware of these painful histories and the reverberating effects of the boarding school system, most settler Americans are woefully uneducated about the cultural genocide enacted through this program for more than a century and a half. As Akwesasne Mohawk scholar Scott Manning Stevens notes, students in the United States generally stop learning anything about Native histories and cultures after the fourth grade, and the curricula that do include information about Indigenous Peoples typically consign them to "the distant past."[16] For many settler Americans, it can be shocking to learn how little we know thanks to a broader colonial system of education that is designed to erase Native cultures and perpetuate settler ignorance. It is even more difficult—and therefore urgently necessary—for educators to acknowledge the fact that our institutions, fields of study, and pedagogical approaches are fundamentally rooted in systems of ongoing coloniality. As Eugenia Zuroski writes in a reflection on her commitments to anticolonial scholarship and pedagogy in Canada, "those of us who have benefitted from settler colonialism in North America must commit to learning how the cruelties of colonialism are sustained in our own ways of knowing, our ways of pursuing our own well-being."[17] By leveraging the institutional power, cultural capital, and legacies of Shakespeare to tell the story of the Indian boarding school system, Reinholz's *Off the Rails* opens up space to begin the work of committing ourselves to learning the truth and creating the structural conditions under which Indigenous communities and stories can thrive.

THE TRUTH ABOUT SHAKESPEARE

The particular choice to use a Shakespeare play to shine a light on the obscured histories of the Indian boarding school system is a rather vexed—and in some ways radical—one. As Mohegan playwright, director, and scholar Madeline Sayet has noted in both her critical and creative work, Shakespeare's plays and poems had a prominent place in the curriculum and activities at many of these institutions.[18] "One way we know Shakespeare was taught at Carlisle Indian School," Sayet explains in her solo performance piece *Where We Belong*, "is that one student – when forced to give up his name and for a new English name – picked Will Shakespeare."[19] That student was a Northern Arapaho boy called Red Turtle who entered the school in 1881 at the age of sixteen and left in 1883 due to poor health.[20] He would go on to work as an interpreter, tribal police officer, farmer, and herder on the Wind River Indian Reservation in Wyoming.[21] One of his sons, also named William (Strikes Again) Shakespeare, explains that his father "took the name of William Shakespeare because the agent told him it was a very distinguished name of a great English writer."[22] When the younger William, more commonly known as Bill, went away to boarding school himself, he "had a chance to read some Shakespeare and realized [he] had a good name," so he decided to keep it with pride.[23] As an adult, Bill toggled uneasily between Wind River and the world beyond, spending time in Europe, appearing in Western films with actor Tim McCoy, and serving as a language consultant or informant for anthropologists who sought to study Arapaho language and culture. Although members of the Wind River Arapaho were suspicious of his affiliations with outsiders and ambivalent about his efforts to establish himself as a tribal historian using the methods of anthropology, Bill Shakespeare demonstrated a deep desire to learn about and preserve his tribe's history throughout the course of his life after boarding school.[24]

Further evidence of the English playwright's legacy at Carlisle abounds in the pages of the various institutionally sanctioned and often propagandistic newspapers produced by the students for the Carlisle Press and sent to the school's supporters.[25] In 1903, for instance, it was reported in *The Red Man and Helper* that graduating seniors presented a "Shakespearean symposium," featuring quotations, scene performances, music, and an essay on Shakespeare.[26] In 1914 and 1915, students received visits from a professor named Charles Richmond, who declared that "Shakespeare's works came next to the Bible" as he read passages from the plays and extracted lessons for moral improvement from the characters' actions and behaviors.[27] Carlisle superintendent Oscar Lipps aligned Richmond's views on Shakespeare with the school's mission, assuring students that "a knowledge of Shakespeare's works will help you to obtain a better position after you leave Carlisle."[28] To know Shakespeare was to know white Christian culture. And to know white Christian culture, according to the colonial logic of the boarding school system, was to know success.[29]

Nowhere were these assimilationist ideologies more clearly on display than in Carlisle's contribution to the worldwide tercentenary celebrations of Shakespeare's death in 1916. That year, *The Carlisle Arrow* reported on and published images of students who had dressed up as "famous Shakespearian characters" (as well as Shakespeare himself) to create living pictures and to perform various scenes and speeches during the school's annual closing-week exercises under the direction of Mrs. Emma H. Foster (see Figure 1.1).[30] As Mashpee student Lyman Madison explained, "The Tercentenary Anniversary of Shakespeare's death is being observed all over the country, so it was considered appropriate that the

Figure 1.1 Carlisle students dressed up as famous Shakespearean characters on the occasion of the tercentenary of Shakespeare's death in 1916. *The Carlisle Arrow* 13, no. 1, July 21, 1916. Courtesy of the Carlisle Indian School Digital Resource Center.

Carlisle Indian School should participate in this memorial celebration."[31] Group photographs and portraits featured Native students in the roles of Shakespeare and Queen Elizabeth I, Macbeth and Lady Macbeth, Caesar and Volumnia, Brutus and Cassius, Romeo and Juliet, Shylock and Portia, Cardinal Wolsey, Henry VIII, Ophelia, Hamlet, Richard III, Cleopatra, Nerissa, Viola, Cordelia, Miranda, a Page, and seven witches around a cauldron. Other students served as singers, speakers, and announcers in this large-scale entertainment.

Coverage of these closing exercises in various mainstream newspapers throughout the Northeast and beyond reflected a broader investment in the Shakespeare tercentenary as an occasion through which to affirm a white supremacist Anglo-American national identity.[32] On May 26, 1916, for instance, Philadelphia's *Evening Ledger* reported on the performance by "copper-colored Indian youths and maidens," characterizing it rather condescendingly as a "tribute to the hitherto almost unsuspected powers of dramatic characterization possessed by Indians."[33] Beneath the widely circulated group photograph of the Carlisle student performers was a caption that referred to them as "modern Hiawathas and Minnehahas," an allusion to the main characters in Henry Wadsworth Longfellow's 1855 epic poem *The Song of Hiawatha*, which further reflected a desire to see Indigenous Peoples through the stereotypes perpetuated by white Anglo-American literary traditions.[34]

The assimilationist agenda of Carlisle and the system of schools it inspired were touted once more on June 4, 1916, when *The Sun* in New York published the same photograph of the Carlisle students in their Shakespearean costumes with the headline "Real North American Indians Celebrate Shakespeare with Pageant" and the following blurb:

> An all-American Indian cast composed of students of the Carlisle Indian School at Carlisle, Pa., gave recently what is probably unique among the flood of Shakespearian pageants that this tercentenary year has brought forth. Every member of the cast was an Indian, although the white strain is predominant among many of them. The programme shows the remarkable extent to which the Indians are adopting sterling English surnames.[35]

Much like the "sterling English surnames" that were undoubtedly forced upon these Native students, their Shakespearean performance is presented here as evidence of the success of the assimilatory program at Carlisle. However, as Monika Smialkowska observes, this mainstream coverage also reflects an "ambivalent oscillation between approval of Native Americans' ability to act like white Americans and a simultaneous insistence on their 'essential' difference."[36] Even as it seems to celebrate the students' performance, the headline exoticizes the children as "Real North American Indians," and the blurb makes racialized assumptions about their phenotypic appearances, revealing the casual and colonial nature of public discourses about Indigenous individuals.[37]

For settlers—including myself—who benefit from Shakespeare and the cultural capital he has accrued in the United States and globally, the time has come for a long overdue reckoning with the role his works have played in this history of cultural genocide and its lasting impacts. As I detailed in this book's Introduction, the use of Shakespeare as a weapon of assimilation is not separable from his outsized presence in school curricula, theater programming, and funding opportunities. Shakespeare as we know it today, Sayet contends, is a system that is bound up with histories of oppression and domination, and we must interrogate "what it means for all of us artists, educators, and administrators to be upholding that system."[38]

Asking such questions can (and should) be deeply unsettling. As historian Margaret Jacobs writes, "it can unsettle us—literally—to realize that our settler histories of triumph are inextricably intertwined with Indigenous histories of theft."[39] We cannot understand Shakespeare's place in American culture without acknowledging the role he played in the boarding school systems, and we certainly cannot understand Native appropriations of Shakespeare without first learning about how his works were employed in these larger efforts to suppress Native languages and cultures. Scott Manning Stevens has noted on several occasions that it is only when we take time to reckon with the weaponization of Shakespeare in the boarding school curricula that we can see just how radical it is for Native artists to remake his plays to tell their stories.[40] For Randy Reinholz and the Native Voices company, *Measure for Measure* proved to be a usefully imperfect vehicle for redirecting the capital—both cultural and financial—that Shakespeare has accrued toward forms of storytelling that allow obscured truths to shine forth and lead the way toward healing.

PRESERVING, PERSEVERING

Given the vastness and reach of the U.S. federal Indian boarding school system, Reinholz's adaptation of *Measure for Measure* could have been set in many different locations. When he began developing the concept for the play that would come to be titled *Off the Rails*, the setting shifted among several schools, including Carlisle, but Genoa became the clear choice for both historical and contemporary reasons. Newly admitted as a state in 1867, Nebraska was a growing site of settlement in the late nineteenth century as American and European immigrant settlers moved west and railroad companies expanded their vast networks, often with the help of land grants from the federal government that depended on the violent dispossession of Indigenous Peoples.[41] For Reinholz, setting his play in 1880s Nebraska offered an opportunity to counteract the typically whitewashed narratives of westward expansion that too often neglect the experiences and voices of Native communities.[42]

The particular setting of Genoa also connected Reinholz's play to the remarkable work of the Genoa Indian School

Foundation, a non-profit organization that seeks to preserve the history of the school and to create space for learning and healing. Established by members of the local Genoa community, the foundation has sponsored annual reunions for survivors and their descendants since 1990—a tradition that began in response to requests from former students who wished to reconnect with their classmates and share stories about the place where they had spent years of their childhood. After purchasing the school's manual training building from the town, these settler community volunteers created a museum and interpretive center designed to give Native people a place to understand what their ancestors endured and to provide opportunities for settlers to learn about this difficult history and its legacies (Figure 1.2). Over the years,

Figure 1.2 A remaining portion of the stile and gate outside the Genoa U.S. Indian Industrial School. Genoa, Nebraska. April 16, 2022. Photo by Kathryn Vomero Santos.

the volunteers have collected artifacts, documents, oral histories, and the flags of the nations from which the children came. In collaboration with scholars from the University of Nebraska–Lincoln, community advisors from the Omaha, Pawnee, Ponca, Santee Sioux, and Winnebago tribes of Nebraska, and descendants of students enrolled at the school, the foundation has also participated in the creation of the Genoa Indian School Digital Reconciliation Project, which expands access to the archive for those who cannot travel to Genoa and promotes awareness about the history of Indian boarding schools more broadly.[43]

The documents, artifacts, and oral histories collected by the museum volunteers and the families of survivors have allowed for a deeper understanding of students' experiences at Genoa and further insight into the particular ways in which they resisted assimilation. Sidney Byrd, whose testimonies and recollections opened this chapter, was not the only student who would leave Genoa with a complex relationship to their native language and a desire to preserve it. In her study of the literacy practices of students enrolled at the school, historian Amy Goodburn explains that many Native children "used their literacy instruction to question and complicate the institutional values of the Genoa Indian School."[44] In response to the essay prompt "Shall the Indian tongue be preserved?" for instance, some students made arguments about the value of assimilation while others were critical of a white settler society founded on the dispossession of Native Peoples. Goodburn's interview with Genoa survivor Stanford Whitewater offers an especially powerful example of a long-lasting refusal to accept the school's ideology. Upon returning to the Winnebago reservation in Nebraska after twelve years at Genoa, Whitewater became instrumental in the preservation of the Ho-Chunk language by recording elders, creating translations, and offering language classes at Little Priest Tribal College and in his own home.[45] A 1999 obituary for Minnie Greywolf Littlebear, a Winnebago elder who attended the Genoa Indian School as a young teenager, tells a similar story about her secretly speaking Ho-Chunk with friends at school and encouraging tribal members to "reclaim their language and customs" in the years after she returned home to her reservation.[46]

Informed by and infused with these forms of resistance, preservation, and reclamation, Reinholz's *Off the Rails* might thus be understood not simply as an adaptation of *Measure for Measure* set in the late nineteenth-century frontier but as a defiant act of reclaiming the very tools of assimilation in order to highlight the parts of U.S. history that have been deliberately whitewashed out of settler narratives about the American West. By "populat[ing] the stage with lead characters who are Native, and living through the story,"[47] Reinholz repurposes Shakespeare's meditations on morality, sexuality, justice, and mercy to center what White Earth Anishinaabe writer Gerald Vizenor terms "Native survivance," a neologism combining "survival" and "resistance" or "endurance" that names "an active sense of presence over absence, deracination, and oblivion."[48] As theater scholar Julie Burelle observes, *Off the Rails* "moves away from the reductive narratives of Indian victimhood largely available to non-indigenous audiences and privileges instead a variety of speech acts that are primarily resonant and recognizable for Native American actors and spectators and that honor the complexity of their survivance."[49] That complexity becomes especially evident within the framework of *Measure for Measure*, a play that resists the conventions of genre as it blends tragedy with comedy and explores what it means to achieve justice.

WHOSE JUSTICE?

The action of *Off the Rails* opens at the Stewed Prunes Saloon, a brothel owned and operated by a Lakota and French woman named Madame Overdone. Her patrons are eagerly anticipating the arrival of Buffalo Bill, who plans to pass through Genoa to audition performers for his famous Wild West Show.[50] The town's mayor, General Gatt (modeled after Richard Henry Pratt), announces that he will be leaving for a period of time, allegedly to go on a hunt with members of the Sac and Fox Nation. In reality, though, he will be busy negotiating for the Union Pacific Railroad to build a station in Genoa and thereby accelerate white settlement and growth of the town. In his "remove," Gatt appoints Captain Angelo, the superintendent of the Genoa Indian School, as mayor in the hope that he will "bring law and order to the town."[51] Angelo's second-in-command will be Gatt's counselor McDonald, a Choctaw and Scottish lawyer modeled after the historical James McDonald, whom many regard to be the first Native American lawyer trained in the American legal system. When McDonald questions whether Angelo is suited to govern the town given his reputation for being "hard on the pupils of the school," Gatt declares that "discipline provides the path to salvation" (16). "The Indian lands and ways are long gone," he adds. "Forever changed by Manifest Destiny. / They must endure assimilation or die" (17). The drama of Shakespeare's play about justice thus unfolds within a fundamentally unjust legal context in which laws are arbitrarily created, applied, or broken to justify the mistreatment, dispossession, and extermination of Native Peoples.

While the abuse, starvation, and medical neglect that children suffered at the Genoa Indian School and throughout the boarding school system is openly discussed among the characters throughout the play, it is never explicitly represented on stage. Off the Rails repeatedly pulls the audience into the historical and human reality of their experiences, however, through the recurring projection of archival before-and-after photographs onto the backdrop of the stage during transitions between pivotal scenes as the conflict escalates. Often accompanied by somber Native music, these projected images were originally commissioned by Indian boarding and residential school administrators in both the United States and Canada for propagandistic purposes and typically feature tribal youth first in their traditional dress with long hair and then in military uniforms with their hair cut short. The earliest photographs the audience sees are of Thomas Moore Keesick, a young Salteaux boy who attended the Regina Indian Industrial School in Saskatchewan, Canada, and is often referred to as the "face" of residential schools.[52] Over the course of the play, the number of children in the projections increases, illustrating the growing scale and impact of the boarding school system (see Figure 1.3). Images that were once intended to serve as visual evidence of successful assimilation become painful reminders of the very real harm done to thousands of children in Genoa and beyond.

Although the play features a diverse cast of Native characters, and Genoa's historical student body reflected what Ojibwe scholar Brenda J. Child refers to as the "pan-Indianness of boarding school life," Reinholz underscores the connection between the dispossession of land and the forced assimilation of children by placing a pair of Pawnee siblings at the center of Off the Rails.[53] In the play's second scene, we meet Momaday, a sixteen-year-old Pawnee boy currently enrolled at the school, who tells the spirit of his grandfather about the time when their people were removed from their land and

Figure 1.3 *Off the Rails* (2017): Steven Sapp, Cedric Lamar, Stephen Michael Spencer, Jen Olivares, Nancy Rodriguez. Photo by Jenny Graham, Oregon Shakespeare Festival.

forced to relocate to Indian Territory in Oklahoma. Momaday makes particular note of the brutal irony of spending "two moons" walking only to be stolen from his mother and forced to return as a student at the boarding school built on Pawnee land (11). There, his hair was cut short and washed with kerosene. He was forbidden from speaking his native tongue or beaten if he did. Family members who tried to rescue him were imprisoned or hanged. To him, the intention was clear: "To break our family. Destroy our way of life" (11). In spite of these efforts to eradicate his cultural ties, Momaday tells his grandfather that he continues to "practic[e] the way of the Hiruúska (Warrior Society)" through dance when the other children go to sleep (12).

By contrast, Momaday's older sister Isabel regards education as "the new path" to survival under colonialism and a viable alternative to decades of massacre and war (41). Having completed her primary education at the boarding school, she is not a novice nun like her counterpart in Shakespeare's play but rather a student at the normal school in Lincoln, studying to become a teacher herself in an attempt to save her people from complete annihilation.

The arbitrary and often cruel nature of settler colonial laws becomes acutely apparent when Angelo discovers that Momaday's partner, an orphaned Irish American girl named Caitlin, is pregnant. Although the young couple has been married "in the Pawnee way," Angelo regards their union as unlawful precisely because it is interracial (9). Going so far as to accuse Momaday of rape, he sentences him to death the next day, hoping to make an example of him. As the other Native characters in town try to determine precisely which law Momaday has broken and why the punishment is so harsh, they quickly realize that this situation is emblematic of their experiences of the capricious U.S. legal system. "They're just making it up as they go along," says Alexie, son of a Kiowa chief and former Carlisle student. "Like all Indian policy," adds Madame Overdone (32).

If anyone can reason with Angelo, it is Isabel, who has been educated in the white man's ways and is known for her persuasive rhetorical abilities. Despite her disagreement with her brother's refusal to leave "the traditional ways" behind, she agrees to try to save his life with the linguistic skills she honed in school (39). As in Shakespeare's play, Isabel's impassioned and eloquent attempt to advocate for her brother's life awakens Angelo's desire, leading him to offer to spare Momaday's life on the condition that Isabel have sex with him in exchange for the pardon. But the sudden shift we see in Angelo reflects deeper—and ongoing—histories of settler sexual violence against Indigenous women and the eroticization of colonial domination. Although he finds himself moved to pardon Momaday on the basis that Isabel is a "soulless pagan brought / To the light through Christ," and thus an exemplary product of the boarding school he oversees, "the virtue of this Indian maid arouses [him] quite," reflecting the troublingly blurred line between conversion and coercion (63).

When Isabel threatens to tell the world "with an outstretched throat" about Angelo's hypocrisy unless he agrees to sign the pardon that will save her brother's life without any strings attached, Angelo responds with a version of what many have described as one of the most chilling lines in Shakespeare: "Who will believe you, Isabel?" (76). As in *Measure for Measure*, Reinholz's Angelo understands the social and political weight of his word against Isabel's and is wholly prepared to use that disparity to his advantage. Indeed, as Anna Kamaralli explains in her reading of Shakespeare's play, the discrediting of women's voices is a central facet of patriarchal domination because it "contributes to the erasure of women as fully human subjects, and therefore the increased ease of committing more tangible violations against them."[54] As Angelo goes on to outline the oppressive logics undergirding his harrowing question in a lengthy speech, he reveals the ways in which the misogyny of *Measure for Measure* is, as Nora J. Williams contends, fundamentally a structural problem.[55] When we compare Shakespeare's version of that harrowing speech with Reinholz's adaptation thereof, we can see precisely how Angelo's threats of gendered violence are brutally and disproportionately magnified as they intersect with structures of racial and colonial oppression.

Here is Shakespeare's text:

> Who will believe thee, Isabel?
> My unsoiled name, th'austereness of my life,
> My vouch against you, and my place i'th' state
> Will so your accusation overweigh
> That you shall stifle in your own report
> And smell of calumny. I have begun,
> And now I give my sensual race the rein;
> Fit thy consent to my sharp appetite,
> Lay by all nicety and prolixious blushes,
> That banish what they sue for, redeem thy brother
> By yielding up thy body to my will,
> Or else he must not only die the death,
> But thy unkindness shall his death draw out
> To lingering sufferance. Answer me tomorrow,
> Or by the affection that now guides me most,
> I'll prove a tyrant to him. As for you,
> Say what you can, my false o'erweighs your true.
>
> (2.4.154–70)[56]

And here is Reinholz's adaptation of the same speech:

> Who will believe you, Isabel?
> My unsoiled name, and you an Indian.
> My word against yours, my station in town,
> Will so outweigh your accusation,
> That you shall choke in your own report,
> Reeking of squalor and be the squaw that you are.
> Now I give my superior race the rein:
> Fit your consent to my sharp appetite;
> To redeem your brother, thereby

> Yielding up your body to my will;
> Or by your unkindness his death will draw out
> To lingering sufferance. You'll answer me today,
> Or, by the passion that now guides me most,
> I'll torture that boy to make the Sand Creek Massacre
> Look like a Sunday picnic. As for you,
> Say what you can, my false outweighs your true.
>
> (76)

The power differential that animates Angelo's sexual extortion of Isabella in Shakespeare's play is both racialized and underwritten by the authority of the U.S. government in Reinholz's horrific reimagining. Using a slur intended to diminish and dismiss Native women, this Angelo heightens the threats of sexual violence in Shakespeare's version once more as he merges it with the racial violence that settlers enacted upon Indigenous Peoples.[57] As Shakespeare's "sensual race" becomes "superior race," Angelo's white supremacist tyranny promises to exceed the horrors of a real mass murder event that had taken place just over twenty years before the time of this play. The Sand Creek Massacre to which he refers occurred in 1864 when U.S. troops attacked and burned a Cheyenne and Arapaho village at Sand Creek in the Colorado Territory, brutally murdering at least 150 people, most of whom were women and children.[58] Angelo's threat to outdo such gruesome acts in torturing Momaday—a child enrolled at the school he oversees—makes it abundantly clear that the boarding school system was part of a continuum of violence against Native Peoples.

In the face of this ever-present threat of extermination, the siblings at the heart of Reinholz's play find themselves alienated from each other and in disagreement about what it means to endure within systems of colonial oppression. For Momaday, speaking the Pawnee language, praying into the wind, practicing traditional dances, and "choos[ing] to hold onto the old ways" are all forms of resistance (82). While his sister's name means "pledged to God" and is associated with "a Christian queen from the other world," Momaday's name is Native, implying that he has rejected whatever English name may have been forced upon him in the boarding school (78). More specifically, his name also connects him to a larger tradition of Native resistance, as Reinholz named the character after the Pulitzer Prize–winning Kiowa writer N. Scott Momaday (Navarre Scott Mammedaty), whose 1994 play *The Indolent Boys* commemorates the tragic deaths of three boys who froze to death while attempting to run away from the Kiowa Boarding School in 1891.[59] While we do not know whether the Momaday in *Off the Rails* has ever tried to run away from Genoa, his decision to make a family with Caitlin is, in his view, a radical act of hope, a way to combat the loneliness of life in a boarding school town and to imagine a future for himself in his ancestral homeland.

Isabel, however, sees her brother's behavior as selfish and reckless. She accuses him of behaving like the "savage" the white men believe him to be, arguing that when he defies settler laws and regulations, he not only exposes himself to risk but also undermines other Native people and her efforts to save them (82). In Momaday's eyes, Isabel is upholding "the white man's rules," and her refusal to "sacrifice [her] morals, to save a person" is evidence that she has "become one of them, a Christian" (82–3). Becoming a Christian and participating in the colonial education system, he harshly reminds her, provides only a false sense of belonging and security within a rigid settler racial hierarchy:

> They don't want you. They will hate you because
> You are dark, and dirty, an Indian.
> You will never be smart enough, or white enough.
> And they will never let you forget.

(83)

What Momaday perhaps cannot fully understand, though, are the particular vulnerabilities his sister faces as a Native woman in white settler society. Madame Overdone's Stewed Prunes Saloon, after all, offers a "safe place" for sex workers who have no other choice but to trade in their own bodies and are often subjected to the violent coercion of men (117). We might read Isabel's refusal to comply with Angelo's demands in much the same way that Katherine Gillen reads Isabella's commitment to chastity in Shakespeare's play: as a refusal to participate in a system that treats women as consumable and disposable.[60] In contrast to the hope that Momaday finds in reproduction, Isabel regards the threat of impregnation with "that white man's bastard" as yet another form of settler violence and erasure (88).

As Isabel mourns the impossibility of her dilemma and the impending death of her brother, Madame Overdone emerges with a plan to save Momaday's life while protecting Isabel from Angelo's predatory demands. By shifting this critical plotline away from Shakespeare's Duke Vincentio and giving it instead to a Native woman, Reinholz turns the play's resolution into an act of resistance that manipulates power structures rather than one that comes from the seat of state power itself. The plan remains much the same as it is in the source text: Isabel will agree to Angelo's demands and make arrangements to meet him at night, but in her stead will be Mariana, Angelo's erstwhile fiancée whom he abandoned after her dowry was lost with the death of her brother who worked with the Lakota on the Pine Ridge Reservation. While Shakespeare's Isabella finds some degree of comfort in the plan to escape Angelo's sexual coercion by having Mariana's body stand in for hers and thus forcing Angelo to uphold his agreement to marry the woman he jilted, Reinholz's Isabel initially refuses to be "part of these lies" (88). Overdone counters by explaining that this act of deception is a strategy for survival in a society built on the lies of white men:

> Whose lies? Do you trust the laws of these men, who have proclaimed themselves proprietors of this stolen land? I don't. They buy influence with profits from the labor of slaves and indentured servants. None of their laws are fair, so it's all a bunch of lies, and until they confess their sins, we will do all we must to survive.
>
> (88)

Madame Overdone does not present the so-called "bed-trick" as a morally neutral tactic as Duke Vincentio does, nor does she deny the fact that this plan involves dishonesty. As several critics have noted, the non-consensual sex that Angelo has with Mariana creates an uncomfortable parallel between him and the woman he thinks he has just coerced.[61] In other words, the would-be rapist experiences a form of rape himself. Overdone's response to Isabel's objection to the plan, however, acknowledges that it is difficult and potentially fatal to take the moral high ground within a system that rewards white men for their acts of exploitation and offers women—especially Native women—few options for recourse.

It is this larger system that Overdone also seeks to address as she pushes the play toward a communal reckoning with the physical, sexual, and emotional abuse happening at the Genoa Indian School. When she enters the school to confront Angelo after he orders Momaday's execution despite the fact that Mariana-as-Isabel has satisfied his demands, Overdone sees that the students have been subjected to one of the most infamous forms of school discipline and humiliation: writing lines. Responding to the violence of the repeated phrase "I will not speak Pawnee" on the chalkboard, she picks up the eraser and drags it along the word "not" in each line, leaving its positive opposite behind: "I will speak Pawnee" (115). Overdone's clever remix of a familiar convention becomes another act of resistance as she affirms a future in which Pawnee is spoken, including in this very play.

Upon finding McDonald at the school instead of Angelo, Overdone seizes this opportunity to highlight what she perceives as his complicity, suggesting that he has betrayed his own identity and responsibilities as a Native person by participating in this abusive system even though he claims to be able to change it from within:

> Real Indians know about abuse at the
> Boarding schools, others like you turn a blind eye.
> While the children of this school go hungry,
> You buy new pants because the old ones
> Won't fit around your growing belly.
> Meanwhile the teachers bring "visitors"
> To the students in the night.
>
> (116)

McDonald counters Overdone's critique by pointing to the fact that she makes money from the sexual vulnerability of

Native women, just as her "friend Buffalo Bill" has profited enormously from the Native performers who reenact battles in his Wild West shows (117). In both cases, McDonald and Overdone believe that they are doing what they can to shield other Native people from further harm within systems designed to exploit them. As we once again witness two Native characters struggling with what it means to survive within settler institutions, the play forces us all to confront our own complicity in those same structures of power, including those that govern the theater and the Shakespeare system itself.

Despite Overdone's valid critiques of McDonald, it turns out that his working within the system of the boarding school is ultimately what leads to Angelo's downfall. Although he has been telling General Gatt about the abuse throughout the play, accountability only becomes possible when McDonald is able to uncover evidence that Angelo, like his historical counterpart Genoa Superintendent Horace R. Chase, has been embezzling money from the school.[62] Drawing the line at financial harm to the institution, Gatt can no longer overlook Angelo's crimes and proposes a solution of retributive justice: in his view, it is only fitting that Angelo should be hanged from the same gallows where he condemned the young Momaday to die. Madame Overdone, however, sees this moment as an opportunity to end the cycle of violence by moving toward systemic change rather than taking revenge against the individual offender:

> No, we need to fix this. Angelo is hardly unique.
> There are "Angelos" all over this country.
> The Ponca Chief Standing Bear once said,
> "Our hands are not the same color, but if
> You pierce yours or I pierce mine we both feel pain.

> The blood that flows is the same color.
> God made us all." Isabel, must we hang Angelo?
>
> (138)

As she makes the case for sparing Angelo's life, Overdone turns to the words of Chief Standing Bear (Maⁿchú-Naⁿzhíⁿ), who was arrested for leading a small group of Poncas back to their homeland in present-day Nebraska in order to bury his son Bear Shield, who died after government officials had arbitrarily removed them to Indian Territory in 1877. With the help of General George Crook, the man ordered to detain and return him to Indian Territory, and journalist Thomas Henry Tibbles, Standing Bear was able to secure legal representation and sue the federal government for a writ of *habeus corpus*. During the resulting federal court trial, *United States, ex rel. Standing Bear v. George Crook*, Standing Bear's lawyers set out to argue against the U.S. government's claims that Native Americans were not considered citizens or persons under the law.

After the formal legal proceedings had concluded, Judge Elmer S. Dundy allowed Standing Bear himself to address the audience in the courtroom. As he rose to speak, the chief held his right hand out and then turned to the bench to address the judge, delivering the words that Overdone quotes with the aid of an Omaha interpreter named Bright Eyes (Inshata-Theumba), also known as Susette La Flesche.[63] For readers and audiences familiar with Shakespeare, Standing Bear's appeal to a shared sense of humanity despite racial and cultural differences will undoubtedly resonate with Shylock's famously moving speech in *The Merchant of Venice* in which he asks, "If you prick us do we not bleed?" (3.1.58).[64] After all, Shylock, too, lives in a white Christian society that has denied him full personhood under the law. In a landmark decision,

Judge Dundy ruled "that an Indian is a person within the meaning of the laws of the United States" and that Standing Bear and his people should be released and allowed to return to their land.⁶⁵ Standing Bear's trial, along with a subsequent lecture tour in the eastern states, led to a campaign that would eventually expand into a larger movement to reform federal Indian policy.⁶⁶

What do we make of the fact, then, that Overdone uses the words of a powerful advocate for Native American civil rights to plead for mercy on behalf of someone who has actively dehumanized Native people? As she argues, hanging this Angelo does nothing to fix the problem of all the other Angelos operating within the larger system, nor does it change the beliefs of those who uphold or benefit from white settler supremacist structures of power. When Isabel responds to affirm Overdone's calls for mercy, she makes it clear that "forgiveness reveals a path from madness," and that such a path involves making the truth known to those who have refused to acknowledge it: "We will speak together so that he comes / To know the loss of those he has harmed. / Mistake me not, he will learn the truth" (139). It is clear, however, that Angelo is far from the only one who has learning to do both inside and outside the world of the play. It is also clear that learning is only a first step toward meaningful reform.

As in the final scene of Shakespeare's play, Isabel's call for mercy ushers in a rapid conclusion to *Off the Rails* that feels deeply unsatisfying. Thanks to Madame Overdone's crafty scheming, Momaday was not in fact executed and is reunited with his family. Angelo is pardoned, but Reinholz's Mariana chooses not to marry him after all in light of his actions. And General Gatt does not propose to Isabel as the Duke troublingly does in the source text but rather appoints Isabel as head of the boarding school and agrees to use the profits from the railroad to fund it.

If this ending seems uncomfortably and implausibly tidy, that's because it is. The final scene of Off the Rails acutely reminds us why scholar Frederick S. Boas designated *Measure for Measure* a "problem play" in 1896: "at the close our feeling is neither of simply joy nor pain; we are excited, fascinated, perplexed, for the issues raised preclude a completely satisfactory outcome."[67] This complicated feeling is only magnified by an adaptation that seeks to shed light on nineteenth-century history while ultimately underscoring the lack of resolution for present-day Indigenous Peoples who continue to live under settler colonialism and still feel the lasting pain of the boarding school system. Julie Burelle sees the conclusion of *Off the Rails* as emblematic of the difficulties and risks of reconciliation: "Reinholz's ending, featuring settlers easily absolved in an openly far-fetched and frustrating set of wrap-ups, calls attention to the ways in which reconciliation can become yet another settler colonial tactic aimed at silencing First Peoples."[68] In this regard, the uneasy conclusion of Shakespeare's "problem play" becomes an asset as it shows audiences that healing cannot be achieved within the space of a few hours, a few days, or even a few years. The problem cannot be solved by attending, reading, or teaching a play. It cannot be solved with Shakespeare.

The palpable tension that hangs in the air as *Off the Rails* reaches its hastily happy ending soon gives way to a powwow, led in the 2017 OSF production by the drumming of Brent Florendo (Confederated Tribes of Warm Springs), who was also cast in the role of Isabel and Momaday's grandfather

Figure 1.4 *Off the Rails* (2017): Jen Olivares, Shaun Taylor-Corbett, Lily Gladstone, Román Zaragoza. Photo by Jenny Graham, Oregon Shakespeare Festival.

to meet Reinholz's condition that the part be played by an Indigenous person from the region where *Off the Rails* is performed. As the Native actors take center stage to sing and dance in regalia (see Figure 1.4), they step forward to address the audience and explain the significance of their ability to do so. Although the script assigns these lines to the characters, it is clear that the actors are also speaking as themselves in the present moment:

MOMADAY: In the boarding schools we couldn't sing and dance. NOW WE DO. We have one more special moment on stage. In Pow Wow, we broaden our circle. So we ask some of you here in the front to join us on stage. Raise your hand if you would like to join our circle.

> *When MOMADAY completes his line, members of the cast go into the audience to get five or six audience members to join the round dance.*

OVERDONE: We have these dances because of the resilience of those boys and girls AND the caring families and elders who practiced their traditions.

ISABEL: And we celebrate these living cultures and traditions with you.

(146–7)

As they break the fourth wall—as well as the boundaries between Native and non-Native people, between past and present—Shakespeare recedes into the background of a much larger effort to tell the truth about the boarding school system and to celebrate the fact that Native languages, cultures, and communities are still alive in spite of concerted efforts to eradicate them. As Choctaw theater scholar Bethany Hughes concludes in her review of the OSF production, "Off the Rails is not Shakespeare with Indians nor an educational tool to teach white audiences about Native American history. It is a decolonial act of love, of storytelling, of community. It is a Native play."[69]

As I noted earlier in this chapter, Off the Rails became the first play by a Native writer to be produced by the Oregon Shakespeare Festival since it began in 1935, just one year after the Genoa Indian Industrial School officially closed due to a lack of funding and shifting federal Indian policy.[70] Because the play requires at least seven Native actors to be cast, those actors became part of that season's repertory company, thus gaining important professional experience that enhanced their careers. Other Native artists worked on the production as choreographers, dramaturgs, and consultants. In other words, the capital generated by Shakespeare was deliberately used to pay and support Native creators in the telling of their stories. Perhaps more significant than the fact that *Off the Rails* was the first Native play at OSF in its eight-decade-long history, however, is that it has not been the *last*. Since 2017, OSF has produced *Manahatta* by Cherokee playwright Mary Kathryn Nagle and *Between Two Knees* by the intertribal sketch comedy troupe the 1491s, whose members would go on to create the popular Native-centered television shows, *Reservation Dogs* and *Rutherford Falls*. In 2021, OSF launched the Visual Sovereignty Project, which commissions and showcases Native digital storytelling, and the festival's 2023 season included a production of Madeline Sayet's *Where We Belong*.[71]

Despite these important developments at OSF and other major theater organizations such as The Public in New York City, Shakespeare still occupies an outsized place in American theater and education. Sayet poignantly observes that it is "no accident" that we have a profound lack of knowledge about the Peoples and stories of these lands while we continue to overvalue Shakespeare:

> This land has an abundance of rich and complex Indigenous storytelling traditions, but Native people in America were stolen from their homes, taken to boarding schools, forced to give up their languages, and made to learn Shakespeare. ... We live in a place where policies have been written that have made Indigenous art illegal and learning

Shakespeare mandatory, and to be honest a quick look at current school curriculums would show that not much has changed. This is the foundation of Shakespeare in America. It is as rotten as the foundation of America itself.[72]

To interrogate the Shakespeare system, as Sayet implores us to do, we must take the time to understand precisely how it interlocks with the complex and enduring legacies of the boarding school system. And while *Off the Rails* offers a compelling example of how Shakespeare can be repurposed by Native artists to tell that story and to imagine a path toward justice, it also serves as a reminder of the limitations of Shakespeare as a vehicle for decolonial artmaking. As Sayet notes, Shakespeare's plays "are finite and do not represent all of us," and "if his plays are going to continue to be done, it's important that Shakespeareans spend as much time learning about the world we are in today and how we got here."[73]

PATHS FORWARD

In June 2021, during the National Congress of American Indians' Mid-Year Conference, U.S. Secretary of the Interior Deb Haaland (Pueblo Laguna) announced the creation of the Federal Indian Boarding School Initiative. According to the press release that accompanied her address, the goal was to undertake "a comprehensive review of the troubled legacy of federal boarding school policies" in the United States.[74] The resulting two-volume report, produced under the leadership of Assistant Secretary of Indian Affairs Bryan Newland (Ojibwe) and in collaboration with the National Native American Boarding School Healing Coalition, confirmed that for over 150 years, the United States operated or supported "417 Federal schools across 37 states or then-territories, including 22 schools in Alaska and 7 schools in Hawai'i,"[75] and "directly targeted American Indian, Alaska Native, and Native Hawaiian children in the pursuit of a policy of cultural assimilation that coincided with Indian territorial dispossession."[76] This investigation, which began in the wake of the devastating discovery of hundreds of unmarked graves on the sites of the Kamloops and Marieval Indian Residential Schools in Canada, also identified at least seventy-four marked and unmarked burial sites and accounted for at least 973 documented child deaths across the U.S. Indian boarding school system.[77] Even as the numbers increased in the second volume of the report, the Department of the Interior acknowledges that this information is incomplete and that "the actual number of children who died while in Indian boarding schools is greater."[78]

As the first Native American cabinet member whose own grandparents and great-grandparents were taken from their families as children and sent to boarding schools, Haaland has framed the Federal Indian Boarding School Initiative as a significant effort to "shine a bright and undeniable spotlight" on these dark histories in order to promote healing and future growth in Indigenous communities:

> The federal policies that attempted to wipe out Native identity, language, and culture continue to manifest in the pain tribal communities face today, including cycles of violence and abuse, disappearance of Indigenous people, premature deaths, poverty and loss of wealth, mental health disorders, and substance abuse. Recognizing the impacts of the federal Indian boarding school system cannot just be a historical reckoning. We must also chart a path forward to deal with these legacy issues.[79]

That path forward, Haaland explains, will require creating space for the voices of survivors and descendants; listening and learning on the part of all Americans; and making meaningful policy changes that mobilize the resources of the federal government and other institutions to provide support services and trauma-informed care to Native communities. It will also be essential to collect a permanent oral history and to sustain cultural and linguistic revitalization efforts. "The [Interior] Department's work thus far," she continues, "shows that an all-of-government approach is necessary to strengthen and rebuild the bonds within Native communities that federal Indian boarding school policies set out to break."[80] Despite bipartisan support and advocacy from Indigenous leaders, Congress has yet to pass legislation that would establish a U.S. Truth and Healing Commission on Indian Boarding Schools much like the one formed in Canada in 2008 as part of a legal settlement with residential school survivors. According to the National Native American Boarding School Healing Coalition, which formed in 2012 in part to advocate for this legislation, such a federal commission would do the following:

- Locate church and government records
- Examine the location of children forcibly placed in U.S. Indian boarding schools
- Hold culturally appropriate public hearings to collect testimony from survivors and descendants
- Gather institutional knowledge from subject matter experts
- Document the boarding schools' ongoing impacts
- Tell the truth by sharing findings publicly with cultural sensitivity
- Provide a final report with a list of recommendations for healing.[81]

Passing this bill into law would mark a major shift in this country's relationship to its own history. While Secretary Haaland's Federal Indian Boarding School Initiative has done important work to begin a comprehensive study of the boarding school system, only Congress or the President can act on those findings. In late 2024, President Joe Biden made a monumental gesture in issuing an official apology for the U.S. government's role in the systemic abuse of Native American children, but as many survivors and descendants have rightly insisted, sustained action must follow.

All Americans have the capacity to use their voices to persuade their elected officials to back the proposed legislation and future efforts to allocate government resources to cultural revitalization, support services, and healing programs. Both individually and collectively, we can make a sustained effort to learn about the Indigenous Peoples who lived or currently live on the lands where we reside and work, and we can actively support the lifeways of Native communities by listening to their needs and finding ways to meet them. As Jane Griffith writes, settlers have a responsibility "for the attempted eradication of Indigenous languages and the theft of land that such attempts helped to facilitate."[82] It is up to us to see "that such responsibility translates into tangible and concrete restitution in ways that Indigenous peoples determine."[83] Brenda J. Child reminds us that true restitution also requires giving land back: "We can't change the past. We can't change the experience of assimilation. But what we can do is restore land to Native people who were dispossessed. And if you would ask Indians, they would tell you exactly what land they want restored."[84] A play like *Off the Rails* is one place to start the conversation, but we must continue the work of unsettling our knowledge of the past and looking well beyond Shakespeare so that we can better understand the present and actively create a future in which Native Peoples, lands, languages, stories, and cultures flourish.

NOTES

1 Sidney Byrd, "Boarding School Days," *Flandreau Santee Sioux Tribe Monthly Newsletter*, July 2011, 9.
2 Civilization Fund Act, Public Law 15-85, 3 Stat. 516, March 3, 1819. Although records indicate that the earliest boarding school for Native children was opened in 1801, federal funding was not allocated until 1819.
3 United States Indian Peace Commission, "Report to the President by the Indian Peace Commission," January 7, 1868, H. Exec. Doc. No. 97, 40th Cong., 2nd Sess., 17.
4 There are many histories of the boarding school system and of specific boarding schools, several of which I cite throughout this chapter. For one detailed overview, see David Wallace Adams, *Education for Extinction: American Indians and the Boarding School Experience, 1875–1928*, 2nd ed. (University Press of Kansas, 2020).
5 Richard Henry Pratt, "The Advantages of Mingling Indians with Whites," in *Proceedings of the National Conference of Charities and Correction*, ed. Isabel C. Barrows (Boston: George H. Ellis, 1892), 46.
6 For more about the Friends of the Indian, see Margaret D. Jacobs, *After One Hundred Winters: In Search of Reconciliation on America's Stolen Lands* (Princeton University Press, 2021), 126–64. See also Frederick E. Hoxie, *A Final Promise: The Campaign to Assimilate the Indians, 1880–1920* (University of Nebraska Press, 1984).
7 Patrick Wolfe, "Settler Colonialism and the Elimination of the Native," *Journal of Genocide Research* 8, no. 4 (2006): 401.
8 Byrd, "Boarding School Days," 10.
9 Byrd, "Boarding School Days," 10. Byrd also recounts this story in a documentary entitled *In the White Man's Image*, dir. Christine Lesiak. Public Broadcasting Service (PBS), 1992.
10 Byrd went on to become a Presbyterian minister and civil rights activist who marched across the Edmund Pettus Bridge in Selma, Alabama, with Martin Luther King, Jr. in 1965.

11 K. Tsianina Lomawaima, *They Called It Prairie Light: The Story of Chilocco Indian School* (University of Nebraska Press, 1994), xii. For other stories of resistance and preservation of Native cultures, see Clifford E. Trafzer, Jean A. Keller, and Lorene Sisquoc, eds., *Boarding School Blues: Revisiting American Indian Educational Experiences* (Bison Books, 2006).

12 There are many studies and accounts of the residential schools in Canada, the boarding schools and missions in Australia, and the native schools in Aotearoa New Zealand. For one overview of the Canadian system, see J. R. Miller, *Shingwauk's Vision: A History of Native Residential Schools* (University of Toronto Press, 1996). On the Stolen Generations in Australia, see Anna Haebich, *Broken Circles: Fragmenting Indigenous Families, 1800–2000* (Fremantle Arts Centre Press, 2000). For a multifaceted study of the state schooling system for Māori children, see *A Civilising Mission? Perceptions and Representations of the New Zealand Native Schools System*, ed. Judith Simon and Linda Tuhiwai Smith (Aukland University Press, 2001).

13 See Ruth Spack, *America's Second Tongue: American Indian Education and the Ownership of English, 1860–1900* (University of Nebraska Press, 2002); Amelia V. Katanski. *Learning to Write "Indian": The Boarding-School Experience and American Indian Literature* (University of Oklahoma Press, 2005); and Arnold Krupat, *Boarding School Voices: Carlisle Indian School Students Speak* (University of Nebraska Press, 2021).

14 Oregon Shakespeare Festival, "Off the Rails," accessed October 23, 2024, https://www.osfashland.org/en/productions/2017-plays/off-the-rails.aspx.

15 Oregon Shakespeare Festival, "Playwright and Dramaturg Interview: OFF THE RAILS (The Play)," September 16, 2016, YouTube video, 10:28, https://youtu.be/xe8p9CE8lDc?si=F50uO84uAjmG4SE2.

16 Scott Manning Stevens, "On Native American Erasure in the Classroom," in *Teaching Race in Perilous Times*, ed. Jason E. Cohen, Sharon D. Raynor, and Dwayne A. Mack (SUNY Press, 2021), 25.

17 Eugenia Zuroski, "This Ship We're In," *The Rambling*, August 7, 2020, https://the-rambling.com/2020/08/07/issue9-zuroski/.

18 Madeline Sayet, "Interrogating the Shakespeare System," HowlRound, August 31, 2020, https://howlround.com/interrogating-shakespeare-system.

19 Madeline Sayet, *Where We Belong* (Methuen, 2022), 37–8.

20 The school records for the Arapaho boy who took the name William Shakespeare and other documents related to his life after Carlisle can be found at the Carlisle Indian School Digital Resource Center.

21 For further information about William Shakespeare (Red Turtle) and a collection of some of his writings about his time at the school and his life thereafter, see Krupat, *Boarding School Voices*, 153–57. Western film star Tim McCoy also records an interaction with William Shakespeare in his autobiography, *Tim McCoy Remembers the West* (University of Nebraska Press, 1988), 54–5. William's brother George Shakespeare taught McCoy Plains Indians Sign Language, a tool that McCoy then used to recruit Native American actors to appear in Westerns such as *The Covered Wagon* (1923).

22 Thomas H. Johnson and Helen S. Johnson, "A Visit with Bill Shakespeare," in *Two Toms: Lessons from a Shoshone Doctor* (University of Utah Press, 2011), 58.

23 Johnson and Johnson, "A Visit with Bill Shakespeare," 58. According to Loretta Fowler, the younger William Shakespeare was enrolled in several on- and off-reservation schools, including the Genoa U.S. Indian Industrial School between 1918 and 1919 under the name Alfonzo Shakespeare. See Loretta Fowler, "Oral Historian or Ethnologist? The Career of Bill Shakespeare," in *American Indian Intellectuals of the Nineteenth and Early Twentieth Centuries*, ed. Margot Liberty (University of Oklahoma Press, 2002), 256–73.

24 Fowler, "Oral Historian or Ethnologist?"

25 Ojibwe scholar Brenda J. Child advises approaching these newspapers "with a measure of skepticism" due to the fact that they "reflected the culture of the boarding schools" and were "destined for a public audience." Child, *Boarding School Seasons: American Indian Families, 1900–1940* (University of Nebraska Press, 1998), xii. Jacqueline Emery's recent collection of Native student writings for various boarding school presses reveals that these publications also included writings that challenged stereotypes about Native communities and presented critical perspectives on the schools' assimilationist agendas. See Jaqueline Emery, ed., *Recovering Native American Writings in the Boarding School Press* (University of Nebraska Press, 2017). For a study of Canadian residential school newspapers, see Jane Griffith, *Words Have a Past: The English Language, Colonialism, and the Newspapers of Indian Boarding Schools* (University of Toronto Press, 2019).

26 "The Seniors Give Their Last Entertainment for the Season," *The Red Man and Helper* 3, no. 25, May 15, 1903, 3.

27 "General School News," *The Carlisle Arrow* 11, no. 7, October 16, 1914, 3. For details about Richmond's 2015 visit, see Rose Thelma Snow, "A Shakespearian Evening," *The Carlisle Arrow* 11, no. 38, June 4, 1915, 37.

28 "General School News," 3.

29 In the published transcript of the 1919 hearings before the U.S. House of Representatives Committee on Indian Affairs, one boarding school superintendent lamented that "they have acquired more knowledge of Shakespeare and the higher arts than they have of the homely art of physical labor." United States Congress House Committee on Indian Affairs, *Indians of the United States: Hearings Before the Committee on Indian Affairs*, vol. 1 (Government Printing Office, 1919), 1266.

30 *The Carlisle Arrow* 13, no. 1, July 21, 1616, 3.

31 Lyman Madison, "Shakespearean Entertainment," *The Carlisle Arrow* 12, no. 37, June 2, 1916, 4.

32 For studies of the tercentenary celebrations in the United States, see Thomas Cartelli, *Repositioning Shakespeare: National Formations, Postcolonial Appropriations* (Routledge, 1999), 63–83; Coppélia Kahn, "Caliban at the Stadium: Shakespeare and the Making of Americans," *The Massachusetts Review* 41, no. 2 (2000): 256–84; and Monika Smialkowska, *Shakespeare's Tercentenary: Staging Nations and Performing Identities in 1916* (Cambridge University Press, 2024).

33 *Evening Ledger*, May 26, 1916, 11.

34 *Evening Ledger*, May 26, 1916, 22. Mohawk scholar Louellyn White explains that *The Song of Hiawatha* was also taught at Carlisle. At the Lincoln Institute in Philadelphia, an urban boarding school where her grandfather and great uncle were enrolled, students were compelled to perform a theatrical version of this poem and thus forced to embody stereotypical versions of Indianness and to perpetuate the idea of the vanishing Indian. See White, "White Power and the Performance of Assimilation: Lincoln Institute and Carlisle Indian School," in *Carlisle Indian Industrial School: Indigenous Histories, Memories, and Reclamations*, ed. Jacqueline Fear-Segal and Susan D. Rose (University of Nebraska Press, 2016), 116–18.

35 *New York Sun*, n.p.

36 Smialkowska, *Shakespeare's Tercentenary*, 239. In her study of this event, Smialkowska notes that the record for Daniel Chase, the Mandan student

who played Shakespeare himself, indicates that he ran away from Carlisle twice in 1916. Daniel Chase Student Information Card, Carlisle Indian School Digital Resource Center, accessed September 30, 2024, https://carlisleindian.dickinson.edu/student_files/daniel-chase-student-information-card.

37 There is evidence of other Shakespeare performances in the boarding schools. In 1927, for instance, students at the Haskell Institute in Lawrence, Kansas, performed *A Midsummer Night's Dream* under the direction of Dakota Sioux educator Ella Cara Deloria. See Susan Gardner, "Subverting the Rhetoric of Assimilation: Ella Cara Deloria (Dakota) in the 1920s," *Hecate* 39, no. 1/2 (2013): 8–31.

38 Sayet, "Interrogating the Shakespeare System."

39 Jacobs, *After One Hundred Winters*, 7.

40 See, for instance, Scott Manning Stevens, "Native America and Shakespeare in the Gilded Age," Gilding the Guilt: Buffalo Folger Workshop, April 27, 2023, YouTube video, 20:18, https://www.youtube.com/watch?v=3fmloEEZCzc. See also Stevens, "Shakespeare Studies and the Indigenous Turn," in *Histories of the Future: On Shakespeare and Thinking Ahead*, ed. Carla Mazzio (University of Pennsylvania Press, 2024), 108–14.

41 On the imperial dimensions and impacts of the transcontinental railroad system, see Manu Karuka, *Empire's Tracks: Indigenous Nations, Chinese Workers, and the Transcontinental Railroad* (University of California Press, 2019).

42 Randy Reinholz, email message to author, March 15, 2022.

43 The website for the Genoa Indian School Digital Reconciliation Project is genoaindianschool.org.

44 Amy Goodburn, "Literacy Practices at the Genoa Industrial Indian School," *Great Plains Quarterly* 19, no. 1 (1999): 46.

45 Goodburn, "Literacy Practices," 42–4. See also Elaine Rice, "College Honors Stanford Whitewater, Sr.," *Tribal College: Journal of American Indian Higher Education* 15, no. 1 (2003), https://tribalcollegejournal.org/college-honors-stanford-whitewater-sr/.

46 Erin Grace, "Littlebear Services Set for Today," *Omaha World-Herald*, March 23, 1999.

47 Randy Reinholz, "The Current State of Native Theatre," *HowlRound*, February 24, 2015, https://howlround.com/current-state-native-theatre.

48 Gerald Vizenor, "Aesthetics of Survivance: Literary Theory and Practice," in *Survivance: Narratives of Native Presence*, ed. Gerald Vizenor (University of Nebraska Press, 2008), 1.
49 Julie Burelle, "Off the Rails at the Autry: What Can Shakespeare Tell Us about Indian Boarding Schools?" *Theatre Annual* 69 (2016): 4.
50 On Buffalo Bill and his employment of Native performers, see Linda Scarangella McNenly, *Native Performers in Wild West Shows: From Buffalo Bill to Euro Disney* (University of Oklahoma Press, 2012) and L. G. Moses, *Wild West Shows and the Images of American Indians, 1883–1933* (University of New Mexico Press, 1999).
51 Randy Reinholz, *Off the Rails* (OSF Scripts, 2017), 16–17. All subsequent references to page numbers this edition will be cited within the text. Where relevant, I refer to the Oregon Shakespeare Festival's archival recording from September 9, 2017. I have also consulted earlier drafts of the script in the Native Voices at the Autry archive at the Autry Museum.
52 For more about Keesick and the legacy of the photographs taken of him, see *I Am a Boy: Thomas Moore Keesick*, a short 2015 documentary directed by Louise BigEagle.
53 Child, *Boarding School Seasons*, xiv.
54 Anna Kamaralli, "Putting on the Destined Livery: Isabella, Cressida, and our Virgin/Whore Obsession," in *A Feminist Companion to Shakespeare*, ed. Dympna Callaghan, 2nd ed. (Blackwell, 2016), 397.
55 Nora J. Williams, "Incomplete Dramaturgies," *Shakespeare Bulletin* 40, no. 1 (2022): 1–22.
56 All citations of *Measure for Measure* are from William Shakespeare, *Measure for Measure*, ed. A. R. Braunmuller and Robert N. Watson, The Arden Shakespeare Third Series (Bloomsbury, 2020).
57 While the S-word has roots in the Algonquin word for "woman," it has been used over time as a racialized and gendered slur. In 2022, U.S. Secretary of the Interior Deb Haaland banned use of the term to name geographic features of federal lands and in related communications.
58 For more on the Sand Creek Massacre and its legacies, see Ari Kelman, *A Misplaced Massacre: Struggling over the Memory of Sand Creek* (Harvard University Press, 2013).
59 This tragedy and others like it echo throughout the play, as we learn that children have increasingly attempted to run away from Genoa

since Angelo took over the school. Among them are "two indolent boys" who "headed hundreds of miles south to Kiowa country" (54).

60 Katherine Gillen, *Chaste Value: Economic Crisis, Female Chastity and the Production of Social Difference on Shakespeare's Stage* (Edinburgh University Press, 2017), 38.

61 See, for instance, Marliss C. Desens, *The Bed-Trick in English Renaissance Drama: Explorations in Gender, Sexuality, and Power* (University of Delaware Press, 1994), 85, 116. See also Connie Scozzaro, "Rape's Hypothetical in Shakespeare's *Measure for Measure*," *Shakespeare Quarterly* 70, no. 4 (2019): 270–94.

62 As Wilma A. Daddario explains in her account of the Genoa school, Chase "was suspended for financial irregularities in 1889." Daddario, "'They Get Milk Practically Every Day': The Genoa Indian Industrial School, 1884–1934," *Nebraska History* 73 (1992): 9.

63 For a full account of Standing Bear's statement, see Joe Starita, "The Case of Standing Bear: Establishing Personhood under the Law," *Court Review: The Journal of the American Judges Association* 45, no. 1/2 (2009): 4–11. Reinholz's quotation in *Off the Rails* is slightly different from the translation of the words recorded in this account. In 2011, Cherokee playwright and attorney Mary Kathryn Nagle composed a play about the trial titled *Waaxe's Law*. Madeline Sayet played the role of Bright Eyes in a 2012 performance at the Newseum in Washington, DC.

64 William Shakespeare, *The Merchant of Venice*, ed. John Drakakis, The Arden Shakespeare Third Series (Bloomsbury, 2010).

65 Quoted in Starita, "The Case of *Standing Bear*," 10.

66 For more on the Standing Bear trial and its consequences, see Valerie Sherer Mathes and Richard Lowitt, *The Standing Bear Controversy: Prelude to Indian Reform* (University of Illinois Press, 2003). The shift in federal Indian policy that this trial ushered in would eventually lead to the Dawes Act of 1887, which put tribal land into individual ownership, allowing for the breaking up of reservations and the further dispossession of Native Peoples.

67 Frederick S. Boas, *Shakespere and His Predecessors* (London: John Murray, 1896), 345.

68 Julie Burelle, "*Off the Rails* at the Autry," 20.

69 Bethany Hughes, "*Off the Rails*: Look at Shakespeare, See a Native Play," *HowlRound*, January 22, 2018, https://howlround.com/rails.

70 Under the leadership of Commissioner John Collier, the Bureau of Indian Affairs (BIA) closed several off-reservation boarding schools and

opened dozens of day schools on reservations. Soon after the Genoa Indian School was closed in 1934, the Indian Reorganization Act was passed in an attempt to reverse the allotment and assimilation policies. The act promoted Native self-government under federal supervision and restored some control over tribal lands and education. That same year, the Johnson–O'Malley Act allowed the BIA to enter into contracts with states to educate Native children in public schools. It was only in 1975, after decades of Native activism, that the Indian Self-Determination and Education Assistance Act granted federally recognized tribes control over the services they provide to their communities.

71 Sayet herself has made a conscious effort to leverage the financial and cultural capital associated with Shakespeare to support Native communities and to mitigate colonial harm by requiring any theaters that produce her play to sign an accountability rider in which they agree "to develop a plan to authentically engage in a continuous, long-term relationship with the Indigenous people whose land they occupy and/or the urban Indian/local Native population." Sayet, *Where We Belong*, n.p.

72 Sayet, "Interrogating the Shakespeare System."

73 Sayet, "Interrogating the Shakespeare System."

74 United States Department of the Interior, "Secretary Haaland Announces Federal Indian Boarding School Initiative," news release, June 22, 2021, https://www.doi.gov/pressreleases/secretary-haaland-announces-federal-indian-boarding-school-initiative.

75 Bryan Newland, *Federal Indian Boarding School Investigative Report*, vol. 2 (United States Department of the Interior, 2024), 12, https://www.bia.gov/sites/default/files/media_document/doi_federal_indian_boarding_school_initiative_investigative_report_vii_final_508_compliant.pdf.

76 Bryan Newland to Deb Haaland, April 1, 2022, in Bryan Newland, *Federal Indian Boarding School Investigative Report*, vol. 1 (United States Department of the Interior, 2022), n.p., https://www.bia.gov/sites/default/files/dup/inline-files/bsi_investigative_report_may_2022_508.pdf.

77 Newland, *Federal Indian Boarding School Investigative Report*, vol. 2, 15–16. On the discovery of unmarked graves in Canada, see Tristin Hopper, "How Canada Forgot about More than 1,308 Graves at Former Residential Schools," *Ottawa Citizen*, July 13, 2021, https://ottawacitizen.com/news/canada/how-canada-forgot-about-more-than-1308-graves-at-former-residential-schools.

78 Newland, *Federal Indian Boarding School Investigative Report*, vol. 2, 16.

79 United States Department of the Interior, "Federal Boarding School Initiative Press Conference," May 11, 2022, YouTube video, 31:18, https://www.youtube.com/watch?v=b8jcBxie3HI.

80 United States Department of the Interior, "Federal Boarding School Initiative Press Conference."

81 National Native American Boarding School Healing Coalition, "Progress on S.1723: Senators to Lead Floor Block on Truth & Healing Commission Bill," July 24, 2024, https://boardingschoolhealing.org/progress-on-s-1723-senators-to-lead-floor-block-on-truth-healing-commission-bill/.

82 Griffith, *Words Have a Past*, 250.

83 Griffith, *Words Have a Past*, 250.

84 Quoted in Olivia B. Waxman, "The History of Native American Boarding Schools Is Even More Complicated than a New Report Reveals," *Time*, May 17, 2022, https://time.com/6177069/american-indian-boarding-schools-history/.

REFERENCES

Adams, David Wallace. *Education for Extinction: American Indians and the Boarding School Experience, 1875–1928*. 2nd ed. University Press of Kansas, 2020.

BigEagle, Louise, dir. *I Am a Boy: Thomas Moore Keesick*. RIIS Media Project. October 28, 2015. YouTube video, 11:53. https://www.youtube.com/watch?v=74qL_OomdeE.

Boas, Frederick S. *Shakespere and His Predecessors*. London: John Murray, 1896.

Burelle, Julie. "Off the Rails at the Autry: What Can Shakespeare Tell Us about Indian Boarding Schools?" *Theatre Annual* 69 (2016): 1–24.

Byrd, Sidney. "Boarding School Days." *Flandreau Santee Sioux Tribe Monthly Newsletter*, July 2011.

"Carlisle Indians Play Shakespearean Roles." *Evening Ledger* (Philadelphia), May 26, 1916. Night Extra.

Cartelli, Thomas. *Repositioning Shakespeare: National Formations, Postcolonial Appropriations*. Routledge, 1999.

Child, Brenda J. *Boarding School Seasons: American Indian Families, 1900–1940*. University of Nebraska Press, 1998.

Civilization Fund Act. Public Law 15–85. 3 Stat. 516. March 3, 1819.

Daddario, Wilma A. "'They Get Milk Practically Every Day': The Genoa Indian Industrial School, 1884–1934." *Nebraska History* 73 (1992): 2–11.

Daniel Chase Student Information Card. Carlisle Indian School Digital Resource Center. Accessed September 30, 2024. https://carlisleindian.dickinson.edu/student_files/daniel-chase-student-information-card.

Desens, Marliss C. *The Bed-Trick in English Renaissance Drama: Explorations in Gender, Sexuality, and Power.* University of Delaware Press, 1994.

Emery, Jaqueline, ed., *Recovering Native American Writings in the Boarding School Press.* University of Nebraska Press, 2017.

Fowler, Loretta. "Oral Historian or Ethnologist? The Career of Bill Shakespeare." In *American Indian Intellectuals of the Nineteenth and Early Twentieth Centuries*, edited by Margot Liberty. University of Oklahoma Press, 2002.

Gardner, Susan. "Subverting the Rhetoric of Assimilation: Ella Cara Deloria (Dakota) in the 1920s." *Hecate* 39, no. 1/2 (2013): 8–31.

"General School News." *The Carlisle Arrow* 11, no. 7. October 16, 1914.

Gillen, Katherine. *Chaste Value: Economic Crisis, Female Chastity and the Production of Social Difference on Shakespeare's Stage.* Edinburgh University Press, 2017.

Goodburn, Amy. "Literacy Practices at the Genoa Industrial Indian School." *Great Plains Quarterly* 19, no. 1 (1999): 35–52.

Grace, Erin. "Littlebear Services Set for Today." *Omaha World-Herald*, March 23, 1999.

Griffith, Jane. *Words Have a Past: The English Language, Colonialism, and the Newspapers of Indian Boarding Schools.* University of Toronto Press, 2019.

Haebich, Anna. *Broken Circles: Fragmenting Indigenous Families, 1800–2000.* Fremantle Arts Centre Press, 2000.

Hopper, Tristin. "How Canada Forgot about More than 1,308 Graves at Former Residential Schools." *Ottawa Citizen*, July 13, 2021. https://ottawacitizen.com/news/canada/how-canada-forgot-about-more-than-1308-graves-at-former-residential-schools.

Hoxie, Frederick E. *A Final Promise: The Campaign to Assimilate the Indians, 1880–1920.* University of Nebraska Press, 1984.

Hughes, Bethany. "Off the Rails: Look at Shakespeare, See a Native Play." *HowlRound*, January 22, 2018. https://howlround.com/rails.

Jacobs, Margaret D. *After One Hundred Winters: In Search of Reconciliation on America's Stolen Lands.* Princeton University Press, 2021.

Johnson, Thomas H., and Helen S. Johnson. "A Visit with Bill Shakespeare." In *Two Toms: Lessons from a Shoshone Doctor.* University of Utah Press, 2011.

Kahn, Coppélia. "Caliban at the Stadium: Shakespeare and the Making of Americans." *The Massachusetts Review* 41, no. 2 (2000): 256–84.

Kamaralli, Anna. "Putting on the Destined Livery: Isabella, Cressida, and our Virgin/Whore Obsession." In *A Feminist Companion to Shakespeare*, edited by Dympna Callaghan. 2nd ed. Blackwell, 2016.

Karuka, Manu. *Empire's Tracks: Indigenous Nations, Chinese Workers, and the Transcontinental Railroad*. University of California Press, 2019.

Katanski, Amelia V. *Learning to Write "Indian": The Boarding School Experience and American Indian Literature*. University of Oklahoma Press, 2005.

Kelman, Ari. *A Misplaced Massacre: Struggling over the Memory of Sand Creek*. Harvard University Press, 2013.

Krupat, Arnold. *Boarding School Voices: Carlisle Indian School Students Speak*. University of Nebraska Press, 2021.

Lesiak, Christine, dir. *In the White Man's Image*. Public Broadcasting Service, 1991.

Lomawaima, K. Tsianina. *They Called It Prairie Light: The Story of Chilocco Indian School*. University of Nebraska Press, 1994.

Madison, Lyman. "Shakespearean Entertainment." *The Carlisle Arrow* 12, no. 37, June 2, 1916.

Mathes, Valerie Sherer, and Richard Lowitt. *The Standing Bear Controversy: Prelude to Indian Reform*. University of Illinois Press, 2003.

McCoy, Tim, with Ronald McCoy. *Tim McCoy Remembers the West: An Autobiography*. University of Nebraska Press, 1988.

McNenly, Linda Scarangella. *Native Performers in Wild West Shows: From Buffalo Bill to Euro Disney*. University of Oklahoma Press, 2012.

Miller, James Rodger. *Shingwauk's Vision: A History of Native Residential Schools*. University of Toronto Press, 1996.

Moses, Lester George. *Wild West Shows and the Images of American Indians, 1883–1933*. University of New Mexico Press, 1999.

National Native American Boarding School Healing Coalition. "Progress on S.1723: Senators to Lead Floor Block on Truth & Healing Commission Bill." July 24, 2024. https://boardingschoolhealing.org/progress-on-s-1723-senators-to-lead-floor-block-on-truth-healing-commission-bill/.

Newland, Bryan. *Federal Indian Boarding School Investigative Report*, vol. 1. United States Department of the Interior, 2022. https://www.bia.gov/sites/default/files/dup/inline-files/bsi_investigative_report_may_2022_508.pdf.

Newland, Bryan. *Federal Indian Boarding School Investigative Report*, vol. 2. United States Department of the Interior, 2024. https://www.bia.gov/sites/default/files/media_document/doi_federal_indian_boarding_school_initiative_investigative_report_vii_final_508_compliant.pdf.

Oregon Shakespeare Festival. "Off the Rails." Accessed October 23, 2024. https://www.osfashland.org/en/productions/2017-plays/off-the-rails.aspx.

Oregon Shakespeare Festival. "Playwright and Dramaturg Interview: OFF THE RAILS (The Play)." September 16, 2016. YouTube video, 10:28. https://youtu.be/xe8p9CE8lDc?si=F50uO84uAjmG4SE2.

Pratt, Richard Henry. "The Advantages of Mingling Indians with Whites." In *Proceedings of the National Conference of Charities and Correction*, edited by Isabel C. Barrows. Boston: George H. Ellis, 1892.

"Real North American Indians Celebrate Shakespeare Tercentenary with Pageant." *The Sun* (New York), June 4, 1916. Fourth Section, Pictorial Magazine.

Reinholz, Randy. "The Current State of Native Theatre." HowlRound, February 24, 2015. https://howlround.com/current-state-native-theatre.

Reinholz, Randy. *Off the Rails*. OSF Scripts, 2017.

Rice, Elaine. "College Honors Stanford Whitewater, Sr." *Tribal College: Journal of American Indian Higher Education* 15, no. 1 (2003). https://tribalcollegejournal.org/college-honors-stanford-whitewater-sr/.

Sayet, Madeline. "Interrogating the Shakespeare System." HowlRound, August 31, 2020. https://howlround.com/interrogating-shakespeare-system.

Sayet, Madeline. *Where We Belong*. Methuen, 2022.

Scozzaro, Connie. "Rape's Hypothetical in Shakespeare's *Measure for Measure*." *Shakespeare Quarterly* 70, no. 4 (2019): 270–94.

"The Seniors Give Their Last Entertainment for the Season." *The Red Man and Helper* 3, no. 25. May 15, 1903.

Shakespeare, William. *Measure for Measure*. Edited by A. R. Braunmuller and Robert N. Watson. The Arden Shakespeare Third Series. Bloomsbury, 2020.

Shakespeare, William. *The Merchant of Venice*. Edited by John Drakakis. The Arden Shakespeare Third Series. Bloomsbury, 2010.

Simon, Judith, and Linda Tuhiwai Smith, eds. *A Civilising Mission? Perceptions and Representations of the New Zealand Native Schools System*. Aukland University Press, 2001.

Smialkowska, Monika. *Shakespeare's Tercentenary: Staging Nations and Performing Identities in 1916*. Cambridge University Press, 2024.

Snow, Rose Thelma. "A Shakespearian Evening." *The Carlisle Arrow* 11, no. 38. June 4, 1915.

Spack, Ruth. *America's Second Tongue: American Indian Education and the Ownership of English, 1860–1900*. University of Nebraska Press, 2002.

Starita, Joe. "The Case of *Standing Bear*: Establishing Personhood under the Law." *Court Review: The Journal of the American Judges Association* 45, no. 1/2 (2009): 4–11.

Stevens, Scott Manning. "Native America and Shakespeare in the Gilded Age." Gilding the Guilt: Buffalo Folger Workshop. April 27, 2023. YouTube video, 20:18. https://www.youtube.com/watch?v=3fmloEEZCzc.

Stevens, Scott Manning. "On Native American Erasure in the Classroom." In *Teaching Race in Perilous Times*, edited by Jason E. Cohen, Sharon D. Raynor, and Dwayne A. Mack. SUNY Press, 2021.

Stevens, Scott Manning, "Shakespeare Studies and the Indigenous Turn." In *Histories of the Future: On Shakespeare and Thinking Ahead*, edited by Carla Mazzio. University of Pennsylvania Press, 2024.

Trafzer, Clifford E., Jean A. Keller, and Lorene Sisquoc, eds. *Boarding School Blues: Revisiting American Indian Educational Experiences*. Bison Books, 2006.

United States Congress, House Committee on Indian Affairs. *Indians of the United States: Hearings Before the Committee on Indian Affairs*, vol. 1. Government Printing Office, 1919.

United States Department of the Interior. "Federal Boarding School Initiative Press Conference." May 11, 2022. YouTube video, 31:18. https://www.youtube.com/watch?v=b8jcBxie3HI.

United States Department of the Interior. "Secretary Haaland Announces Federal Indian Boarding School Initiative." News release. June 22, 2021. https://www.doi.gov/pressreleases/secretary-haaland-announces-federal-indian-boarding-school-initiative.

United States Indian Peace Commission. "Report to the President by the Indian Peace Commission." January 7, 1868. H. Exec. Doc. No. 97, 40th Cong., 2nd Sess.

Vizenor, Gerald. "Aesthetics of Survivance: Literary Theory and Practice." In *Survivance: Narratives of Native Presence*, edited by Gerald Vizenor. University of Nebraska Press, 2008.

Waxman, Olivia B. "The History of Native American Boarding Schools Is Even More Complicated than a New Report Reveals." *Time*, May 17, 2022. https://time.com/6177069/american-indian-boarding-schools-history/.

White, Louellyn. "White Power and the Performance of Assimilation: Lincoln Institute and Carlisle Indian School. In *Carlisle Indian Industrial School: Indigenous Histories, Memories, and Reclamations*, edited by Jacqueline Fear-Segal and Susan D. Rose. University of Nebraska Press, 2016.

William Shakespeare Student Information Card. Carlisle Indian School Digital Resource Center. Accessed September 30, 2024. https://carlisleindian.dickinson.edu/student_files/william-shakespeare-student-file.

Williams, Nora J. "Incomplete Dramaturgies." *Shakespeare Bulletin* 40, no. 1 (2022): 1–22.

Wolfe, Patrick. "Settler Colonialism and the Elimination of the Native." *Journal of Genocide Research* 8, no. 4 (2006): 387–409.

Zuroski, Eugenia. "This Ship We're In." *The Rambling*, August 7, 2020. https://the-rambling.com/2020/08/07/issue9-zuroski/.

Being Now Awake

Two

In the late 1960s, a UC Berkeley Linguistics graduate student named Richard B. Applegate took a part-time job that, in his words, "changed the course of [his] life and the lives of many other people."[1] Working on behalf of the Survey of California and Other Indian Languages, Applegate was tasked with cataloging boxes of materials gathered in the early twentieth century by linguist and ethnologist John Peabody Harrington under the aegis of the Smithsonian's Bureau of American Ethnology. Harrington had spent over fifty years meticulously documenting more than a hundred different Native American languages during a critical moment when many were on the verge of dormancy after centuries of colonial dispossession, massacre, and forced assimilation on the part of the Spanish, Mexican, and U.S. governments. In the face of this dire reality, Harrington approached his work with a feverish urgency. As he once wrote in a letter to his young assistant Jack Marr,

> You know how I look at this work, you and I are nothing, we'll both of us soon be dust. If you can grab these dying languages before the old timers completely die off, you will be doing one of the FEW things valuable to the people of the REMOTE future. The time will come and SOO[N] when there won't be an Indian language left in California, all the languages developed for thousands of years will be ASHES, the house is AFIRE, it is BURNING.[2]

DOI: 10.4324/9781003292838-3

While Harrington periodically sent reports back to his colleagues in Washington, DC, his extensive notes and audio recordings were stored away in basements, warehouses, and even chicken coops throughout the country, remaining scattered and untouched for decades until after his death in 1961.[3]

From among the stacks and stacks of boxes that eventually ended up in the basement of Dwinelle Hall at UC Berkeley on loan from the Smithsonian, Applegate's professor Mary Haas randomly assigned him to work on those related to Samala, the language of the Santa Ynez Band of Chumash Indians, also called Ineseño by the Spanish missionaries.[4] In the process of sorting through thousands of pages of Harrington's notes in English, Spanish, and a phonetic script that scrupulously documented the sounds of Samala, Applegate quickly recognized how valuable these documents were for providing insight into the sonic, syntactic, and semantic details of the language as well as into the cultural practices, storytelling traditions, and histories of the Indigenous Peoples of California's Central Coast. As Applegate continued to decipher the notes, it also became clear to him that Harrington's informants understood that they were doing important work to protect their peoples' languages during a critical moment. Indeed, the single most important informant for Harrington was a woman named María Ysidora del Refugio Solares (Qilikutayiwit), the only surviving child of nine siblings who devoted much of her time between the years 1914 and 1919 to speaking with Harrington in great detail. Throughout their conversations, Solares recounted stories about her childhood, shared the details of Chumash folkways and land-based rituals, provided an account of the Chumash Revolt of 1824, and sang traditional tribal songs that Harrington also captured on wax cylinders. "Like the flower of this earth," she told him, "is our Samala language."[5] Solares was well aware that she was actively preserving knowledge not just of the language but of the land itself.

Applegate did not stop at organizing and cataloging the boxes. In fact, he became so fascinated with Samala that he ended up writing his doctoral dissertation on the language.[6] But this was no easy task. In the absence of living native speakers or any kind of key from Harrington, Applegate had to rely on sporadic translations of words and phrases scattered throughout the notes in order to reconstruct a grammar and compile a dictionary. Because Harrington's recordings of Solares primarily involved singing rather than speaking, Applegate modeled his phonetic pronunciation guide to Samala on Harrington's recordings of a Šmuwič (Barbareño) Chumash woman named Mary Yee, the last fluent first-language speaker of any Chumash language who died in 1965.[7] After completing this dissertation project, Applegate published a handful of articles on Samala and other Chumash languages documented by Harrington and moved on to new projects, never thinking that his graduate research would be of interest to the descendants of the people who spoke the language he studied.[8]

More than thirty years later, however, Applegate was presented with an opportunity to shepherd that language back to the community from which it came when leaders of the Santa Ynez Chumash sought to revitalize Samala in the early 2000s and turned to him as an expert and knowledge bearer.[9] Over the next several years, Applegate collaborated with tribal members to create a comprehensive dictionary and pronunciation guide featuring photographs of the community and their ancestors. Soon after the *Samala–English*

Dictionary was published in 2007, the tribe continued their collaborations with Applegate to develop an apprentice program for learners and aspiring teachers of Samala.[10] They also successfully advocated for the passage of California Assembly Bill 544, a law that allows teachers to be credentialed to teach Native languages in public schools so that they can work with children during the school day and use the very same educational systems that were once responsible for taking their language away to advance their cultural reclamation.[11] As former vice chairman of the tribe Richard Gomez noted in 2012, "Samala was and is not lost. Instead, it's making a comeback through a multi-pronged cultural and educational program of the Santa Ynez Band of Chumash Indians. Today tribal members are speaking and singing in Samala, and we've only just begun."[12]

It was not long after the publication of the *Samala–English Dictionary* and the development of the corresponding educational program that Samala would make its debut on a professional stage—not in a play by a Chumash storyteller but in a new multilingual adaptation of Shakespeare's *The Winter's Tale* by Chicano playwright José Cruz González. Commissioned by Artistic Director Mark Booher of the Pacific Coast Repertory (PCPA), whose theater is situated on the ancestral lands of the Chumash Peoples, González's *Invierno* was developed in consultation with Santa Ynez Chumash cultural director Nakia Zavalla along with Richard Applegate himself, who helped González, Booher, and members of the cast to incorporate Samala and various elements of Chumash culture into the production. Through these shared efforts, they demonstrated the power of the central belief animating Shakespeare's late tragicomic romance: that what is thought to have been lost can be found again.

Just as we saw with Randy Reinholz's strategic embrace of the ambivalent qualities of *Measure for Measure* to highlight the contours of Native survivance in the previous chapter, González's *Invierno* mobilizes the generic hybridity and temporal instability of *The Winter's Tale* to participate in the creation of what Chicana historian Emma Pérez theorizes as a "decolonial imaginary"—"a rupturing space, the alternative to that which is written in history."[13] González activates this rupturing space by constructing a new dramatic frame in which a pair of contemporary characters fall back into the world of the nineteenth-century land-grant rancho system in California and bear witness to the political and personal conflicts of the colonial past that have shaped their present. *Invierno* thus invites audiences into a space of temporal suspension and connection, or what Pérez characterizes as "that time lag between the colonial and postcolonial, that interstitial space where differential politics and social dilemmas are negotiated."[14] It is here, in the liminality between the no longer and the not yet, between tragedy and comedy, that *Invierno* draws upon *The Winter's Tale*'s own ideas about resilience, revitalization, and repair to encourage us to listen for the gaps and silences that "interrupt the linear model of time" and point toward ways of knowing and being that can bring about the futures colonization attempted to foreclose.[15]

TINY CRACKS, SMALL OPENINGS

When the Samala language apprentices began working with children in their community, they noticed that tribal elders started to feel more comfortable speaking up and sharing what they knew about the language but had repressed during their time in Indian boarding schools and in California public schools.[16] This newfound comfort prompted one elder to step forward during the tribe's annual Chumash Culture Day and share a lullaby. "We were all in tears," recalls Nakia Zavalla, "because it was the first time we've ever heard a song like that before."[17] Such embodied evidence of linguistic survival through a deep intergenerational connection between mothers and their babies confirmed for Zavalla, a woman who traces her lineage six generations back to María Solares, that Samala "was never put to rest. It lies within us. It's part of us."[18]

Given the tenderness and intimacy of this moment for the Santa Ynez Chumash community, it is especially meaningful that the first thing the audience hears from offstage in Invierno's Prelude is a Samala lullaby sung by Paulina, a Chumash healer woman who functions as a storyteller, a bridge between past and present, and a voice of Indigenous resistance and protection throughout the play:

> We' we' kice' (Sleep, sleep little one)
> Ksuyuwanin (I love you)
> Ma k'ayapis i pi' (You are my heart)
> We'n a čʰoho (Sleep well)
> We' we' kice' (Sleep, sleep little one)
> Ksuyuwanin (I love you)
> Ma k'ayapis i pi' (You are my heart)
> We'n a čʰoho (Sleep well)[19]

Shortly after singing this song, Paulina comes upon a contemporary young couple in a state of crisis standing before an oak tree on a sacred site. "Carved into the tree," the stage directions indicate, "is the shape of a woman" who we will later learn is Hermonia, the half-sister of Paulina (171). She died of grief after her husband Don León accused her of having an affair with his friend Don Patricio, banished their newborn infant Alegría, and thus caused the grief-stricken death of their son Maximino. The Young Woman, a Latina teenager named Aly who has discovered that she is pregnant, attempts to hang herself on this tree but is stopped by the Young Man, a light-skinned teenager named A.J. who struggles to process the news that his girlfriend has apparently "been with somebody else" (172). Just when the Young Man starts to strike the tree with a knife in anger, Paulina appears, identifying herself as "Wind Woman," first in Samala, then in English. As she invites the distressed teens to join her on a journey back in time so that they can learn from the traumas that transpired on this land in order to begin healing themselves and changing their collective future, she welcomes them and the audience into a space ungoverned by a linear sense of time: "Sometimes," Paulina says, "there are tiny cracks, small openings, allowing the past to live differently in the present and the present to become truthful because of the past, joining us together in ways we never thought possible" (174). In recasting Paulina as the embodiment of the Samala language and its enduring survival, *Invierno* activates the decolonial imaginary that Pérez describes, rupturing colonial timelines, worldviews, and stories to create space to live and think otherwise.

When the Young Woman and Young Man enter the world of the nineteenth-century California ranchos approximately sixteen years prior to the U.S. war against Mexico that would end with the Mexican cession of over half of its territory, including Alta California, to the United States, they find that the conflicts around issues of land, language, race, and reproduction unfolding before them resonate in unexpected and sometimes uncomfortable ways with their contemporary situation. They are quickly disabused of their assumption that they will be mere observers to the past, moreover, when Don León Cervantes Mejía, a prominent Californio and el gran don del Rancho Las Mariposas, picks the Young Woman up and places her in a wheelchair, casting her in the role of his son Maximino. Just as Leontes does in his conversation with Mamillius in *The Winter's Tale*, Don León asks Maximino to affirm that he is indeed his son, but the question becomes even more fraught with racial tension in the colonial context of nineteenth-century California and in light of the Young Woman's own pregnancy. As a pregnant Hermonia enters with Don Patricio, an Irishman and close childhood friend of Don León who runs the Rancho Los Molinos, Don León asserts the importance of continuing the colonizer bloodline through his son, declaring, "You are my blood. De sangre de conquistadores. A proud lineage going back to Spain!" (178).[20] But his bombastic paternal self-assurance quickly descends into colonial paranoia as he suspects, erroneously, that Hermonia is pregnant with his best friend's child.

Indeed, Don León's suspicions about Hermonia's fidelity and the paternity of his children are bound up with his tenuous claims to the land as the beneficiary of the land-grant system that began with the Spanish crown and continued with the Mexican government after independence from Spain. Don León first expresses his concerns about faithfulness in racial and linguistic terms when he laments that the mestizos—that is, people of mixed Indigenous and Spanish heritage—come to work on his rancho without sufficient knowledge of the Spanish language, thereby limiting his ability to surveil and impose demands on them. "How do I even know they're faithful to me?" he worries, foretelling the ways in which he will also come to question whether or not his mestiza wife has been faithful to him (179). When Hermonia attempts to allay his concerns by assuring him that the mestizos of which he speaks are "of [her] blood" (179), we begin to see how Don León's paranoia is that of a colonizer who feels entitled to but ultimately insecure about his control over the land and those who labor on it.

As she is in Shakespeare's play, Paulina is a fierce defender of Hermonia's honor in González's reimagining, but the dynamic between the two women is complicated by the colonial politics that have shaped their kinship ties. While they share a Chumash mother, Paulina reveals in a tense exchange immediately after Hermonia gives birth that Hermonia's own birth was the result of rape, an act committed by her Spanish conquistador father who murdered their mother's first husband (Figure 2.1). In Paulina's view, Hermonia has perpetuated the erasure of their people by marrying Don León:

PAULINA: You abandoned your people and your family for him.
HERMONIA: I'm tired.
PAULINA: Look how these Spaniards treat us! They're burying us alive!
HERMONIA: Enough, I will not be buried nor will my children be!
PAULINA: Then they will become just like him!
HERMONIA: No, I'll teach them what's important.
PAULINA: And what's that?
HERMONIA: That we survive! The old ways are broken. The pieces that remain are what we are.
PAULINA: No!
HERMONIA: It's true. We are connected by blood or love. You cling to the past, but I look toward the future!

(204–5)

Figure 2.1 Catalina Maynard as Paulina and Leah Dutchin Okada as Hermonia in *Invierno*, dir. Mark Booher, Pacific Conservatory Theatre (PCPA), 2010. Photo by Luis Escobar, Reflections Photography Studio. Copyright © 2010 PCPA.

From Hermonia's perspective, a future under colonialism means leaving the past behind in order to preserve the "pieces that remain" and pass "what's important" on to the next generation. But for Paulina, to live under colonial rule is to experience a slow death. Reproduction that involves intermarriage with colonizers is, to her, an insufficient, if not counterproductive, approach to sustaining Chumash life. Survival is not possible, Paulina maintains, without "the old ways" of knowing, being, and doing that have long sustained their ancestors on this land. In the colonial contexts of California, the concerns about fidelity and futurity that drive the plot of *The Winter's Tale* have much deeper roots and far higher stakes.

As the Young Woman and Young Man bear witness to the tragic events of the past, they resist making direct connections to their own lives despite the resonances that become increasingly apparent as *Invierno*'s first act reaches its tragic peak. Like that of Hermonia and Don León, their relationship has been poisoned by fears of infidelity heightened by a pregnancy. They, too, find themselves at an impasse, unable to communicate or trust in a moment of crisis. But what the events of the past ultimately bring to the surface is a deeper truth about the intergenerational impacts of trauma. Such legacies manifest most clearly in Hermonia's decision to give her baby the name Alegría after Paulina insists, in a departure from Shakespeare's version of the story, that the infant "must have one" (208). What is initially an act of hope that Hermonia's "joyful little one" will be the thing that brings her family back together, however, becomes a poignant marker of loss when her happiness—her Alegría—is quite literally stripped from her (208).

As Aly's name takes on new, or perhaps old, meaning in light of these revelations about the tragic past, she recognizes that she has a clear purpose to reclaim her own joy while looking toward a future that has not yet been written. This realization crystalizes when she serves as both witness and interlocutor in González's reimagining of Antigonus's "dream" encounter with the spirit of Hermione. In Shakespeare's play, Antigonus reports that, while he was traveling from Sicilia to Bohemia to carry out Leontes's orders to abandon his infant daughter in "some remote and desert place" (2.3.174), Hermione's ghost came to him in a dream and insisted that he name the child Perdita, "for the babe / Is counted lost forever" (3.3.31–2).[21] In González's version, by contrast, the appearance of Hermonia is not merely reported but staged, and Aly finds herself unexpectedly on the receiving end of the message clearly meant for Alejandro after he has been tasked with bringing the infant Alegría northward to Los Molinos, the location of Don Patricio's rancho:

> HERMONIA: Fate has chosen you.
> YOUNG WOMAN: Me?
> HERMONIA: My sweet Alegría is lost forever.
> YOUNG WOMAN: No.
> HERMONIA: Never will you know love.
> YOUNG WOMAN: That's not true!
> HERMONIA: Never will you see tomorrow.
> YOUNG WOMAN: The future's not decided!
>
> (224–5)

While she may not initially be the intended audience for these words, Aly needs to hear them in order to find the strength to break intergenerational cycles of trauma and to reject the idea of a future defined only by loss.[22] Like his Shakespearean counterpart, Alejandro meets his untimely exit, pursued by a bear—in this case when the sacred oak tree undergoes an ursine transformation. Within the multifaceted timeline of *Invierno*, however, the infant for whom Alejandro sacrifices his life is taken up into the protective arms of Aly, whose cross-temporal presence ushers in the play's shift from a tragic register to a comic one in which accountability and healing become possible. By emphasizing this maternal lineage across generations, González subtly but powerfully shows that the personification of Father Time that Shakespeare brings on stage between the two parts of *The Winter's Tale* is not the bridge these characters need to heal.

COLONIAL PASTS, UNDECIDED FUTURES

The shift in genre becomes apparent at the outset of *Invierno*'s second act, which opens with Aly still holding baby Alegría, singing a lullaby in English, and wearing the seashell necklace that Hermonia had placed on the infant before Don León ordered her to be sent away. For Paulina, the transfer of this object from Alegría to Aly represents the merging of temporalities that she sees as necessary for healing to occur: "It's happening," she declares. "We move forward. The past and the present become one" (228). Within the fiction of the play, we are told that this necklace was made by Paulina and Hermonia's grandfather (K-iš-popoč') when Hermonia was born. In the realm of the play's twenty-first-century production, however, this necklace was, in fact, loaned to the theater company by the Samala Chumash, reflecting the continuation of their coastal lifeways and lending an even deeper resonance to Paulina's line about the past and the present moving together toward future healing. But before the past and the present can become one, Aly must confront loss head-on and step into the role of Perdida, the teenage version of the abandoned infant who was raised by Vaquero, a sheepherding cowboy who cared for the "little lost one" upon discovering her after Alejandro's demise (228).

As the nineteenth-century plot of *Invierno* leaps sixteen years forward and A.J. is thrust into the role of Florentino, the teenage son of Don Patricio who falls in love with Perdida, González retains the famous "gap of time" that transpires between the third and fourth acts of *The Winter's Tale*. In this context, however, the temporal jump also maps onto a deeply consequential rupture in the politics of Alta California. The United States has officially declared war against Mexico, and a small group of Euro-American settlers "illegally" present in the region have mounted a revolt against Mexican authorities (246). "California is under attack," a frantic Californio lancer informs the young couple. "American immigrants called the

Bear Flaggers are marching against our homeland" (234). Named after their makeshift flag featuring the image of a grizzly bear and lone red star, the Bear Flaggers took inspiration from the Republic of Texas and aimed to seize Mexican territory in order to establish their own republic rather than becoming citizens of Mexico. In the context of González's multitemporal reimagining of *The Winter's Tale*, the violence represented by the bear flag not only resonates with the gruesome death of Alejandro at the end of act one, but it also reflects the fact that a greater ursine threat continues to loom over the land. Although the flag of the California Republic was replaced by the American stars and stripes when the U.S. Army invaded and occupied the territory soon after the Bear Flag incident, a version of this symbol of settler violence currently flies over the land today thanks to the Native Sons of the Golden West, an anti-immigrant, white supremacist organization who resurrected the rebel bear flag as their marching banner and lobbied for the California legislature to adopt it as the state's official flag in 1911.[23]

By the time the play reaches its conclusion, the war has ended and "Los Americanos" have won, seizing half of Mexico's territory and creating an uncertain future for those living in Alta California as a result. News of the 1848 Treaty of Guadalupe Hidalgo, which redefined the border between the two countries at the war's conclusion, is delivered rather comedically by Afilado, the play's Autolycus figure, who has assumed the identity of the notorious bandido and folk hero Joaquín Murrieta as he repeatedly steals from Vaquero throughout the comic subplot.[24] "They've taken half of México's land, including California," he reports. "They made out like bandits" (277).[25] As they discuss the treaty's provision to make them citizens of the United States, Afilado predicts the linguistic consequences of this new reality: "Better learn English," he advises, anticipating the ways in which Spanish would eventually shift from a colonial language with political power in California to one that has been subordinated to English and stigmatized as foreign and not white (278).²⁶ While the first California state constitution was printed in both English and Spanish and guaranteed Spanish translations of all laws, decrees, regulations, and provisions, it was rewritten just three decades later to include an amendment that required all governmental proceedings and communications to be conducted only in English. As Rosina Lozano explains in her book *An American Language: The History of Spanish in the United States*, "the decline of translations follows a larger historical trajectory that redefined what it meant to be American and who should be excluded."²⁷ By putting this dialogue about property, citizenship, and language in the mouths of the play's most comedic characters, González creates a poignant moment of levity around another heavy truth about the layers of colonization that have shaped California and the Southwest more broadly.

For one particular character, however, the U.S. invasion of Mexico and the resulting changes coincide with another type of shift—a shift toward atonement for past actions and beliefs. At the start of the play, Don León embraces a worldview that is governed by what Pérez terms—in contradistinction to the decolonial imaginary—the colonial imaginary.²⁸ Like Aly, he sees the future as undecided but for an entirely different reason. In his mind, it is full of endless financial opportunity and potential profit to be extracted from the land and its people: "The future is unwritten," he tells his counselor Caspian. "This land is abundant. Riches we can't even imagine. All you have to do is seize it, and it is yours. It takes vision, and the will to act upon it" (191–2). But as Don León atones for his actions against his wife and children in the years that pass between the play's first and second acts, he starts to see just how fragile and destructive such claims to the land and the future really were. While other Californios are horrified by the potential loss of their land as the invasion escalates, Don León poignantly admits, "It was never truly mine. My grandfather was deeded this grant by the Spanish crown. And that piece of paper determined the fate of thousands. Now, I am witness to the destruction that has come to this place and its people" (269–70). As he loses his desire and his capacity to own both property and persons, he begins to own his actions instead, taking responsibility for the harm that he and his ancestors have caused.

When Aly and A.J.—both as themselves and in their roles as Perdida and Florentino—seek refuge from the war at Rancho Las Mariposas, they find a penitent Don León, who has spent the last sixteen years praying for forgiveness at a shrine of his own creation: the tree carving of Hermonia that we saw in the Prelude (Figure 2.2). Rooted in the same earth where Maximino and Hermonia are buried, this carving is materially and ontologically different from the statue that Paulina reveals to Leontes and Perdita at the end of Shakespeare's play. Whereas the lifelike rendering of Hermione is reported to have been made "by that rare Italian master Giulio Romano" (5.2.94–5), it is Don León who "spent years carving the very likeness of [Hermonia] into this grand tree" (279). Just like Hermonia and her children, this creation is of the sacred land of the Chumash Peoples, and it is blessed by Paulina in Samala, but it is only when Don León addresses 'Eneq a saxtak^{h}it (Wind Woman) in her language and truly acknowledges the consequences of his attempts to control the land and its inhabitants that the wind begins to stir his carving to life.

Figure 2.2 The sacred tree in *Invierno*, dir. Mark Booher. Scenic design by Tim Hogan. Pacific Conservatory Theatre (PCPA), 2010. Photo by Luis Escobar, Reflections Photography Studio. Copyright © 2010 PCPA.

For Shakespeare scholars, the parallel moment of miraculous reanimation in *The Winter's Tale* has prompted many questions. Is it actually a statue or Hermione pretending to be a statue? If it is a statue, does it come to life through some kind of magical forces? Or is this all an elaborate theatrical spectacle orchestrated by Paulina in order to reawaken Leontes's faith and bring about reunion and forgiveness?[29] By reimagining the statue as the product of Don León's penance, González eliminates the ambiguity around its creation while retaining a sense of spiritual wonder as Hermonia lives and breathes once more. It is crucially not Don León alone who brings about Hermonia's reanimation, however. As the wind moves through the tree following the Samala blessing of the Wind Woman herself, Paulina and Aly begin to sing their respective lullabies in Samala and English, prompting Hermonia to join them in Spanish. Together, they form a chorus of women across languages, cultures, and generations that becomes symbolic of the reunion between Samala and its speakers and the reawakening of a language that was not, in fact, lost forever.

In the process of facilitating the reunion within the nineteenth-century plotline, Aly and A.J. also undergo their own healing journeys throughout the course of *Invierno*'s second act. Following her realization that she has more control over the future than she had imagined, Aly is finally able to confide in A.J. and reveal that her pregnancy was not the result of a consensual sexual relationship but rather an outcome of the abuse she has suffered at the hands of her uncle. Her joy—her own sense of self—has been stolen from her, too. As they work through the implications of this revelation for their relationship, the young couple turns to Shakespeare's *Romeo and Juliet* as a point of reference, but they reject the predetermined tragic ending implicit in the act of comparing themselves to teenage lovers whose deaths were brought about by the world around them:

YOUNG MAN: Look, I'm no Romeo—
YOUNG WOMAN: Stop.
YOUNG MAN: —but you're my Juliet.

> YOUNG WOMAN: That's so corny.
> YOUNG MAN: I know, it's stupid.
> YOUNG WOMAN: Their story ends badly.
> YOUNG MAN: Yeah, well, ours won't.
> YOUNG WOMAN: What makes you so sure?
> YOUNG MAN: 'Cause when I'm with you I don't feel so hopeless.
>
> (252–3)

As they reach for a European tale from the past most closely associated with Shakespeare to explain their present, Aly and A.J. find that this canonical story of teenage love and death ultimately fails to capture the tragicomic nature of their narrative and their newfound hope about what remains unwritten. "I don't know about the future," Aly declares in the Epilogue, "but I'm going to walk through it knowing I can" (283). Accepting A.J.'s offer to keep her company on this journey, she looks down at the seashell necklace still around her neck, and the oak tree where she found herself in a moment of crisis at the play's beginning "blooms with light" (283). This ending, which is not an ending so much as it is a continuation of the story unfolding on this land, suggests that the tragic ruptures of the past can illuminate the path toward a future governed by the enduring belief that what was once lost can indeed be found.

LIVING, BREATHING, THINKING

It is this same future-oriented belief that motivates Nakia Zavalla to continue the work of reawakening and reclaiming the Samala language. While she hopes for a day when her community can "bring it really back so that we are living it, breathing it, thinking it," Zavalla acknowledges that her dream for everyone to be speaking the language will not be realized in her own lifetime.[30] As master Samala apprentice and credentialed language teacher Kathleen Marshall explains, this sustained effort to return their language to its speakers is what they owe not only to future generations but also to the ancestors who did everything they could to survive, even if it meant having to let go of their language and culture:

> Learning language isn't just about learning words or a word list. It's actually in each and every one of us. It grows in us. It tells stories. It tells culture. It sings songs. It has taught us so much about where to gather, where our villages were, who was in those villages, and about our existence. Our language is the core of who we are, and my ancestors clearly didn't want it to happen this way, but it did. Culture and language did not become number one anymore. They had to survive, and they had to assimilate. And that's what they did. They did that to protect us. So now it's our job, now that we are in this stable place, now that we have support, it is our job to bring back this language. It is our job to bring back the culture. It is our job to help bring this back to our people.[31]

Not unlike the shepherd who finds the baby on the shores of Bohemia in *The Winter's Tale* or Vaquero who finds Alegría abandoned near Rancho Los Molinos in *Invierno*, Richard Applegate found Samala stowed away in boxes in a basement at UC Berkeley, and when called upon, he did everything he could with his training as a linguist to return the language back to its rightful inheritors. Thanks to María Solares and her contributions to Harrington's notes, Samala was never actually gone. "It was all sitting there waiting for us," says Zavalla.[32] In the years since the *Samala–English Dictionary* was published, members of the tribe have taken the reins, coining new words, expanding access to learners of all ages, and ensuring that their work is archived and recorded so that it can be taken up by future generations.

The open-ended nature of *Invierno*'s contemporary framing reminds us that one function of the decolonial imaginary is to create possibility that exceeds the limitations imposed by colonial narratives, histories, and worldviews. As Catherine E. Walsh argues, decoloniality "is not a static condition, an individual attribute, or a lineal point of arrival or enlightenment. Instead, decoloniality seeks to make visible, open up, and advance radically distinct perspectives and positionalities that displace Western rationality as the only framework and possibility of existence, analysis, and thought."[33] When mobilized toward such ends, embodied performance has the power to generate what Chela Sandoval, Arturo J. Aldama, and Peter J. García describe as "a pause in the activity of coloniality," creating space to reactivate Indigenous timelines and ways of living, breathing, and thinking.[34] By incorporating the Samala language and culture into his multitemporal reimagining of *The Winter's Tale*, González did far more than acknowledge the original inhabitants of the land on which his play was set and staged. He used Shakespeare's play about betrayal, loss, and rebirth to pry open the "tiny cracks, small openings" between the past and the present to tell a truthful story of resilience, hope, and liberation.

NOTES

1 For Applegate's account of his work on Samala, see Richard B. Applegate and Nakia Zavalla, "From Shore to Sea Lecture: Bringing Back the Chumash Language," Channel Islands National Park, April 8, 2010, YouTube video, 1:10:07, https://youtu.be/JAfGWamdLR4.

2. John P. Harrington to John P. Marr, January 22, 1941, emphasis original, National Museum of Natural History, National Anthropological Archives, https://sova.si.edu/record/naa.1976-95/ref16046.
3. For more on Harrington, see Jane MacLaren Walsh, *John Peabody Harrington: The Man and His California Indian Fieldnotes* (Ballena Press, 1976). See also "John P. Harrington and His Legacy," edited by Victor Golla, special issue, *Anthropological Linguistics* 33, no. 4 (1991).
4. The Spanish name Ineseño is derived from the Mission Santa Inés (sometimes spelled Ynez), which was established by Franciscan priests in 1804. For a study and compilation of some of the stories that Harrington recorded during his time with the Chumash Peoples, see Thomas C. Blackburn, *December's Child: A Book of Chumash Oral Narratives* (University of California Press, 1975). For a study of Chumash cultures and societies at the time of European contact, see Lynn H. Gamble, *The Chumash World at European Contact: Power, Trade, and Feasting Among Complex Hunter-Gatherers* (University of California Press, 2008).
5. Advocates for Indigenous California Language Survival (AICLS), "Samala Language Revitalization & Language Teacher Credentialing," Breath of Life 2021 Online Symposium, November 19, 2021, YouTube video, 1:28:14, https://www.youtube.com/watch?v=L0iZfJAsIe0.
6. Richard B. Applegate, "Ineseño Chumash Grammar" (PhD diss., UC Berkeley, 1972).
7. Harrington worked with several members of Yee's family, including her grandmother Luisa Ygnacio and her mother Lucrecia Garcia. For more on Harrington's multigenerational work with this family, as well as Yee's own documentation of Barbareño and her daughter Ernestine Ygnacio-De Soto's first-hand memories, see the documentary *6 Generations: A Chumash Family's History*, dir. Paul Goldstein, script by Ernestine De Soto and John R. Johnson (Santa Barbara Museum of History, 2011).
8. See, for instance, Richard B. Applegate, "Chumash Placenames," *The Journal of California Anthropology* 1, no. 2 (1974): 187–205 and Richard B. Applegate, "Chumash Narrative Folklore as Sociolinguistic Data," *The Journal of California Anthropology* 2, no. 2 (1975): 188–97.
9. For an overview of how the Santa Ynez Band of Chumash Indians revitalized their language in collaboration with Applegate, see Chumash Life, "A Linguistic Rebirth," December 4, 2014, YouTube video, 4:06,

https://www.youtube.com/watch?v=8k3uQzqI1lE. On the revitalization of Indigenous languages, see Serafín M. Coronel-Molina and Teresa L. McCarty, eds., *Indigenous Language Revitalization in the Americas* (Routledge, 2016) and Leanne Hinton, Leena Huss, and Gerald Roche, eds., *The Routledge Handbook of Language Revitalization* (Routledge, 2018).

10 Santa Ynez Band of Chumash Indians, *Samala–English Dictionary: A Guide to the Samala Language of the Ineseño Chumash People* (Santa Ynez Band of Chumash Indians, 2007).

11 For detailed information about the range of strategies and approaches used to develop language revitalization programs and to train teachers, see Leanne Hinton and Ken Hale, eds., *The Green Book of Language Revitalization in Practice* (Brill, 2001).

12 Richard Gomez, "Chumash Language Goes to the Next Stage," *Santa Ynez Valley News*, October 25, 2012, https://syvnews.com/news/opinion/commentary/chumash/chumash-language-goes-to-the-next-stage/article_46f9198e-1dbc-11e2-b46d-0019bb2963f4.html.

13 Emma Pérez, *The Decolonial Imaginary: Writing Chicanas into History* (Indiana University Press, 1999), 6.

14 Pérez, *The Decolonial Imaginary*, 6.

15 Pérez, *The Decolonial Imaginary*, 5.

16 For more information and resources about the Indian boarding school system, see Chapter 1 of this book. Several Chumash children were taken to the Sherman Institute in Riverside, California. For a history of the Sherman Institute, see Diana Meyers Behr, *The Students of Sherman Indian School: Education and Native Identity since 1892* (University of Oklahoma Press, 2014). For an account of one Chumash elder who attended, see Chumash Life, "Memories of Sherman School," YouTube video, 5:03, December 11, 2017, https://www.youtube.com/watch?v=lcOB6NufW-A.

17 Applegate and Zavalla, "From Shore to Sea Lecture."

18 Applegate and Zavalla, "From Shore to Sea Lecture."

19 José Cruz González, *Invierno*, in *The Bard in the Borderlands: An Anthology of Shakespeare Appropriations en La Frontera*, vol. 2, ed. Katherine Gillen, Adrianna M. Santos, and Kathryn Vomero Santos (ACMRS Press, 2024), 171. All subsequent references to page numbers in this edition will be cited within the text. English translations of Samala words and phrases are provided in parentheses throughout the script.

20. Don Patricio's name and Irish identity appear to be a reference to the San Patricios, a group of Irish and European immigrants who defected from the U.S. Army and fought on the side of the Mexico during the Mexican–American war. González's play about this military unit, titled *The San Patricios*, premiered at PCPA in 2014. On the history and legacy of the San Patricios, also known as the St. Patrick's Battalion, see Robert Ryal Miller, *Shamrock and Sword: The Saint Patrick's Battalion in the U.S.-Mexican War* (University of Oklahoma Press, 1989).
21. All quotations of *The Winter's Tale* are from William Shakespeare, *The Winter's Tale*, ed. John Pitcher, The Arden Shakespeare Third Series (Bloomsbury, 2010).
22. On the question of temporality and Antigonus's reported dream, see Lauren Robertson, "'Ne'er Was Dream so Like a Waking': The Temporality of Dreaming and the Depiction of Doubt in *The Winter's Tale*," *Shakespeare Studies* 44 (2016): 291–315.
23. On the racist history of California's state flag, see Aaron Brick, "'No Cause for Celebration': The White Supremacist Message of California's Bear Flag and Seal," *Southern California Quarterly* 105, no. 3 (2023): 243–77. On the Bear Flag incident and contemporary resistance to whitewashed Euro-American narratives in California, see L Heidenreich, *"This Land Was Mexican Once": Histories of Resistance from Northern California* (University of Texas Press, 2007), 75–92.
24. While biographical details remain sparse, Murrieta was the subject of many legends and came to be known as "the Robin Hood of the West." Cherokee author John Rollin Ridge's 1854 book *The Life and Adventures of Joaquín Murrieta: The Celebrated California Bandit* was the first novel published by a Native American.
25. For an overview of this history, see Richard Griswold del Castillo, *The Treaty of Guadalupe Hidalgo: A Legacy of Conflict* (University of Oklahoma Press, 1990).
26. For more on this trajectory, see Rosina Lozano, *An American Language: The History of Spanish in the United States* (University of California Press, 2018).
27. Lozano, *An American Language*, 66.
28. Pérez, *The Decolonial Imaginary*, 5.
29. For scholarly commentary on the statue's materiality and animation, see Jill Delsigne, "Hermetic Miracles in *The Winter's Tale*," in *Magical*

Transformations on the Early Modern English Stage, ed. Lisa Hopkins and Helen Ostovich (Routledge, 2014). See also Jennifer Waldron, "Of Stones and Stony Hearts: Desdemona, Hermione, and Post-Reformation Theater," in *The Indistinct Human in Renaissance Literature*, ed. Jean E. Feerick and Vin Nardizzi (Palgrave, 2012) and Kenneth Gross, *The Dream of the Moving Statue* (The Pennsylvania State University Press, 1992).

30 Kenny Chism and Allison Lewis-Towbes, hosts, "Nakia Zavalla (Extended)," *The Human Family Podcast*, March 3, 2021, podcast, 59:00.
31 Santa Ynez Chumash, "The Chumash People – A Living History," June 21, 2021, Vimeo video, 11:01, https://vimeo.com/565834077.
32 Chism and Lewis-Towbes, hosts, "Nakia Zavalla (Extended)."
33 Catherine E. Walsh, "The Decolonial For: Resurgences, Shifts, and Movements," in *On Decoloniality: Concepts, Analytics, Praxis*, ed. Walter D. Mignolo and Catherine E. Walsh (Duke University Press, 2018), 17.
34 Chela Sandoval, Arturo J. Aldama, and Peter J. García, "Toward a De-Colonial Performatics of the US Latina and Latino Borderlands," in *Performing the US Latina and Latino Borderlands*, ed. Arturo J. Aldama, Chela Sandoval, and Peter J. García (Indiana University Press, 2012), 3.

REFERENCES

Advocates for Indigenous California Language Survival (AICLS). "Samala Language Revitalization & Language Teacher Credentialing." November 19, 2021. YouTube video, 1:28:14. https://www.youtube.com/watch?v=L0iZfJAsIe0.

Applegate, Richard B. "Chumash Placenames." *The Journal of California Anthropology* 1, no. 2 (1974): 187–205.

Applegate, Richard B. "Chumash Narrative Folklore as Sociolinguistic Data." *The Journal of California Anthropology* 2, no. 2 (1975): 188–97.

Applegate, Richard B. "Ineseño Chumash Grammar." PhD diss., University of California, Berkeley, 1972.

Applegate, Richard B., and Nakia Zavalla. "From Shore to Sea Lecture: Bringing Back the Chumash Language." Channel Islands National Park. April 8, 2010. YouTube video, 1:10:07. https://www.youtube.com/watch?v=JAfGWamdLR4.

Behr, Diana Meyers. *The Students of Sherman Indian School: Education and Native Identity since 1892*. University of Oklahoma Press, 2014.

Blackburn, Thomas C. *December's Child: A Book of Chumash Oral Narratives*. University of California Press, 1975.

Brick, Aaron. "'No Cause for Celebration': The White Supremacist Message of California's Bear Flag and Seal." *Southern California Quarterly* 105, no. 3 (2023): 243–77.

Chism, Kenny, and Allison Lewis-Towbes, hosts. "Nakia Zavalla (Extended)." *The Human Family Podcast*, March 3, 2021. Podcast, 59:00. https://podcasts.apple.com/us/podcast/nakia-zavalla-extended/id1552939866.

Chumash Life. "A Linguistic Rebirth." December 4, 2014. YouTube video, 4:06. https://www.youtube.com/watch?v=8k3uQzqI1lE.

Chumash Life. "Memories of Sherman School." December 11, 2017. YouTube video, 5:03. https://www.youtube.com/watch?v=lcOB6NufW-A.

Coronel-Molina, Serafín M., and Teresa L. McCarty, eds. *Indigenous Language Revitalization in the Americas*. Routledge, 2016.

Delsigne, Jill. "Hermetic Miracles in *The Winter's Tale*." In *Magical Transformations on the Early Modern English Stage*, edited by Lisa Hopkins and Helen Ostovich. Routledge, 2014.

Gamble, Lynn H. *The Chumash World at European Contact: Power, Trade, and Feasting Among Complex Hunter-Gatherers*. University of California Press, 2008.

Goldstein, Paul, dir. *6 Generations: A Chumash Family's History*. Script by Ernestine De Soto and John R. Johnson. Santa Barbara Museum of History, 2011.

Golla, Victor, ed. "John P. Harrington and His Legacy." Special Issue. *Anthropological Linguistics* 33, no. 4 (1991).

González, José Cruz. Invierno. In *The Bard in the Borderlands: An Anthology of Shakespeare Appropriations en La Frontera*, vol. 2, edited by Katherine Gillen, Adrianna M. Santos, and Kathryn Vomero Santos. ACMRS Press, 2024.

Gomez, Richard. "Chumash Language Goes to the Next Stage." *Santa Ynez Valley News*, October 25, 2012. https://syvnews.com/news/opinion/commentary/chumash/chumash-language-goes-to-the-next-stage/article_46f9198e-1dbc-11e2-b46d-0019bb2963f4.html.

Griswold del Castillo, Richard. *The Treaty of Guadalupe Hidalgo: A Legacy of Conflict*. University of Oklahoma Press, 1990.

Gross, Kenneth. *The Dream of the Moving Statue*. The Pennsylvania State University Press, 1992.

Harrington, John P. John P. Harrington to John P. Marr, January 22, 1941. National Museum of Natural History. National Anthropological Archives. https://sova.si.edu/record/naa.1976-95/ref16046.

Heidenreich, L. *"This Land Was Mexican Once": Histories of Resistance from Northern California*. University of Texas Press, 2007.

Hinton, Leanne, and Ken Hale, eds. *The Green Book of Language Revitalization in Practice*. Brill, 2001.

Hinton, Leanne, Leena Huss, and Gerald Roche, eds. *The Routledge Handbook of Language Revitalization*. Routledge, 2018.

Lozano, Rosina. *An American Language: The History of Spanish in the United States*. University of California Press, 2018.

Miller, Robert Ryal. *Shamrock and Sword: The Saint Patrick's Battalion in the U.S.-Mexican War*. University of Oklahoma Press, 1989.

Pérez, Emma, *The Decolonial Imaginary: Writing Chicanas into History*. Indiana University Press, 1999.

Robertson, Lauren. "'Ne'er Was Dream So Like a Waking': The Temporality of Dreaming and the Depiction of Doubt in *The Winter's Tale*." *Shakespeare Studies* 44 (2016): 291–315.

Sandoval, Chela, Arturo J. Aldama, and Peter J. García. "Toward a De-Colonial Performatics of the US Latina and Latino Borderlands." In *Performing the US Latina and Latino Borderlands*, edited by Arturo J. Aldama, Chela Sandoval, and Peter J. García. Indiana University Press, 2012.

Santa Ynez Band of Chumash Indians. *Samala–English Dictionary: A Guide to the Samala Language of the Ineseño Chumash People*. Santa Ynez Band of Chumash Indians, 2007.

Santa Ynez Chumash. "The Chumash People – A Living History." June 21, 2021. Vimeo video, 11:01. https://vimeo.com/565834077.

Shakespeare, William. *The Winter's Tale*. Edited by John Pitcher. The Arden Shakespeare Third Series. Bloomsbury, 2010.

Waldron, Jennifer. "Of Stones and Stony Hearts: Desdemona, Hermione, and Post-Reformation Theater." In *The Indistinct Human in Renaissance Literature*, edited by Jean E. Feerick and Vin Nardizzi. Palgrave, 2012.

Walsh, Catherine E. "The Decolonial For: Resurgences, Shifts, and Movements." In *On Decoloniality: Concepts, Analytics, Praxis*, edited by Walter D. Mignolo and Catherine E. Walsh. Duke University Press, 2018.

Walsh, Jane MacLaren. *John Peabody Harrington: The Man and His California Indian Fieldnotes*. Ballena Press, 1976.

The Oppressor's Wrong
Three

"To be a Pocha or not to be."

Serving as both title and refrain, this unmistakable riff on Hamlet's famously introspective question pulses through a stirring poem by Iris De Anda, a Los Angeles-based writer and activist of Mexican and Salvadoran descent.[1] Rather than reproducing the Danish prince's interrogative mode of thinking, however, "To be a Pocha or not to be" redirects his iconic query toward a radical statement of being, or what Olga García Echeverría describes as an "anthem to Pocha reality."[2] To be a Pocha is to be "neither / from here nor there" and to "speak both languages / with a flair." To be a Pocha is to have "roots that extend / reaching out to faraway lands / faraway sands" beyond and beneath geopolitical borders. To be a Pocha is to cross those borders "every time [one] speak[s]."[3] To disparage or dismiss such lived experiences, De Anda's anthem declares, is to deny her existence altogether. To be a Pocha or not to be.

As scholars such as Luis Leal and Spencer Herrera have detailed in their work, the word "pocha/o/x" has a long and complicated history in North America.[4] Often deployed pejoratively, it is a term used to describe a person of Mexican descent who has been Americanized or assimilated into U.S. culture. The word came into popular use during the 1920s and 1930s following a surge of emigration from Mexico to

DOI: 10.4324/9781003292838-4

the United States in the wake of the Mexican Revolution. Writing in 1936, José Vasconcelos defined "pocho" as "[una] palabra que se usa en California para designar al descastado que reniega de lo mexicano aunque lo tiene en la sangre y procura ajustar todos sus actos al mimetismo de los amos actuales de la región" ["a word used in California to designate the ungrateful Mexican who denies his Mexican background although he carries it in his blood, and in his acts tries to ape the present masters of the region"].[5] By that point, the border had already crossed thousands of Mexican and Indigenous people living in the California region and what is now known as the Southwestern United States. The seismic geopolitical shift brought about by the signing of the Treaty of Guadalupe Hidalgo in 1848—in which Mexico was forced to cede more than half of its territory to the United States at the conclusion of the war between the two nations—not only created a rupture in the citizenship of the peoples living in that territory but, as we saw in Chapter 2, also led to the marginalization of their cultures and languages as white Anglo settlers moved in and laid claim to land north of the new border.[6] Indeed, the most distinctive marker of pochxs was, and continues to be, their vexed relationship to Spanish, manifesting either as "incorrect" Spanish, Spanglish, or little to no Spanish at all.

Self-proclaimed pocho poet Américo Paredes articulated his sense of linguistic insecurity in the prologue to his 1937 collection *Cantos de adolescencia* (*Songs of Youth*). Owing to his education in English and lack of access to books "en la lengua de Cervantes" during his childhood in Brownsville, Texas, Paredes lamented that he felt "más seguro de mí mismo en la lengua de Shakespeare que en la mía," or, "more comfortable with myself in the language of Shakespeare than in my own."[7] Beyond the familiar colonial conflation of English with "la lengua de Shakespeare" and Spanish with "la lengua de Cervantes," Paredes's description of linguistic ownership, (dis)comfort, and alienation speaks powerfully to the cultural dilemmas at the heart of pochx identity. For many Mexican Americans, particularly those living in the U.S.–Mexico Borderlands, the tension is bidirectional. As Ruben Espinosa notes, the experience of being "rendered inadequate on both sides" can create a sense of linguistic insecurity among Borderlands residents, leaving them suspended between two languages and not fully at home in either.[8]

This suspension and the linguistic hybridity it creates is precisely what Gloria E. Anzaldúa explores in her essential essay "How to Tame a Wild Tongue," where she rehearses the accusations so frequently directed at Mexican Americans: "Pocho, cultural traitor, you're speaking the oppressor's language by speaking English, you're ruining the Spanish language."[9] In this catalog of insults, we can see precisely how complicated it is to be caught in the middle of two colonial tongues. To speak English is to speak the language of the current oppressor, but to speak Spanish in ways that deviate from what is considered standard or correct is to "ruin" the language of an earlier oppressor. The emergence of a vibrant hybrid tongue in response to such pressures, Anzaldúa contends, is hardly surprising. When a people is forced to live at the intersection of two languages that cannot fully reflect who they are, who they were, and who they could be, "what recourse is left to them but to create their own language?"[10] The "living language" of pochxs is one "which they can connect their identity to, one capable of communicating the realities and values true to themselves—a language with terms that are neither *español ni inglés*, but both."[11]

In more recent decades, Mexican Americans have actively reclaimed the term "pocho/a/x," embracing its power as what Cruz Medina calls a "symbol for resistance against enduring rhetoric of cultural deficiency and colonial narratives."[12] One of the most full-throated statements of reclamation took the form of a manifesto published in the 1990 inaugural issue of *Pocho Magazine*, a publication created by Lalo Alcaraz and Esteban Zul.[13] Fueled by a "deep burning resentment of cultural imperialism from both sides of the imaginary border," Alcaraz and Zul declare: "We at *Pocho Magazine* accept Pocho as a term of empowerment for tacky, uncultured, fucked-up-Spanish-speaking Pochos everywhere."[14] To be a pochx according to this revised definition is to take pride in a linguistic identity that is rebellious and even playful in its unapologetic hybridity.

So, what's Hamlet to pochxs, or they to him?[15]

The answers to these questions are not immediately obvious. Perhaps more than any other character in any other play in the Western canon, Shakespeare's Hamlet has long been held up by critics as the "universal human"—the mirror in which we should all see ourselves reflected. As Ian Smith astutely notes, however, much of the commentary on the play has assumed and privileged a default but unspoken whiteness. The outsized prominence of *Hamlet* in Shakespearean scholarship, Smith argues, is emblematic of "the open secret of dominant white culture."[16] Indeed, while "we" are all expected to identify with Hamlet and his personal and political dilemmas, this supposedly "universal" play does little on its own to reflect the experiences of the marginalized and the subaltern.

But for the pochx poet-performers I discuss in this chapter, the Danish prince's inner-most musings are ripe for radical acts of decolonial resistance that use Hamlet's ontological questioning to reckon with the ongoing colonization, linguistic terrorism, and white supremacist racism that have shaped their existence en La Frontera. Embracing what Anzaldúa has theorized as a "mestiza consciousness" or a "consciousness of the Borderlands," these artists seize the dramatic, poetic, and rhetorical function of the soliloquy to perform selfhood as they explore the inner-most thoughts and struggles of a border subject who must develop a "tolerance for ambiguity" in the face of violent policies, pressures to assimilate, and intergenerational trauma.[17] A border Hamlet does not—cannot—choose between opposing sides but stands "on both shores at once" and "stradd[les] two or more cultures."[18] A border Hamlet dwells in the liminal space that Anzaldúa terms "nepantla," a Nahuatl word meaning "tierra entre medio," or the "land in-between."[19] A border Hamlet often does not have the luxury of querying whether or not to be but rather must constantly ask what it means to be someone whose existence is made vulnerable precisely because it exceeds the increasingly policed boundaries of nation, language, race, and gender. What happens when we follow this line of inquiry instead, directing our attention beyond the abstract "slings and arrows of outrageous fortune" (3.1.57) and shining a spotlight on "th'oppressor's wrong[s]" (3.1.70) that created the conditions for such harms to occur? *That* is the question of this chapter.

WHAT COUNTRY, FRIENDS, IS THIS?

Let us begin at an artificial point of origin: Border Field State Park, located on the ancestral and current homeland of the Kumeyaay/Kumiai Nation at the southwestern-most edge of the present-day U.S.–Mexico border that runs between the cities of Imperial Beach, California, and Tijuana, Baja California.[20] On this site sits Monument No. 258, a fourteen-foot marble obelisk erected atop a coastal mesa in 1851. Originally labeled Monument No. 1, this marker represents the "initial point" of the newly surveyed boundary that was redrawn with the signing of the Treaty of Guadalupe Hidalgo in 1848.[21] The half-acre immediately around the obelisk is presently known as Friendship Park, a location that First Lady Pat Nixon envisioned as a destination where friends and families could gather and greet each other across the international borderline when she dedicated Border Field State Park in 1971 (see Figure 3.1).

What was once a rare cross-border meeting place divided only by a few strings of barbed wire has been bisected in the decades since by various types of fencing and an increasingly fortified and surveilled border wall that currently extends

Figure 3.1 The monument marking the Initial Point of Boundary between the United States and Mexico. March 21, 1973. Photo by Joe Burkeholder for the National Park Service.

300 feet into the Pacific Ocean, making the monument both inaccessible and difficult to see from the U.S. side (see Figures 3.2 and 3.3). In recent years, the most physical contact that could possibly occur through the eighteen-foot steel slats and tight iron mesh constituting the wall at Friendship Park was the touching of fingertips known as "pinky kisses"—that is, only when the San Diego Border Patrol unit opened the gate to a twenty-foot secondary wall during a designated window of time on the weekends, allowing just ten people at a time into the so-called enforcement zone (see Figure 3.4). At the start of the COVID-19 pandemic in early 2020, Border Patrol shut down access to the U.S. side of Friendship Park indefinitely, leaving families and friends with no means of

Figure 3.2 The U.S. side of Friendship Park in 1987. From Peter Goin, *Tracing the Line: A Photographic Survey of the Mexican-American Border, 1985–1987*. Artist Limited Edition. 1987.

Figure 3.3 Friendship Park in 2014. Photo by Julio Blanco. Courtesy of the Friends of Friendship Park coalition.

Figure 3.4 Friendship Park as seen from behind the northern wall on the U.S. side on March 27, 2022. Photo by Kathryn Vomero Santos.

gathering together at the border. As of this writing in 2024—more than fifty years after Pat Nixon expressed her hope that "there won't be a fence too long here"[22]—construction has just been completed on two thirty-foot replacement walls, and it remains unclear whether or when the park will ever reopen (see Figure 3.5).

This fraught and ever-changing location, where the political visibly and violently interrupts the natural, is perhaps best known in Borderlands studies as the site on which Gloria Anzaldúa ruminates in the poem that opens the first chapter of her foundational 1987 text *Borderlands/La Frontera*. As her poem's speaker "stand[s] at the edge where earth touches ocean" at "Border Field Park" and watches the water attack the end of the chain-link fence that terminated on the beach

Figure 3.5 Friendship Park as seen from behind the newly constructed thirty-foot walls on the U.S. side on November 9, 2024. Photo by María Teresa Fernández.

at the time (see Figure 3.6), she presses her "hand to the steel curtain– / chainlink fence crowned with rolled barbed wire," mentally tracing its path "rippling from the sea where Tijuana touches San Diego / unrolling over mountains / and plains / and deserts" and eventually "turning into *el río Grande*," which "empt[ies] into the Gulf."[23] Constructed by the Immigration and Naturalization Service with congressional funding during the Carter administration between the years 1978 and 1979, this fence came to be known derisively in the U.S. media as the "Tortilla Curtain," as it represented a troubling escalation in border enforcement in the face of ongoing federal policy failures and a surge in undocumented immigration from Mexico in the second half of the twentieth century.[24]

Figure 3.6 The end of the chain-link border fence in 1987. From Peter Goin, *Tracing the Line: A Photographic Survey of the Mexican-American Border, 1985–1987*. Artist Limited Edition. 1987.

For Anzaldúa's speaker, the boundary that this "steel curtain" demarcates reflects a much longer and deeply personal history:

> 1,950 mile-long open wound
> dividing a *pueblo*, a culture,
> running down the length of my body,
> staking fence rods in my flesh
> splits me splits me
> *me raja me raja*[25]

As a queer Chicana who grew up in the Borderlands, she experiences the split marked by this fence, and the violence it represents, within herself, feeling the *herida abierta* of the border as an open wound in her body. "Borders," Anzaldúa goes on to write in the paragraph that immediately follows this poem, "are set up to define the places that are safe and unsafe, to distinguish us from them. A border is a dividing line, a narrow strip along a steep edge. A borderland is a vague and undetermined place created by the emotional residue of an unnatural boundary."[26]

Just one year after the publication of Anzaldúa's *Borderlands/La Frontera*, the decidedly "unnatural boundary" on the beach that inspired her book's opening poem would become the setting of another poetic text about the "emotional residue" produced by lines designed to divide: "El Border Hamlet" or "El Hamlet Fronterizo," a bilingual performance poem written and rewritten by Mexican/Chicano performance artist Guillermo Gómez-Peña beginning in 1988. In its most recent iteration, which was revised in 2010 and published in 2021, "El Hamlet Fronterizo" opens by situating its speaker both geographically and temporally in a very specific pose:

(Playas de Tijuana, 1988. Rewritten in 2010.)

The context

Border State Park;
Facing the formidable Pacific Ocean
w/one foot on each country
I talk to my other self
a dos voces interiores:

me ama/no me ama
me caso/no me caso
me canso/no me canso
chicano/mexicano
que soy o me imagino
regreso o continúo
me mato/no me mato
en Mexico/in Califas
to write or to perform
en Inglés or in Spanish...

I hate you; no, I forgive you,
no, I crave for you, mi loca
ansiosamente tuyo,
de nadie más
frontera mediante...
te espero, mi chuca,
te sigo esperando...
you are it, tu llanto,
tu make-up, tus cicatrices,
(*pause*)
no, you are definitely not it
you don't even exist yet[27]

It is perhaps not difficult to see why the fraught setting of this poem might prompt the kind of existential thinking we have come to associate with Hamlet. His "To be or not to be" soliloquy is, after all, a performance poem about straddling borders of many kinds, and it is a text that has been reanimated and repurposed on countless occasions to reflect internal conversations with the self about the nature of human existence and the unknowability of what comes after life. But what I find most haunting about the opening lines of the 2010 version of "El Hamlet Fronterizo" is that they, along with the time and place markers, were not always part of the poem. In fact, such contextual details were only added once it was no longer possible to stand with "one foot on each country," thus making the text that follows an ever-evolving meditation on what it means to be a border subject as this political and physical landscape has changed dramatically since Gómez-Peña first began to write the poem in 1988.

In the early 1990s, the chain-link fence that ended at the sea's edge was largely replaced with a ten-foot wall that started in the ocean and extended fourteen miles east. Built by the Army Corps of Engineers, this barrier was made up of steel pilings driven into the sand and corrugated steel landing pads recycled from Vietnam War–era aircraft carriers. In the case of the cross-border meeting place at Friendship Park, the chain-link fencing on either side of Monument No. 258 was replaced with panels of metal grate that allowed for what activist, pastor, and historian John Fanestil describes as "a clear line of sight and immediate physical contact for visitors," even as it reflected a hardening of the border.[28] While this border wall and the attendant security measures introduced by Border Patrol's Operation Gatekeeper program in 1994 were not successful in stopping migration, they did have several adverse effects in the region and beyond as they divided friends, families, and Indigenous nations from each other; disturbed sensitive ecosystems; and forced would-be crossers into remote, harsh, and fragile environments such as the Sonoran Desert, where many migrants perished.[29] As San Diego–based human rights advocate Pedro Rios explains, "Operation Gatekeeper introduced the modern era of deadly border enforcement measures, where migrant deaths were an expected and calculated outcome, intended to deter migration to the United States, but which only exacerbated human suffering."[30]

Attempts to build more border infrastructure and to further criminalize immigration only intensified in the following years. With the help of a rider attached to the Real ID Act of 2005 and the Secure Fence Act of 2006, the newly formed Department of Homeland Security was able to waive all federal, state, and local laws to seize land by eminent domain in order to build the secondary wall 150 feet north of the border. Although this secondary wall did not extend all the way into the ocean, Border Patrol enforced an imaginary line in the sand, preventing anyone from approaching the actual border on the U.S. side of the beach. Soon after construction on the new wall was completed in 2009, Customs and Border Protection closed access to the U.S. portion of Friendship Park altogether, and it was not until 2011 that, thanks to the tireless activism of a grassroots coalition called the Friends of Friendship Park, they agreed to open the "enforcement zone" between the walls to small groups of people during specific hours on the weekend.[31] The deliberate positioning of "El Hamlet Fronterizo" and its speaker on this specific site and in this now-impossible border-straddling pose in the 2010 revision, then, has the dual effect of inviting a contemplation of the increasingly hardened international boundary while also conjuring the time and place where Gómez-Peña began to develop what he describes as his "artistic sensibility as a deterritorialized Mexican American artist living a permanent border experience."[32]

Born in Mexico City, Gómez-Peña moved to California in 1978 at the age of twenty-five, thus beginning his self-described "irreversible process of Pocho-ization or de-Mexicanization."[33] In 1984, he co-founded the Border Art Workshop/Taller de Arte Fronterizo (BAW/TAF) with a binational, interracial group of artists and activists who, in the words of Coco Fusco, "claimed the border as an intellectual laboratory."[34] Beginning with exhibitions, installations, and site-specific performances such as the *Border Tableau* and *End of the Line*, both of which took place at the end of the chain-link fence on the same beach where Anzaldúa began to compose her influential poem in 1983, they collaboratively created a series of cultural interventions at the U.S.–Mexico border. As Ila Nicole Sheren notes, "BAW/TAF pioneered the use of performance art to comment on the international border," engaging in "an aesthetic occupation of space."[35] During the period when BAW/TAF was actively using the border fence on the beach as a site of performance and artistic commentary, Gómez-Peña and the U.S.-born artist Emily Hicks performed *The Border Wedding* at the end of the line in February 1988 (see Figure 3.7).[36] As the two exchanged vows through the border fence, their guests moved fluidly along the transnational strip of sand that surrounded it, crossing into each other's countries during the ceremony. For both the central couple and the participant-attendees, this border performance reflected the ways in which the location has long been, as Gómez-Peña himself once put it, "extremely charged with political, legal and cultural meaning."[37]

Figure 3.7 *The Border Wedding*. Guillermo Gómez-Peña and Emily Hicks. Border Field State Park/Playas de Tijuana. February 1988. Photo courtesy of Guillermo Gómez-Peña.

Following his work with the BAW/TAF, Gómez-Peña would go on to become the founder and artistic director of La Pocha Nostra, a collaborative and transdisciplinary arts organization based in San Francisco that develops "multi-centric narratives and large-scale performance projects from a border perspective."[38] In collaboration with members of La Pocha Nostra, and as a solo artist, Gómez-Peña has generated a series of performance practices and pieces that bring together spoken word, multilingual poetry, music, and interactive rituals in order to explore the many facets of his transborder identity. It is in these artistic, activist, and philosophical contexts that Gómez-Peña's border Hamlet character repeatedly enters the scene, becoming one among several personae that he assumes to reenact his recursive journey across the border, across languages, and across identities.[39]

While the 2010 revision of "El Hamlet Fronterizo" opens with the image of the speaker straddling the physical borderline on the beach at Border Field State Park, the lines that follow manifest the psychic experience of occupying that space at the level of form and grammar. By using a slash to separate a series of Spanish verbs from their negative opposite, the printed poem presents a Hamlet who is not just introspective but one who necessarily has "*dos voces interiores*" and who can talk to his "other self":[40]

```
me ama/no me ama
me caso/no me caso
me canso/no me canso
```

The palpable insecurity of this particular internal dialogue indicates, however, that these *dos voces interiores* are not always at one with each other. Although the first-person pronoun "me" remains constant in these lines, the subjects and objects of the verbs are slippery, shifting between first and third person, between non-reflexive and reflexive.

Take the line "me ama/no me ama," for example. Given Hamlet's focus on the inner self, we might be inclined to read or hear this line as a fittingly reflexive statement at first: "me amo/no me amo" ["I love myself/I don't love myself"]. But that's not what this border Hamlet says. The third-person agent of the verb is external to the "me" who receives the action: "me ama/no me ama" ["He loves me/He loves me not"]. Who is the "he" (or she, or they) here? Is it the other self? The feelings of love and its absence are importantly not experienced by a single self or expressed by a single voice but are instead fractured across two selves, dos voces, created and separated by the border. The verb of the second line, "casarse," is a reflexive one, but it is unclear to whom the speaker is getting married (or not) when he says "me caso/no me caso." Is this a reference to the border wedding performed on the same beach in 1988? Is the speaker attempting to marry the two selves that have been split by the border? The subtle addition of the letter "n" to "caso" to create "me canso/no me canso"—"I get tired/I don't get tired"—creates a visual and sonic link between the verbs, suggesting that the speaker is exhausted by repeated attempts to wed or reconcile the two interior voices.

The recurring slash between these verbs and their negatives reads a bit differently when it divides the speaker's identity in the next lines:

chicano/mexicano
que soy o me imagino
regreso o continúo
me mato/no me mato

What, the speaker seems to ask, is the appropriate term for someone who has moved to the United States but retains connections to Mexico? Can a "mexicano" become "chicano"? Does becoming "chicano" necessarily mean leaving the "mexicano" behind? Must he be one or the other? Is it possible to occupy the space between them? Or does the slash indicate a split—an irreconcilable border—between the two? These questions about who he is prompt an existential crisis: does the speaker really exist ("que soy") or does he imagine that he exists ("o me imagino")? Does he turn back to Mexico ("regreso") or continue ("continúo") on his journey North, in his "irreversible process of Pocho-ization"? The intensity of the dilemmas expressed by these successive pairs builds up to the line that most clearly echoes Hamlet's famous query about whether or not to be. Here, it is not the infinitive verb "ser" but the violently reflexive "matarse," or "to kill oneself," in the first person: "me mato/no me mato" ("I kill myself/I don't kill myself"). Although the pressures of crossing the border may prove too much to bear for the speaker, Hamlet's line of inquiry ultimately proves insufficient for capturing the complexity and vulnerability of straddling this particular international boundary, where the existential problem for the border subject is how to navigate such a treacherous environment without killing oneself or being killed by the agents, technologies, and laws that police the line.

As Gómez-Peña's speaker ponders his location "en Mexico/in Califas," the slash that we saw in earlier lines seems to mark the geopolitical boundary on the page, but the term "Califas"—the Chicano Caló name for California—signals that the histories of this region run far deeper than the border as it was redrawn in 1848. "Califas" was once part of Mexico, and it remains the homeland of several Indigenous nations, including the Kumeyaay/Kumiai, who have been divided by the current border that is so hostilely marked and policed on their land.[41] When the speaker ponders whether "to write or to perform" and whether to do so "en Inglés or in Spanish," he similarly blurs the line between languages by referring to Inglés en español and to Spanish in English while calling attention to the present and persistent hierarchy between these two colonial tongues and their users. As Gómez-Peña has noted of his own experiences crossing "the linguistic border," "the border crosser develops two or more voices. For the Mexican writers who come to the United States, this is a very frequent experience. We develop different speaking selves that speak for different aspects of our identity."[42] These different speaking selves are reflected in his border Hamlet poem, where the self is not merely divided but necessarily multiple and multilingual.

The capacity to move among several languages—including Spanish, English, Spanglish, Ingleñol, Gringoñol, Franglé, Robo-Esperanto, and fake Nahuatl—has been central to Gómez-Peña's artistic politics and practice. While his use of multiple and often hybrid tongues is an expression of what he calls the "transnational zones within [his] identity," it is also a reflection of his investment in "subverting English structures, infecting English with Spanish," and "finding new possibilities of expression within the English language that English speaking people don't have."[43] With his outsider's ear and tongue, Gómez-Peña is able to hear inside of English, to render it strange, and to create new meanings that a native monolingual speaker of the language could not. In his reflections on a conversation with Gómez-Peña, Latino philosopher Eduardo Mendieta regards this practice as an example of "linguistic rebellion" on the part of the subaltern:

> What happens when the language of the master has been appropriated by the subaltern, and the conquered, and turned into a tool to curse and slander the master? There is no language that is not contaminated by a history of conquest and inequity, but there is also no language that does not bear within its lexical and semantic sedimentations the traces of a memory of resistance and hope. Not even the master owns the language of conquest and control. Resistance to domination is partly enacted through linguistic rebellion. Linguistic incipience augurs dawns of consciousness.[44]

Mendieta's commentary, of course, calls to mind Caliban's powerful line about cursing the colonizer in the tongue that has been violently imposed upon him in *The Tempest*: "You taught me language, and my profit on't / Is I know how to curse" (1.2.364–5).[45] Indeed, as we saw in the Introduction and will see in Chapter 4, Caliban continues to serve as a powerful symbol of resistance to ongoing colonization among Caribbean, Latin American, and North American writers, many of whom find that speaking back in the colonizer's language is the only option they have. "¿Qué otra cosa puede hacer Calibán," asks Cuban author Roberto Fernández Retamar, "sino utilizar ese mismo idioma—hoy no tiene otro—para maldecirlo …?"[46] ["What else can Caliban do but use that same language—today he has no other—to curse him …?"].[47] Both in his performance and in his writing, Gómez-Peña undoubtedly channels the experiences and forms of resistance that Caliban has come to represent, but his repeated return to Hamlet offers a different kind of anticolonial answer to Shakespeare and to Anglo-American cultural hegemony as it is experienced on and across the border. To appropriate the language and persona of Hamlet—to speak back through this canonical figure of white European selfhood—is to force the white gaze out of its self-centered mode of introspection so that it must bear witness to the racist colonial harm that has been inflicted on people of color who are deemed expendable, exploitable, and not worthy of humanity.

Appropriating Hamlet at the border and for the border citizen also has the effect of turning the white gaze back on itself. A Hamlet fronterizo is poised to perform an act of what Gómez-Peña terms "reverse anthropology," a practice that centers the marginalized culture and "treat[s] the dominant culture as if it's exotic and unfamiliar."[48] It is thus no small coincidence that Hamlet also makes an appearance in La Pocha Nostra's El *Mexterminator Project*, a late-1990s interactive online performance series based on "an 'ethnographic questionnaire' asking Internet users to share their projections and preconceptions about Latinos and indigenous people."[49] The anonymous responses to this online survey were used to generate living performance dioramas featuring composite "ethno-cyborg" personae that reflected and refracted "the intercultural fantasies and nightmares of [their] audiences."[50] Among such personae was El Dr. Fritz Mangole, "a Chicano paleontologist" who "discovers the skull of an early Caucasian."[51] Holding what appears to be an animal skull before him just as Hamlet holds that of poor Yorick in the play's gravedigger scene, La Pocha Nostra member Roberto Sifuentes assumes a familiar pose in his performance of the paleontologist persona and his "discovery" (see Figure 3.8). This Hamlet, however, is not using the skull to contemplate the temporariness of life as Shakespeare's character does but to reverse the anthropological gaze and to challenge the racist ideas perpetuated by eighteenth- and nineteenth-century race scientists such as Johann Friedrich Blumenbach and Samuel George Morton, who (mis)measured human skulls to affirm beliefs about racial intellectual capacity.[52] Portraying the supposedly superior Caucasian skull as that of an animal, this performance photo of "El Dr. Fritz Mangole" exaggerates the supposed physiological differences between the "Chicano" and the "Caucasian" and uncomfortably literalizes the dehumanizing logics that have been used to justify colonialism, racism, and the violent demarcation of borders.

By inverting the cultural, racial, and linguistic hierarchies upheld by a play that occupies an outsized place of privilege in Anglo-American, and indeed global, culture, Gómez-Peña

Figure 3.8 Roberto Sifuentes as El Dr. Fritz Mangole in *El Mexterminator Project*. Photo by Eugenio Castro, 1999.

and his artistic collaborators in La Pocha Nostra do not simply offer their spin on *Hamlet*. They break this iconic text open to modes of performance that center Borderlands ontologies—ways of knowing and thinking about what it means to be outside the dominant white Western worldview, to be deemed "illegal" as a border crosser, to be illegible because you don't fit neatly into the rigid categories of race, gender, and language that have been established and policed without your humanity in mind. Indeed, it is fitting that "El Hamlet Fronterizo" ends with the speaker continuing to search for the other self at the border as he expresses hatred, forgiveness, and desire but ultimately concludes, "you don't even exist yet." The poem thus imagines forth a kind of borderless future in which that self can truly come into being. The most urgent question for el Hamlet fronterizo is not whether or not he should be but why it is that his very being—as an immigrant, as a border subject, as a human—is not treated with the dignity it deserves. He demands that his audiences join him in staring straight into the face of "th'oppressor" and begin to reckon with the wrongs they continue to commit.

SPLIT FOREVER INTO ONE

In much the same way that Gómez-Peña has adopted a "Hamlet fronterizo" persona to explore how the shifting politics and landscapes of the U.S.–Mexico border have shaped his identity and lived experiences from the 1970s to the present, Iris De Anda repurposed the prince's introspective inquiry to express her own internal dilemmas during a moment when the border came under intense scrutiny in the early decades of the twenty-first century. Her poem "To be a Pocha or not to be," which I introduced at the outset of this chapter, became part of a poetic movement that began after nine college students chained themselves to the doors of the Arizona State Capitol on April 20, 2010, in protest of Senate Bill 1070. Their aim was to urge Governor Jan Brewer to veto this blatantly anti-immigrant legislation, whose most controversial provision—Section 2(B)—would have required police officers to make an attempt to determine an individual's immigration status during routine traffic stops if they had "reasonable suspicion" to believe that the person in question was "an alien" who was "unlawfully present in the United States."[53] Because this "show me your papers" provision was intended to enable, if not mandate, racial profiling on the basis of skin color and language, many vocal opponents flagged it as a civil rights violation and rightfully feared that it would inspire copycat legislation in other states. In a press release with the headline "SB 1070: Arizona's Apartheid State is 'In Plain Sight,'" the student protestors made the symbolism of their action clear: "Today we are chained to the Capitol, just like our community is chained by this legislation."[54] When the students refused to leave, Capitol Police officers removed their chains with bolt cutters and promptly took them into custody.[55] Governor Brewer signed the bill into law three days later.[56]

Upon seeing the news of these students' brave action, Chicano poet and UC Davis professor Francisco X. Alarcón wrote a poem in both Spanish and English entitled "Para Los Nueve del Capitolio/For the Capitol Nine" and posted it to his own Facebook wall, inviting other poets to join him in responding. The response was so overwhelming that he soon formed a separate Facebook page, "Poets Responding to SB 1070," which received thousands of submissions, quickly becoming what Norma Elia Cantú has described as a "social media movimiento" in the years that followed.[57] Indeed, as Alarcón and Odilia Galván Rodríguez explain in their introduction to *Poetry of Resistance: Voices for Social Justice*—the 2016 anthology that documented the power of this multigenerational, multilingual poetic movement—the online community space "was created to encourage poets, writers, artists, activists, and the general public to respond to and keep informed about the challenges of this historically racist legislation."[58] It was, and continues to be, "an open forum where poetics and politics engage in exciting and groundbreaking new ways."[59] As Christopher Carmona observes, "Poets Responding to SB 1070" was part of a new wave of Chicanx poetry, "a new civil rights movement, and a new sense of the importance of the arts."[60]

Iris De Anda was among the contributors who shared her poetry in the wake of SB 1070, and she would go on to become one of the moderators of the page in the following years. Although "To be a Pocha or not to be" was neither the first nor the last poem she shared in this digital space, it was the one chosen for inclusion in the 2016 *Poetry of Resistance* anthology, and it has featured prominently throughout her artistic and activist work in Los Angeles in the years since she shared it with the "Poets Responding" community in 2011. In addition to publishing the poem in several places, including her own 2014 collection *Codeswitch: Fires from Mi Corazon*, De Anda has performed "To be a Pocha or not to be" in various public settings and, perhaps most notably, on the Hulu original television series *East Los High*, a teen "edutainment" drama designed to educate Latinx youth on issues related to mental, sexual, and reproductive health.[61] Her "anthem to Pocha reality," in other words, demonstrates the power of poetry to play a key role in movements for social change.

Like Gómez-Peña's "El Hamlet Fronterizo," De Anda's "To be a Pocha or not to be" begins by situating its speaker geographically:

> because I'm neither
> from here or there
> I speak both languages
> with a flair
> born in Los Angeles
> with roots that extend
> reaching out to faraway lands
> faraway sands, faraway from here

because I'm my father's daughter
drowning in alcohol
seeking the metaphysical
calling back in time
my family line
a forgotten leaf
on the familia's tree
to be a Pocha or not to be

because I'm my mother's daughter
drowning in depression
seeking a connection
recovering memories
of a tierra I never knew
a forgotten trace
of ancestors in me
to be a *pocha* or not to be

because I'm not good enough
for here or there
i love to hate my flag &
hate to love my creation
ashamed of spanish in the 1st grade
i'm sorry mami i never meant to hurt you
ashamed of english in abuela's embrace
i know you never meant to hurt me

because I'm merging culturas
every time I breathe
crossing borders
every time I speak
split forever into one
at the edge of two worlds

>   the edge of possibility
>   to be a Pocha or not to be
>
>   because I'm finding a balance
>   of this cosmic raza
>   a fusion of color
>   for this mestiza
>   things to learn
>   and things to teach
>   the little ones in front of me
>   to be a Pocha or not to be[62]

Within the first four lines, we can feel the tension inherent in the experience of living in one place while having cultural and familial connections to another. Even as the first line spills over into the second, and the second into the third, the word "neither" temporarily halts that enjambment, performing the very suspension it names. For De Anda's speaker, the notion of being "from" a place, especially a place like Los Angeles, cannot fully capture who she is and how she expresses herself through spoken word. With the repetition of "faraway" and the internal rhyme of "lands" and "sands," the stanza's final lines become the roots she invokes, extending far beyond and far deeper than the limits imposed by geopolitical boundaries.

As the poem's speaker follows these transnational roots in the next two stanzas, she articulates the sense of profound loss and sadness that such genealogical thinking can provoke. "Calling back in time," she feels herself "seeking a connection" to the various branches of her "familia's tree," but describes herself as "a forgotten leaf." Searching for the "forgotten trace of ancestors" in herself, she discovers both the power and the difficulty of "recovering memories / of a tierra [she] never knew." The speaker more closely resembles Shakespeare's "poor Ophelia / Divided from herself and her fair judgement" (4.5.84–5) as she realizes that she has inherited her parents' traumas and finds herself "drowning in alcohol" like her father and "drowning in depression" like her mother. But it is also here in the poem's second and third stanzas that she introduces and begins to repeat her refrain: "to be a Pocha or not to be." The seemingly simple insertion of "a Pocha" between the infinitive verb and its negative works to reframe Hamlet's question as a non-negotiable annunciation of being. By virtue of where she was born and when and to what parents, she is a pocha, or she does not exist.

Embracing her pocha identity has not always been easy, however. Echoing the poem's opening lines, De Anda's speaker explores the feelings of shame and anger she experienced as a child growing up between cultures in the fourth stanza. National and institutional pressures to assimilate create a rift within the speaker as a young girl, who is ashamed of her family's home language in school and her school language at home. Because she is suspended between "here" and "there" and feels "not good enough" for either, she finds it difficult to love and be loved across generations in ways that affirm who she is.

The suspension "at the edge of two worlds" that caused so much pain in her youth is precisely what situates her on what she refers to as "the edge of possibility" in the penultimate stanza. She comes to accept the multiplicity within herself—not as a sign of irreparable brokenness but as a way of understanding her whole being, her at-oneness with herself. Because she is "merging culturas" with every breath she takes and "crossing borders" with every word she speaks, she learns to celebrate the fact that she is not divided into two, but "split forever into one." As De Anda noted in a 2020 interview, she embraces the liminality of nepantla, embodying the "tierra entre medio" or "land in-between" that Anzaldúa describes: "I have always navigated cultures, tongues, borders," De Anda explains. "In the style of Anzaldúa, I live nepantla in my body every day, neither here nor there, not American enough, not Salvadoran enough, not Mexican enough, but always human enough."[63] As she does in her poem, De Anda redirects her feelings of not being "enough" for any single category by naming and claiming her full humanity outside those boundaries.

Indeed, as Anzaldúa writes, nepantleras—or those who dwell in nepantla—inhabit "states of mind that question old ideas and beliefs, acquire new perspectives, change worldviews, and shift from one world to another."[64] Hamlet may seem like an unlikely interlocutor for nepantleras, but what better way to question old ideas and beliefs than through the language of the character who has long been assumed to represent "the human condition"? By converting Hamlet's question into a declaration of being, De Anda not only changes the narrative about herself and other pochxs like her but also brings an entirely different worldview—a consciousness of the Borderlands—to Shakespeare's famous character and the white male concerns he has been made to reflect for centuries.

The final stanza of De Anda's poem is about learning to find balance "for this mestiza," learning to make ambiguity and liminality her home. De Anda's speaker makes it clear, however, that she seeks this balance not just within herself but for the next generation of young people whose identities will be forged at the intersection of different races, cultures, nations, and languages. Having come to terms with her family's intergenerational trauma and its effects on herself, she hopes to break the cycle of hurt. The last line returns to the refrain once more as an open invitation from the speaker to "the little ones in front of me" to join in her journey of ongoing self-understanding, healing, and celebration: "to be a Pocha or not to be."

THIS IS NOT JUST POETRY

In the four centuries since Hamlet's "To be or not to be" soliloquy was first composed and performed, it has become a site for working out existential and ontological questions of many kinds and in many different languages. In this regard, Guillermo Gómez-Peña and Iris De Anda are part of a long tradition of repurposing Hamlet and his iconic question for new political, cultural, and personal contexts. But even as they inscribe themselves into this hyper-canonical text, Gómez-Peña and De Anda radically reimagine Hamlet's interrogative, introspective soliloquy as an opportunity to pursue a decolonial line of inquiry that actively resists binary thinking, rejects strict lines of division, and embraces hybridity and liminality while also contending with the very real effects of border reinforcement in all of its forms.

For both of the poet-performers I have discussed in this chapter, artistic and activist work are not separate endeavors. How could they be? How could their art be anything but political when their very existence has been politicized in this country? As Gómez-Peña himself writes, the inherently activist dimensions of his art became immediately apparent upon his arrival to the United States: "I rapidly learned that to be a 'Mexican artist' in the United States meant—whether I liked it or not—being a member of a culture of resistance."[65]

For her part, De Anda rejects the notion that poetry is an end unto itself. In a poem titled "This is not *Just* Poetry," she reminds us:

> This is not *just* poetry
> it is justice screaming
> thru us in constant
> vowels & soliloquy
>
> [...]
>
> This is not *just* poetry
> it is life revealing itself
> thru spoken word
> this is the sound of urgency[66]

As a canonical poetic form of expression with roots in Roman rhetoric and enduring associations with Shakespearean drama, the soliloquy takes on a new and indeed urgent purpose in the Borderlands, where it is transformed from an individualistic genre into a more collective and political medium through which to call for justice in the face of ongoing oppression.[67] Poetry—particularly as it is spoken, performed, and screamed by those whose lives have been shaped by the physical and psychic realities of the U.S.–Mexico border—becomes a powerfully embodied act of resistance and hope. It is a cry to be heard. A cry to be seen. A cry to be.

NOTES

1 Throughout this chapter, I have privileged the self-identifying terms used by the artists, activists, and scholars whom I cite. When I am not referring to specific individuals or quotations, I use the gender-neutral -x ending for terms such as "Latinx," "Chicanx," and "pochx."

2 Olga García Echeverría, "Codeswitch: The Poetic Fuego of Iris De Anda," August 24, 2014, https://labloga.blogspot.com/2014/08/codeswitch-poetic-fuego-of-iris-de-anda.html. As I will discuss later in this chapter, "To be a Pocha or not to be" was first shared on the "Poets Responding to SB 1070" Facebook page and featured in the December 6, 2011 "On-Line Floricanto" of La Bloga, the "world's longest-established Chicana Chicano, Latina Latino literary blog." The poem would go on to be published in the Fall 2012 issue of LOUDmouth Zine produced by California State University, Los Angeles's Gender and Sexuality Resource Center. It was subsequently reprinted in De Anda's poetry collection Codeswitch: Fires from Mi Corazon (Los Writers Underground Press, 2014), 82–3 and in Poetry of Resistance: Voices for Social Justice, ed. Francisco X. Alarcón and Odilia Galván Rodríguez (University of Arizona Press, 2016), 46–7.

3 Iris De Anda, Codeswitch, 82–3.

4 Luis Leal, "Octavio Paz and the Chicano," Latin American Literary Review 5, no. 10 (1977): 115–23 and Spencer Herrera, "The Pocho Palimpsest in Early 20th Century Chicano Literature from Daniel Venegas to Américo Paredes," Confluencia 26, no. 1 (2010): 21–33.

5 José Vasconcelos, "Asoma el pochismo," in La tormenta, segunda parte de Ulises criollo (Ediciones Botas, 1936), 76. The English translation is quoted in Leal, "Octavio Paz and the Chicano," 115.

6 For a fuller history of the Mexican–American War and its legal aftermaths, see Richard Griswold del Castillo, The Treaty of Guadalupe Hidalgo: A Legacy of Conflict (University of Oklahoma Press, 1990). On the linguistic effects of this political shift, see Rosina Lozano, An American Language: The History of Spanish in the United States (University of California Press, 2018). For an analysis of ongoing coloniality of the border and the border region, see Roberto D. Hernández, Coloniality of the US/Mexico Border: Power, Violence, and the Decolonial Imperative (University of Arizona Press, 2018).

7 Américo Paredes, Cantos de adolescencia: Songs of Youth. (1932–1937), ed. and trans. B.V. Olguín and Omar Vásquez Barbosa (Arte Público Press, 2007), 3, 5. On Paredes's "pocho" poetry, see Herrera.

8 Ruben Espinosa, "Traversing the Temporal Borderlands of Shakespeare," New Literary History 52, no. 3/4 (2021): 617.

9 Gloria E. Anzaldúa, Borderlands/La Frontera: The New Mestiza, 5th ed. (Aunt Lute Books, 2022), 63. Anzaldúa goes on to define "pocho" as "an

anglicized Mexican or American of Mexican origin who speaks Spanish with an accent characteristic of North Americans and who distorts and reconstructs the language according to the influence of English" (64).

10 Anzaldúa, *Borderlands/La Frontera*, 63.

11 Anzaldúa, *Borderlands/La Frontera*, 63.

12 Cruz Medina, *Reclaiming Poch@ Pop: Examining the Rhetoric of Cultural Deficiency* (Palgrave, 2014), 7.

13 The legacy of the magazine lives on at pocho.com and the *Pocho Hour of Power* radio show on KPFK 90.7 FM Los Angeles.

14 Lalo Lopez and Steven Zul, *Pocho Magazine* 1 (1990), n.p. For more on *Pocho Magazine*, see Paloma Martínez-Cruz, "The Intimate Life of the Pocha: A Genealogy of the Self-Ironic Turn in Chican@ Culture," in *The Routledge Handbook of Latin American Culture*, ed. Carlos Manuel Salomon (Routledge, 2018), 347.

15 Here, I am repurposing another question posed by Hamlet when he wonders how an actor can connect emotionally with the plight of the Trojan queen Hecuba: "What's Hecuba to him, or he to her, / That he should weep for her?" (2.2.494–5). All quotations of *Hamlet* are from William Shakespeare, *Hamlet*, ed. Ann Thompson and Neil Taylor, The Arden Shakespeare Third Series, rev. ed. (Bloomsbury, 2016).

16 Ian Smith, "We Are Othello: Speaking of Race in Early Modern Studies," *Shakespeare Quarterly* 67, no. 1 (2016): 105.

17 Anzaldúa, *Borderlands/La Frontera*, 85–6.

18 Anzaldúa, *Borderlands/La Frontera*, 84–5.

19 Gloria E. Anzaldúa, "Preface: (Un)natural bridges, (Un)safe spaces," in *This Bridge We Call Home: Radical Visions for Transformation*, ed. Gloria E. Anzaldúa and AnaLouise Keating (Routledge, 2002), 1.

20 I borrow my subheading for this section from Shakespeare's *Twelfth Night*, when Viola washes up on the shore of Illyria after being shipwrecked and separated from her twin brother Sebastian (1.2.1). William Shakespeare, *Twelfth Night*, ed. Keir Elam, The Arden Shakespeare Third Series (Bloomsbury, 2014).

21 There are 276 of these markers or monuments along the border between the United States and Mexico. The full inscription on the west face of Monument No. 258/1 is in both English and Spanish and divided by a solid line. It reads, "Initial point of Boundary between the United States and Mexico. Established by the joint commission 10 October A.D.

1849 agreeable to the Treaty dated at the City of Guadalupe Hidalgo February 2 A.D. 1848. John B. Weller U.S. Commissioner Andrew B. Gray U.S. Surveyor." The Spanish text lists Pedro García Condea as Mexican commissioner and Jose Salazar Ylarregui as Mexican surveyor. On the two sides of the obelisk's base that face each country, the inscriptions respectively read: "BOUNDARY OF THE UNITED STATES" and "LÍMITE DE LA REPÚBLICA MEXICANA." After the inscriptions became illegible because of vandalism and wear and tear, the obelisk was renovated in 1894.

22 For footage of the 1971 dedication, see the documentary *Too Long Here*, directed by Emily Packer (Marginal Gap Films, 2020). During this event, First Lady Nixon also expressed the following wish: "May there never be a wall between these two great nations. Only friendship." For a detailed account of the shifting landscape, border security infrastructure, and community activism at Friendship Park, see Jill Holslin, "Friendship Park: Environmental Placemaking at the US-Mexico Border," in *The Nature of Hope: Grassroots Organizing, Environmental Justice, and Political Change*, ed. Char Miller and Jeff Crane (University Press of Colorado, 2018).

23 Anzaldúa, *Borderlands/La Frontera*, 16. Anzaldúa began to compose this poem when she visited the site in 1983. For an analysis of Anzaldúa's drafts and revisions of the text, see Marcel Brousseau, "Lines and Fences: Writing and Rewriting the California Fence/Wall," *Boom California*, December 14, 2017, https://boomcalifornia.org/2017/12/14/lines-and-fences/.

24 For a discussion of the construction of and response to the "Tortilla Curtain" within the larger history of boundary making and border conflict between the U.S. and Mexico, see Oscar J. Martinez, "Border Conflict, Border Fences, and the 'Tortilla Curtain' Incident of 1978–1979," *Journal of the Southwest* 50, no. 3 (2008): 263–78.

25 Anzaldúa, *Borderlands/La Frontera*, 16.

26 Anzaldúa, *Borderlands/La Frontera*, 17.

27 Guillermo Gómez-Peña, "El Hamlet Fronterizo: Weird Love Poem in Spanglish," in *Gómez-Peña Unplugged: Texts on Live Art, Social Practice and Imaginary Activism (2008–2020)*, ed. Emma Tramposch and Balitrónica Gómez (Routledge, 2021), 307. This poem has been reproduced with permission from Routledge. Earlier versions of Gómez-Peña's Hamlet

poem were published in *The New World Border: Prophecies, Poems and Loqueras for the End of the Century* (City Lights, 1996); *El Mexterminator: Antropología inversa de un performancero postmexicano* (Editorial Océano de México, 2002); and *Ethno-Techno: Writings on Performance, Activism, and Pedagogy*, ed. Elaine Peña (Routledge, 2005). An audio version was recorded for *Apocalypse Mañana: Opera Electrónica for the New Millennium* (Calaca Press, 2002). The rewriting and incorporating of this poem into various publications and performances is part of what Gómez-Peña describes as his "border-inspired strategy of recycling." *Gómez-Peña Unplugged*, 8. On his "living archive," see *Gómez-Peña Unplugged*, 7–9.

28 John Fanestil, "Performing the Border: Human Behavior at the US–Mexico Border – A Case Study of Friendship Park," unpublished manuscript, May 8, 2014, typescript, 14.

29 For a careful study of the link between U.S. immigration policies and migrant deaths, see Jason De León, *The Land of Open Graves: Living and Dying on the Migrant Trail* (University of California Press, 2015).

30 Quoted in "Operation Gatekeeper and the Birth of Border Militarization, Southern Border Community Coalition, accessed May 5, 2022, https://www.southernborder.org/operation_gatekeeper.

31 The primary wall was replaced with 18-foot steel bollards in 2012, and the part of the wall immediately around the monument was covered with heavy steel mesh. Small numbers of visitors were allowed to return to the "enforcement zone" in October of that year. Reconstruction and extension of the "Surf Fence" in the Pacific Ocean was also completed in 2012.

32 Guillermo Gómez-Peña, "The Multicultural Paradigm: An Open Letter to the National Arts Community," in *Negotiating Performance: Gender, Sexuality, and Theatricality in Latin/o America*, ed. Diana Taylor and Juan Villegas (Duke University Press, 1994), 18.

33 Guillermo Gómez-Peña, "On the Other Side of the Mexican Mirror," in *Ethno-Techno: Writings on Performance, Activism, and Pedagogy*, ed. Elaine Peña (Routledge, 2005), 6. Gómez-Peña has referred to this process elsewhere as his "Chicanization." Gómez-Peña, *The New World Border*, 14, 85.

34 Coco Fusco, "The Border Art Workshop/Taller de Arte Fronterizo: Interview with Guillermo Gómez-Peña and Emily Hicks," *Third Text* 3, no. 7 (2008): 53.

35 Ila Nicole Sheren, *Portable Borders: Performance Art and Politics on the U.S. Frontera since 1984* (University of Texas Press, 2015), 42.

36 Stacy Finz, "Arts Pair Makes Border Their Crossing to Bear," *Los Angeles Times*, March 11, 1988.
37 Quoted in Fusco, "The Border Art Workshop," 57.
38 Guillermo Gómez-Peña, "La Pocha Nostra," accessed June 29, 2021, https://www.guillermogomezpena.com/la-pocha-nostra/.
39 In the process of describing this recursive process of crossing, Gómez-Peña has referred to himself as a "border Sisyphus." *The New World Border*, i.
40 In some earlier versions, Gómez-Peña refers to this "other self" as "myself #2."
41 For an account of how the U.S.–Mexico border has affected Indigenous Peoples and their sovereignty, see Eileen M. Luna-Firebaugh, "The Border Crossed Us: Border Crossing Issues of the Indigenous Peoples of the Americas," *Wicazo Sa Review* 17, no. 1 (2002): 159–81. See also Christina Leza, *Divided Peoples: Policy, Activism, and Indigenous Identities on the U.S.-Mexico Border* (University of Arizona Press, 2019).
42 Quoted in Fusco, "The Border Art Workshop," 73.
43 Quoted in Fucso, "The Border Art Workshop," 74.
44 Eduardo Mendieta and Guillermo Gómez-Peña, "A Latino Philosopher Interviews a Chicano Performance Artist," *Nepantla: Views from the South* 2, no. 3 (2001): 542.
45 William Shakespeare, *The Tempest*, ed. Virginia Mason Vaughan and Alden T. Vaughan, The Arden Shakespeare Third Series (Bloomsbury, 2011).
46 Roberto Fernández Retamar, *Calibán. Apuntes sobre la cultura en nuestra América* (Editorial Diógenes, 1971), 30.
47 Roberto Fernández Retamar, "Caliban: Notes Toward a Discussion of Culture in Our America," trans. Lynn Garafola, David Arthur McMurray, and Roberto Márquez, *The Massachusetts Review* 15, no. 1/2 (1974): 24.
48 Quoted in Evantheia Schibsted, "Confessions of a Webback," *Wired*, January 1, 1997, https://www.wired.com/1997/01/ffpena/.
49 Guillermo Gómez-Peña, "Ethno-cyborgs and Genetically Engineered Mexicans," in *Dangerous Border Crossers: The Artist Talks Back* (Routledge, 2000), 46.
50 Gómez-Peña, "Ethno-cyborgs and Genetically Engineered Mexicans," 49.
51 Guillermo Gómez-Peña, "The New Global Culture: Somewhere between Corporate Multiculturalism and the Mainstream Bizarre (a Border Perspective)," *The Drama Review* 45, no. 1 (2001), 14.

52 Johann Friedrich Blumenbach, *De generis humani varietate nativa*, 3rd ed. (Göttingen: Vandenhoeck, 1795); Samuel George Morton, *Crania Americana, or, A Comparative View of the Skulls of Various Aboriginal Nations of North and South America* (Philadelphia: J. Dobson, 1839).

53 Arizona State Senate, Senate Bill 1070, 49th Legislature, 2nd Regular Session, April 23, 2010, https://www.azleg.gov/legtext/49leg/2r/bills/sb1070s.pdf.

54 "SB 1070: Arizona's Apartheid State is 'in Plain Sight,'" news release, April 20, 2010.

55 The charges against the students were eventually dropped.

56 Since becoming law in 2010, SB 1070 has been challenged in court several times. Although the U.S. Supreme Court struck down the majority of its provisions in 2012, two clauses in Provision 2, including the controversial Section 2(B), were upheld until the state agreed to enter into a settlement agreement with a coalition of civil rights organizations in 2016. At least one news outlet made the "2B or not 2B" pun at the time of the 2012 Supreme Court decision. See Kristen Hare, "Local Legislators, Immigration Advocates Say Nation Needs Comprehensive Reform," *St. Louis Beacon*, June 25, 2012, https://news.stlpublicradio.org/government-politics-issues/2012-06-25/local-legislators-immigration-advocates-say-nation-needs-comprehensive-reform.

57 Norma E. Cantú, "Banning of Ethnic Studies in the United States," *Oxford Research Encyclopedias*, February 28, 2020.

58 Francisco X. Alarcón and Odilia Galván Rodríguez, "Introduction," in *Poetry of Resistance: Voices for Social Justice*, ed. Francisco X. Alarcón and Odilia Galván Rodríguez (University of Arizona Press, 2016), xiii.

59 Alarcón and Galván Rodríguez, "Introduction," xiv.

60 Christopher Carmona, "The Chican@ Nueva Onda as a Poetic Tidal Wave: The Revitalization, Repoliticalization & Redefinition of 'Chican@' Through Poetry," *Diálogo* 17, no. 2 (2014): 49–50.

61 *East Los High*, season 2, episode 4, "The Queen of Ugly the King of Fools," directed by Carlos Portugal, aired July 9, 2014, on Hulu. *East Los High* was the first and thus far only Hulu show to have an all-Latinx cast, and the show's producers collaborated with public health organizations to educate Latinx youth on issues related to sexual and reproductive health. On the show's use of "edutainment" strategies, see Hua Wang and Arvind Singhal, "*East Los High*: Transmedia Edutainment to Promote

Sexual and Reproductive Health of Young Latina/o Americans," *American Journal of Public Health* 106 (2016): 1002–10.

62 Iris De Anda, "To be a Pocha or not to be," in *Codeswitch*, 82–3. This poem has been reproduced with permission from Iris De Anda.

63 "Five Questions with Iris De Anda," *Telejaguar*, February 18, 2020.

64 Anzaldúa, "Preface: (Un)natural Bridges, (Un)safe Spaces," 1.

65 Gómez-Peña, *The New World Border*, 85.

66 Iris De Anda, "This Is not Just Poetry," in *Codeswitch*, 77.

67 For a detailed study of the forms and functions of the soliloquy, see A. D. Cousins and Daniel Derrin, eds., *Shakespeare and the Soliloquy in Early Modern English Drama* (Cambridge University Press, 2018).

REFERENCES

Alarcón, Francisco X., and Odilia Galván Rodríguez, eds. *Poetry of Resistance: Voices for Social Justice*. University of Arizona Press, 2016.

Anzaldúa, Gloria E. *Borderlands/La Frontera: The New Mestiza*. 5th ed. Aunt Lute Books, 2022.

Anzaldúa, Gloria E. "Preface: (Un)natural Bridges, (Un)safe Spaces." In *This Bridge We Call Home: Radical Visions for Transformation*, edited by Gloria E. Anzaldúa and AnaLouise Keating. Routledge, 2002.

Arizona State Senate. Senate Bill 1070. 49th Legislature. 2nd Regular Session. April 23, 2010. https://www.azleg.gov/legtext/49leg/2r/bills/sb1070s.pdf.

Blumenbach, Johann Friedrich. *De generis humani varietate nativa*. 3rd ed. Göttingen: Vandenhoeck, 1795.

Brousseau, Marcel. "Lines and Fences: Writing and Rewriting the California Fence/Wall." *Boom California*, December 14, 2017. https://boomcalifornia.org/2017/12/14/lines-and-fences/.

Cantú, Norma E. "Banning of Ethnic Studies in the United States." *Oxford Research Encyclopedias*. February 28, 2020.

Carmona, Christopher. "The Chican@ Nueva Onda as a Poetic Tidal Wave: The Revitalization, Repoliticalization & Redefinition of 'Chican@' Through Poetry." *Diálogo* 17, no. 2 (2014): 49–56.

Cousins, A. D., and Daniel Derrin, eds. *Shakespeare and the Soliloquy in Early Modern English Drama*. Cambridge University Press, 2018.

De Anda, Iris. *Codeswitch: Fires from Mi Corazon*. Los Writers Underground Press, 2014.

De León, Jason. *The Land of Open Graves: Living and Dying on the Migrant Trail.* University of California Press, 2015.

Espinosa, Ruben. "Traversing the Temporal Borderlands of Shakespeare." *New Literary History* 52, no. 3/4 (2021): 605–23.

Fanestil, John. "Performing the Border: Human Behavior at the US–Mexico Border – A Case Study of Friendship Park." Unpublished manuscript, May 8, 2014, typescript.

Fernández Retamar, Roberto. *Calibán. Apuntes sobre la cultura en nuestra América.* Editorial Diógenes, 1971.

Fernández Retamar, Roberto. "Caliban: Notes Toward a Discussion of Culture in Our America." Translated by Lynn Garafola, David Arthur McMurray, and Roberto Márquez. *Massachusetts Review* 15, no. 1/2 (1974): 7–72.

Finz, Stacy. "Arts Pair Makes Border Their Crossing to Bear." *Los Angeles Times*, March 11, 1988.

"Five Questions with Iris De Anda." *Telejaguar*, February 18, 2020.

Fusco, Coco. "The Border Art Workshop/Taller de Arte Fronterizo: Interview with Guillermo Gómez-Peña and Emily Hicks." *Third Text* 3, no. 7 (2008): 53–76.

García Echeverría, Olga. "Codeswitch: The Poetic Fuego of Iris De Anda." *La Bloga*, August 24, 2014. https://labloga.blogspot.com/2014/08/codeswitch-poetic-fuego-of-iris-de-anda.html.

Gómez-Peña, Guillermo. *Apocalypse Mañana: Opera Electrónica for the New Millennium.* Calaca Press, 2002.

Gómez-Peña, Guillermo. "Ethno-cyborgs and Genetically Engineered Mexicans." In *Dangerous Border Crossers: The Artist Talks Back.* Routledge, 2000.

Gómez-Peña, Guillermo. *Ethno-Techno: Writings on Performance, Activism, and Pedagogy*, edited by Elaine Peña. Routledge, 2005.

Gómez-Peña, Guillermo. *Gómez-Peña Unplugged: Texts on Live Art, Social Practice and Imaginary Activism (2008–2020)*, edited by Emma Tramposch and Balitrónica Gómez. Routledge, 2021.

Gómez-Peña, Guillermo. "La Pocha Nostra." Accessed June 29, 2021. https://www.guillermogomezpena.com/la-pocha-nostra/.

Gómez-Peña, Guillermo. *El Mexterminator: Antropología inversa de un performancero postmexicano.* Editorial Océano de México, 2002.

Gómez-Peña, Guillermo. "The Multicultural Paradigm: An Open Letter to the National Arts Community." In *Negotiating Performance: Gender, Sexuality, and Theatricality in Latin/o America*, edited by Diana Taylor and Juan Villegas. Duke University Press, 1994.

Gómez-Peña, Guillermo. "The New Global Culture: Somewhere between Corporate Multiculturalism and the Mainstream Bizarre (a Border Perspective)." *The Drama Review* 45, no. 1 (2001): 7–30.

Gómez-Peña, Guillermo. *The New World Border: Prophecies, Poems and Loqueras for the End of the Century*. City Lights, 1996.

Gómez-Peña, Guillermo. "On the Other Side of the Mexican Mirror." In *Ethno-Techno: Writings on Performance, Activism, and Pedagogy*, edited by Elaine Peña, Routledge, 2005.

Hare, Kristen. "Local Legislators, Immigration Advocates Say Nation Needs Comprehensive Reform." *St. Louis Beacon*, June 25, 2012. https://news.stlpublicradio.org/government-politics-issues/2012-06-25/local-legislators-immigration-advocates-say-nation-needs-comprehensive-reform.

Hernández, Roberto D. *Coloniality of the U-S/Mexico Border: Power, Violence, and the Decolonial Imperative*. University of Arizona Press, 2018.

Herrera, Spencer. "The Pocho Palimpsest in Early 20th Century Chicano Literature from Daniel Venegas to Américo Paredes." *Confluencia* 26, no. 1 (2010): 21–33.

Holslin, Jill. "Friendship Park: Environmental Placemaking at the US-Mexico Border." In *The Nature of Hope: Grassroots Organizing, Environmental Justice, and Political Change*, edited by Char Miller and Jeff Crane. University Press of Colorado, 2018.

Leal, Luis. "Octavio Paz and the Chicano." *Latin American Literary Review* 5, no. 10 (1977): 115–23.

Leza, Christina. *Divided Peoples: Policy, Activism, and Indigenous Identities on the U.S.-Mexico Border*. University of Arizona Press, 2019.

Lopez, Lalo, and Steven Zul. *Pocho Magazine* 1. 1990.

Lozano, Rosina. *An American Language: The History of Spanish in the United States*. University of California Press, 2018.

Luna-Firebaugh, Eileen M. "The Border Crossed Us: Border Crossing Issues of the Indigenous Peoples of the Americas." *Wicazo Sa Review* 17, no. 1 (2002): 159–81.

Martinez, Oscar J. "Border Conflict, Border Fences, and the 'Tortilla Curtain' Incident of 1978–1979." *Journal of the Southwest* 50, no. 3 (2008): 263–78.

Martínez-Cruz, Paloma. "The Intimate Life of the Pocha: A Genealogy of the Self-Ironic Turn in Chican@ Culture." In *The Routledge Handbook of Latin American Culture*, edited by Carlos Manuel Salomon. Routledge, 2018.

Medina, Cruz. *Reclaiming Poch@ Pop: Examining the Rhetoric of Cultural Deficiency.* Palgrave, 2014.

Mendieta, Eduardo, and Guillermo Gómez-Peña. "A Latino Philosopher Interviews a Chicano Performance Artist." *Nepantla: Views from the South* 2, no. 3 (2001): 539–54.

Morton, Samuel George. *Crania Americana, or, A Comparative View of the Skulls of Various Aboriginal Nations of North and South America.* Philadelphia: J. Dobson, 1839.

Packer, Emily, dir. *Too Long Here.* Marginal Gap Films, 2020.

Paredes, Américo. *Cantos de adolescencia: Songs of Youth (1932–1937),* edited and translated by B. V. Olguín and Omar Vásquez Barbosa. Arte Público Press, 2007.

Portugal, Carlos, dir. *East Los High,* Season 2, episode 4, "The Queen of Ugly the King of Fools." Aired July 9, 2014 on Hulu.

"SB 1070: Arizona's Apartheid State is 'in Plain Sight.'" News release. April 20, 2010.

Schibsted, Evantheia. "Confessions of a Webback." *Wired,* January 1, 1997. https://www.wired.com/1997/01/ffpena/.

Shakespeare, William. *Hamlet.* Edited by Ann Thompson and Neil Taylor. The Arden Shakespeare Third Series. Rev. ed. Bloomsbury, 2016.

Shakespeare, William. *The Tempest.* Edited by Virginia Mason Vaughan and Alden T. Vaughan. The Arden Shakespeare Third Series. Bloomsbury, 2011.

Shakespeare, William. *Twelfth Night.* Edited by Keir Elam. The Arden Shakespeare Third Series. Bloomsbury, 2014.

Sheren, Ila Nicole. *Portable Borders: Performance Art and Politics on the U.S. Frontera since 1984.* University of Texas Press, 2015.

Smith, Ian. "We Are Othello: Speaking of Race in Early Modern Studies." *Shakespeare Quarterly* 67, no. 1 (2016): 104–24.

Southern Border Community Coalition. "Operation Gatekeeper and the Birth of Border Militarization." Accessed May 5, 2022. https://www.southernborder.org/operation_gatekeeper.

Vasconcelos, José. "Asoma el pochismo." In *La tormenta, segunda parte de Ulises criollo.* Ediciones Botas, 1936.

Wang, Hua, and Arvind Singhal. "East Los High: Transmedia Edutainment to Promote Sexual and Reproductive Health of Young Latina/o Americans." *American Journal of Public Health* 106 (2016): 1002–10.

What's Past Is Prologue
Four

On March 12, 2012, a group of writers, educators, and activists calling themselves Librotraficantes gathered in Houston, Texas, to begin a five-day journey to Tucson, Arizona. Along the way, this caravan of book smugglers made stops in San Antonio, El Paso, Mesilla, and Albuquerque, gathering more participants and hundreds of copies of the texts that had been effectively banned earlier that year when the Governing Board of the Tucson Unified School District voted to dismantle its exceptionally successful Mexican American Studies (MAS) program. The stakes of this decision were both ideological and financial. The district stood to lose ten percent of state aid, or nearly $15 million in annual funding, until it came into compliance with House Bill 2281, a 2010 law prohibiting the teaching of courses that:

1. Promote the overthrow of the United States government.
2. Promote resentment toward a race or class of people.
3. Are designed primarily for pupils of a particular ethnic group.
4. Advocate ethnic solidarity instead of the treatment of pupils as individuals.[1]

When the founders of the Librotraficante movement heard reports of books being boxed up and removed from Tucson classrooms—sometimes in front of students during class

DOI: 10.4324/9781003292838-5

time—they immediately recognized HB 2281 for what it was: a targeted effort to stifle the study of Mexican American literature, history, and culture precisely because it was powerful. As a 2011 state-commissioned audit found and a 2012 University of Arizona study later confirmed, the Tucson MAS curriculum increased achievement outcomes and graduation rates among Latinx students enrolled in the program. Such success was attributed to the fact that these students could see themselves reflected in the coursework and were given the tools to critically examine the structures of power that impacted their lives and communities.[2] For Tony Diaz, the leader and spokesperson of the Librotraficantes, it was clear that any legislation designed to destroy such an effective ethnic studies program could only be motivated by white racial fear on the part of Arizona Republican lawmakers: "They were scared of the advancement of our intellectual base. They feared the moment we would not only think for ourselves but act in ways to cultivate and increase our cultural capital."[3]

The Librotraficantes played directly into these anxieties as they mobilized the Mexican American literary community to set up underground libraries along their route and to host Banned Book Bashes with live readings by many of the authors whose work was deemed unsafe to teach in Arizona. One such writer was Chicana Chumash poet, professor, and publisher Lorna Dee Cervantes, who traveled to San Antonio to join the caravan. After learning that several anthologies featuring her poetry had been prohibited, along with books by acclaimed Chicanx writers whose work she once published, Cervantes felt compelled to take action and even composed a poem for the occasion. In "A Chicano Poem," she connects the dismantling of the Tucson MAS program to longstanding and recurring attempts to dispossess the Indigenous Peoples of the present-day U.S. Southwest of their languages, lifeways, and lands:

> They tried to take our words,
> Steal away our hearts under
> Their imaginary shawls, their laws,
> Their libros, their *Líbranos, Señor*.
> No more. They tried to take
> Away our Spirit in the Rock, the Mountain,
> The Living Waters. They tried to steal
> Our languages, our grandmothers' pacts,
> Our magma cartas for their own serfs.
> They razed the land and raised a Constitution,
> Declared others 3/5ths a human being,
> Snapped shackles, cut off a foot,
> Raped our grandmothers into near mute
> Oblivion. They burned the sacred codices
> And the molten goddesses rose anew
> In their flames. They tried to silence a
> Nation, tried to send The People back
> To the Four Corners of the world. They drew
> A line in the sand and dared us to cross it,
> Tried to peel off our skins, Xipe Totec
> Screaming through our indigenous consciousness.
> They tried to brand "America" into our unread
> Flesh, the skull and crossbones flying at
> Half-mast. They tried to put their eggs in
> Our baskets, tried to weave the Native
> Out of us with their drink and drugs, tried to
> Switch their mammy-raised offspring, beaded and
> Unshaven, as the colorless pea under our mattresses
> In a cultural bait and switch, hook and bait.

> They tried to take our words,
> Give us the Spanish translation for
> "Pain," serve us the host of fallow fields on a
> China plate, stripped us of the germ and seed,
> Fed us in a steady diet of disease and famine.
> Where is the word for tomorrow to the dead?
> When is our kingdom come? They claim our
> Reclamations; our reparations, a thing of our
> Imaginations. I discover this truth
> To be self-evident: In the beginning
> We were here.
> I declare us here today
> And speaking.[4]

Linking the history of attempted epistemicide to acts of sexual violation, enslavement, mutilation, massacre, and environmental destruction, Cervantes calls attention to the reality that the United States was built on stolen land with stolen labor. The border, too, as we saw in previous chapters, was a colonial imposition—a "line in the sand" drawn to render certain people "illegal" while making others feel alien in their own homelands. As she riffs on the document that famously declared all men to be created equal while slavery was still legal and referred to Native Americans as "merciless Indian Savages," Cervantes boldly concludes "A Chicano Poem" with a declaration of her own.[5] Hers is not one of independence but one of continued presence in spite of centuries-long efforts to erase, to eradicate, and to expropriate.

As Cervantes's poem so poignantly attests, the dismantling of the Tucson MAS curriculum was about far more than the books themselves. And yet, through the political and performative act of transporting what they cleverly called "wet books" across the highly contested territory of the Southwest, the Librotraficantes demonstrated that texts and the stories they tell matter. They matter because they are witnesses to human experience. They are vessels of ancestral knowledge. And they are conveyors of narratives that shape claims to the truth. By bringing her person *and* her poetry to the caravan of book smugglers who refused to accept this latest attempt to suppress their languages, cultures, and histories, Cervantes embodied the movement's foundation in the power of presence, or what performance studies scholar Diana Taylor has theorized as "¡presente!":

> a war cry in the face of nullification; an act of solidarity as in responding, showing up, and standing with; a commitment to witnessing; a joyous accompaniment; present among, with, and to, walking and talking with others; an ontological and epistemic reflection on presence and subjectivity as process; an ongoing *becoming* as opposed to a static *being*, as participatory and relational, founded on mutual recognition; a showing or display before others; a militant attitude, gesture, or declaration of presence.[6]

The Librotraficantes and those who came out to support their efforts understood how important it was to show up for the young people in Tucson when their education and personhood were under attack. As they made their way to Arizona, where they would host workshops with teachers, students, and members of the community, the Librotraficantes loudly and repeatedly declared: We're here. We've been here. And we stand with you (Figure 4.1).

Despite the fact that the list of libros the caravan carried back to Arizona included many iconic works of Mexican

Figure 4.1 Writer Tony Diaz, El Librotraficante and Director of Nuestra Palabra: Latino Writers Having Their Say, with other members of the Librotraficantes in front of the Alamo in San Antonio, Texas. Photo by Liana Lopez.

American literature—such as *The House on Mango Street* by Sandra Cisneros, *Bless Me, Ultima* by Rudolfo Anaya, and *So Far from God* by Ana Castillo—as well as several books by Black, Indigenous, and other Latinx authors, one text dominated news coverage of HB 2281 and its fallout: Shakespeare's *The Tempest*. "Shakespeare loomed large throughout this episode," writes Ruben Espinosa, "as critics of the law clung to the Bard's iconic status to criticize the misguided nature of the legislation."[7] In the news stories and opinion pieces that proliferated in outlets such as *Salon*, *HuffPost*, *New York Daily News*, the *Daily Mail*, *The Sunday Times*, *The Australian*, and *Telegraph India*, Shakespeare made headlines worldwide. While some commentators tried to make sense of how *The Tempest*, with its themes of colonialism, race, and power, might be in violation of HB 2281, others expressed incredulity that Shakespeare—*even* Shakespeare!—could be caught up in this mess. Still others used Shakespeare's cultural status to illustrate the absurdity of it all. Luis Alberto Urrea, the award-winning Mexican American author of three books prohibited in Arizona, sardonically quipped that Native writers such as Tohono O'odham poet Ofelia Zepeda shared the honor of being outlawed with that "notorious narco, Guillermo Shakespeare."[8]

Rather than seeing *The Tempest* as an outlier among the books prohibited in the wake of HB 2281, however, this chapter will take seriously its inclusion in the Tucson curriculum, exploring the uncanny yet deeply familiar echoes that its outsized presence produced when Shakespeare was not aligned with the white Anglocentric power structures that would otherwise claim him. I do not mean to suggest that we should read the controversy about the MAS curriculum exclusively through the lens of a text written by a white English author in the early seventeenth century. But I do want us to think carefully about why this play about colonialism, linguistic domination, and slavery continues to resonate within larger discussions about the ongoing legacies of Euro-American empire and the disciplinary functions of education that run counter to the liberatory pedagogy upon which the Tucson MAS program was built.

YOU TAUGHT ME LANGUAGE

Early in *The Tempest*, we quickly learn that education is central to Prospero's control of the island and its inhabitants. In the version of the story that he recounts to his daughter Miranda,

Prospero explains that he was unjustly usurped as the Duke of Milan by his brother Antonio, who proceeded to send him and his three-year-old child into exile aboard a "rotten carcass of a butt" that was so unfit for the sea that even "the very rats / Instinctively ha[d] quit it" (1.2.146–8).[9] It was only due to the kindness of his friend Gonzalo that they were accompanied by a selection of books from Prospero's prized library. In the twelve years since they washed up on the shore of this isle, which is situated somewhere in the Mediterranean but imbued with echoes of the Caribbean and the Americas, Prospero has served as Miranda's "schoolmaster," claiming to make her "more profit / Than other princes can that have more time / For vainer hours, and tutors not so careful" (1.2.172–4).[10] Although the language of "profit" was commonplace in early modern English discourses about education, here it seems to be explicitly linked to capital and power as Prospero (whose name connects him to prosperity) seeks to reproduce his ways of knowing and thereby cultivate his daughter's marriageability.[11]

But Miranda is not Prospero's only student, nor is she the only other inhabitant of the island. Through Prospero's conversations with Ariel, the isle's indigenous "brave spirit" (1.2.206) whom he enslaved to do his bidding, we learn about Caliban, a man who was born on this land but is now confined to a rocky cell and forced to labor on behalf of the recent arrivals from Milan.[12] Just as he restricts the movements of Caliban and Ariel, Prospero controls their backstories, describing Caliban's mother Sycorax as a "foul" and "damned witch" who arrived pregnant to the island after she was banished from Algiers for her "mischiefs manifold and sorceries terrible" (1.2.258, 264–5). When Ariel refused to follow her orders, the story goes, she trapped him in a "cloven pine" tree, where he stayed for twelve years until Prospero arrived and used his own magic to free him—only to become his new master (1.2.277). Sometime before she died, Sycorax gave birth to Caliban, or, as Prospero puts it, "littered" a "freckled whelp" on the isle (1.2.282–3). Before we see or hear Caliban, in other words, Prospero has already conjured the image of someone less than human, someone of monstrous birth, a dog.

When Caliban emerges from his confinement, however, we hear a rather different account of Prospero's arrival—one that frames him as a paternalistic teacher figure who used the pretenses of care and education to take advantage of Caliban's knowledge of the land in order to steal it from him:

> This island's mine by Sycorax, my mother,
> Which thou tak'st from me. When thou cam'st first,
> Thou strok'st me and made much of me; wouldst give me
> Water with berries in 't, and teach me how
> To name the bigger light and how the less,
> That burn by day and night. And then I loved thee,
> And showed thee all the qualities o'th' isle:
> The fresh springs, brine pits, barren place and fertile.
> Cursed be I that did so! All the charms
> Of Sycorax – toads, beetles, bats – light on you,
> For I am all the subjects that you have,
> Which first was mine own king; and here you sty me
> In this hard rock, whiles you do keep from me
> The rest o'th' island.
>
> (1.2.332–45)

For Caliban, sovereignty is not just the right to rule the land as he sees fit but also the right to access its resources, which he generously shared with Prospero and is presently denied. It is telling that Prospero, who once relied on Caliban's deep familiarity with "all the qualities o'th' isle" to survive, now keeps his only subject confined away from the land that he inherited through his mother and had used to sustain himself.

As Prospero attempts to take control of the narrative once more, he reveals the dangerous consequences of the patriarchal tyranny with which he rules the island. Calling Caliban a "lying slave," Prospero claims to have "used" him with "humane care" until he sought to "violate / The honour of [his] child," Miranda (1.2.345–9). According to Prospero's logic, he didn't take the island from Caliban. Caliban lost his right to live among the island's occupants when he behaved in a way that disrupted the strict hierarchy of power that Prospero established. By reframing Caliban as a threat to his property in the form of his white daughter's chastity and thus her marriageability, Prospero justifies his acts of dispossession as necessary forms of (self-)protection. Reading Prospero's accusation through the lens of service and education, Tom Lindsay argues that, if it is indeed true that Caliban tried to violate Miranda, it is because he has "learned how to see Miranda as a politically advantageous tool" while under the "humane care" and tutelage of Prospero.[13] The effects of this learning are most evident in Caliban's ambiguous response to Prospero's allegation, which Julia Reinhard Lupton importantly notes is "neither a denial nor a confession."[14] Here, Caliban articulates a violent political fantasy of self-replication that would allow him to ascend in the hierarchy and wrest the island back from Prospero: "O ho, O ho! Would't had been done; / Thou didst prevent me, I had peopled else / This isle with Calibans" (1.2.350–2). Observing that Caliban uses the potential mood to express his ambitions and desires in this moment, Debapriya Sarkar contends that even the act of thinking and speaking speculatively—of plotting—proves to be a threat, not only to Prospero's colonial rule but also to the main plot of the play, both of which depend on "Caliban's unfulfilled futurity."[15]

While Prospero uses the attempted violation of his daughter as the pretext for seizing the island and subjugating its inhabitants with his magic, Miranda herself cites it as evidence that Caliban is incapable of being educated into goodness. Echoing her father's language of slavery and savagery, Miranda enters the conversation to reveal that she, too, had tried to take on the role of teacher in her relationship with Caliban:

> Abhorred slave,
> Which any print of goodness wilt not take,
> Being capable of all ill; I pitied thee,
> Took pains to make thee speak, taught thee each hour
> One thing or other. When thou didst not, savage,
> Know thine own meaning, but wouldst gabble like
> A thing most brutish, I endowed thy purposes
> With words that made them known. But thy vile race,
> (Though thou didst learn), had that in't which good natures
> Could not abide to be with; therefore wast thou
> Deservedly confined into this rock,
> Who hadst deserved more than a prison.
>
> (1.2.352–63)

Reducing Caliban to a "thing most brutish," Miranda reveals that her pedagogy is based on the assumption that his seemingly unintelligible native tongue did not qualify as a language and that he needed her assistance to "know [his] own meaning" or communicate his "purposes." This sense of linguistic and intellectual superiority is in keeping with early modern European colonial beliefs that the languages and cultures of Indigenous Peoples were underdeveloped and therefore waiting to be replaced with supposedly more sophisticated European ways of speaking, knowing, and being. Using the metaphor of imprinting to describe a method of education that replicates through impression, Miranda concludes that Caliban, having failed to receive "any print of goodness," must be inherently ineducable because he is of a "vile race" that is distinct from her own. While Miranda's use of "race" here may not quite carry the same meaning as the term does today, Virginia Mason Vaughan and Alden T. Vaughan have compellingly argued that the pejorative modifier "vile," in tandem with words and phrases such as "slave," "savage," "monster," and "thing of darkness," works to negatively racialize Caliban, placing him in "a distinctly separate and inferior human category from the Europeans who berate and abuse him."[16] He is relegated to what Patricia Akhimie identifies as "an uncultivatable underclass of subhuman who can labor but who cannot improve."[17] As Miranda attributes the cause of Caliban's imprisonment to the stubborn ineducability of his "vile race," she not only perpetuates the notion that her knowledge is universally "good" but also uses what Jonathan Goldberg describes as a "failed pedagogic project" to reinforce a hierarchy of difference and to justify "the unequal distribution of cultural capital" accordingly.[18] When Miranda invokes the idea of "race" to blame Caliban's perceived nature for his confinement, in other words, what she is actually describing is a social practice that we would identify today as racism.

Caliban has come to understand perfectly well that the type of education Miranda describes was not designed for his benefit. "You taught me language," he retorts, "and my profit on't / Is I know how to curse. The red plague rid you / For learning me your language" (1.2.364–6). Reprising the rhetoric of profit that Prospero used earlier to describe the outcome of Miranda's education, Caliban deploys it ironically to speak back to his colonizers. The only profit he has gained from having their language imposed on him is the ability to make his contempt known and to wish them ill in a way that they will understand.

As we learn later in the play, Caliban also recognizes that Prospero derives his power from the books he brought with him to the island. When Caliban enlists the hapless Stephano and Trinculo, who have washed up on the island in the shipwreck caused by Prospero's titular tempest, to help him carry out his violent fantasy of revenge, he repeatedly gives them very specific instructions to "seize[ ]," "possess," and "burn" Prospero's books (3.2.89, 92, 95). In seeking to render Prospero powerless, Caliban rebels against a system of knowledge that has rendered him other, subjugated him, and denied him access to his own land and language. As Nedda Mehdizadeh notes, we are not privy to the exact content of these books, but the play makes it clear that the "white, European ways of knowing" they contain are the means by which Prospero has granted himself "the authority to compel the island natives to perform labor according to his desires, replicating the rhetorical maneuvers of contemporaneous travelogues by white, European travelers who authorized their presence in—and justified the colonization of—foreign lands through acts of writing."[19] These acts of inscription, Mehdizadeh continues, deliberately overwrite traditional knowledge systems "in an effort to delegitimize native claims to their own land" and to deny the right to self-determination and self-representation.[20]

It is indeed telling that Prospero declares that he will "drown [his] book" and renounce the "rough magic" (5.1.57, 50) that allowed him to subjugate the island's inhabitants only after he has successfully orchestrated his return to Milan through the marriage of Miranda to the king's son Ferdinand.

I trace the familiar contours of *The Tempest* to underscore a fundamental tension at the heart of the play: while Prospero seeks to maintain control by imposing dominant narratives, Caliban attempts to harness the power of counternarratives in the interest of finding a more nuanced understanding of the past and the space to imagine a different future. As he gives voice to resistance in the face of linguistic and cultural domination, Caliban disrupts the hierarchical, colonial world order that is invested in keeping him at the bottom and Prospero on top. It is for this reason that Caliban has become a potent symbol of defiance for many readers and writers throughout the Americas and the world more broadly who seek to use the tools of their education to speak back to forces of colonial oppression and reclaim authority over their histories and cultures.[21] "I know no other metaphor more expressive of our cultural situation, of our reality," writes Cuban author Roberto Fernández Retamar. "What is our history, what is our culture if not the history and culture of Caliban?"[22]

Given the colonial dynamics, epistemological struggles, and resistant energies within *The Tempest* and the many afterlives it has inspired, it is certainly not difficult to surmise why this play had a place in a curriculum that emerged from longstanding efforts to reimagine education as a space of liberation, not as a means of oppression or alienation. Founded in 1998, the Tucson MAS program was the outcome of a grassroots effort among a group of community members and teachers who came together to create a series of courses that would validate the experiences of their predominantly Latinx students and help to close the achievement gap that Mexican American Tucsonans had been protesting for decades. In the year following the Chicana/o student walkouts or "blowouts" in East Los Angeles in 1968, a group of undergraduates at the University of Arizona founded the Mexican American Liberation Committee (MALC) and organized a series of walkouts among students in Tucson and Pueblo High Schools in protest of segregation, educational inequality, and a high dropout rate among Mexican American students. They drew attention to the underfunding of largely Mexican American schools on the west side of the city and the funneling of resources to the majority white schools on the east. They demanded Mexican American Studies classes that reflected their history, their literature, and their culture as well as bilingual instruction and "Spanish for Nativos" classes that affirmed the truth that "Spanish is not inferior to English."[23] They wanted an education that prepared them for college, not just for vocational paths. And they advocated for a proportionate number of Chicana/o teachers, administrators, and counselors.[24] As one Tucson High School freshman, Eduardo Rios, lamented in an issue of *Coraje*, the community newspaper published by MALC in 1969, "some of the students at T.H.S. feel that the school system has neglected the pride of Chicanos, their heritage and language; this in itself is the work of an anti-Chicano system in which we are forced to live."[25]

In 1974, the Mexican American Legal Defense and Educational Fund escalated efforts to combat segregation and discrimination in Tucson schools by filing a lawsuit against the Tucson Unified School District that would eventually be combined with a similar lawsuit filed by the National

Association for the Advancement of Colored People on behalf of African American students. Ruling that the district had acted with discriminatory intent, a federal judge ordered the desegregation of schools in 1978 and placed TUSD under court supervision. Inequities and the alarming achievement gap persisted, however, until the teachers who founded the MAS program twenty years later decided to do something about it.[26]

Designed for Mexican American students, Latinx students, and students of color more generally, but open to all, the MAS program, also known as La Raza Studies, strived to create a humane and equitable learning environment and to promote student success through a combination of strategies. The founding teachers drew on Indigenous epistemologies and the frameworks of critical race theory, critical ethnic studies, and social justice pedagogy to construct meaningful counternarratives that spoke to the realities of marginalized peoples and offered more nuanced perspectives on the often-whitewashed versions of history and culture that had been traditionally taught in schools. They developed culturally responsive curricula that focused on the history, literature, and art of Mexican Americans, Indigenous Peoples, and communities of color. And they cultivated social consciousness by encouraging students to use their knowledge to advocate for social change. Graduation rates improved among students enrolled in the classes, and over time, the program expanded to include offerings at all grade levels across several schools in the district. In both theory and practice, the Tucson MAS program was the antithesis of Prospero's approach to education. Unlike Caliban, Tucson students were empowered to embrace their identities and languages and to build futures for themselves that were rooted in justice and equity rather than in revenge. But when Republican lawmakers made it their business to destroy this enormously successful program, *The Tempest* would become even more resonant than anyone could have anticipated.

'BAN, 'BAN, CA-CALIBAN

The attack on the MAS program began in 2006 when conservative state officials caught wind of a speech delivered by Chicana activist Dolores Huerta at Tucson High Magnet School just days after several students walked out in protest of anti-immigrant legislation recently passed by the U.S. House of Representatives. The Border Protection, Antiterrorism, and Illegal Immigration Control Act of 2005 (H.R. 4437), which ultimately failed in the Senate, included provisions to further militarize the border, to make unlawful presence in the United States a felony, and to criminalize the act of providing aid to undocumented immigrants. By joining a nationwide effort to mobilize Latinxs in taking political action against this racist and dehumanizing legislation that would directly impact their communities, Tucson students became part of a long tradition of youth activism, following in the footsteps of those who participated in school walkouts in the 1960s and 1970s.[27] Many educators and administrators expressed concern, however, that they were doing so during school hours and missing key instruction and state-mandated standardized testing. In her address to these students, Huerta encouraged them to stay in class and exercise their political voice in other ways—like starting a postcard campaign to ask the elected officials responsible for this kind of legislation why "Republicans hate Latinos."[28]

It did not take long for Huerta's comment to gain local, state, and even national attention thanks, in large part, to Fox News pundit Bill O'Reilly, who ran an inflammatory segment on his show, *The O'Reilly Factor*. While many Republican elected officials expressed outrage during a special meeting of the Arizona House Select Committee on Government Operations, Performance, and Waste and questioned TUSD officials' decision to invite Huerta in the first place, it was Arizona Superintendent of Instruction Tom Horne who took action by enlisting Deputy Superintendent Margaret Garcia Dugan to plan a rebuttal to Huerta's remarks in which she would tell students why she was "proud to be a Latina and proud to be a Republican."[29] Horne and Dugan were decidedly not interested in what their young audience had to say in response, however. When student requests to hold a question and answer session following Dugan's address were denied, members of the school's chapter of Movimiento Estudiantil Chicano de Aztlán (MEChA) decided to plan a silent protest during the event that would call attention to their silencing. As Dugan extolled the virtues of hard work and individualism from the podium, a group of MEChA students rose from their seats. Some put blue tape over their mouths and raised their right fists in the air while fellow protestors revealed that they were wearing t-shirts that read: "You can silence my voice but not my spirit." Other shirts featured messages such as "Prop 203 is anti-Latino" and "English only is anti-Latino," making clear references to Horne's and Dugan's roles in championing Proposition 203, a successful ballot measure known as "English for the Children" that banned bilingual education for English-language learners and mandated structured English immersion in Arizona.[30] When these students were asked by the principal to sit down, they chose to walk out instead.[31]

Believing that it was their "Raza teachers" who taught them to defy authority in this way, Horne soon after set his sights on destroying the MAS at TUSD. In an open letter to

Tucson residents in 2007, Horne accused the program of teaching "destructive ethnic chauvinism" and thus began his years-long legislative campaign to dismantle it, just as he had worked to end bilingual education in the state.[32] But what Horne perceived as racial resentment toward white people was actually the effect of a curriculum that taught students of color to recognize structural inequities and to use their education to bring about change. As Ruben Espinosa astutely observes, it is clear that what Horne and other legislators "found threatening was not the radical overthrow of the U.S. government, but rather the idea that these young Chicanxs would come to know and understand the power of their political voice."[33] For those who see schools as spaces of discipline and conformity, the idea of an empowered youth—especially youth of color—is terrifying. Henry A. Giroux summarizes this response in the following way:

> The fear is that ethnic studies can be taught in ways that provide a critical reading of history, power, ideas, and institutional mappings. This is viewed as dangerous by conservatives and white supremacists because classroom learning can be used to expose specific modes of racial exclusion, class inequalities, and the ongoing punishment and silencing of the voices of young people. Even though Mexican American students make up the vast majority of public school students in Tucson, a curriculum that addresses their heritage and culture is considered not simply subversive but anti-American.[34]

Horne's insistent claims that the MAS program was anti-American were amplified by his successor, John Huppenthal, who helped to author HB 2281 when he was a state senator and ran for the office of State Superintendent in 2010 on the explicit campaign promise to "stop La Raza." When Huppenthal declared the program to be in violation of the law in early 2011, he willfully ignored the fact that the external audit he commissioned and paid for with state funds found that the program did not violate the terms of the statute. In fact, the report recommended that the program be expanded.[35]

In the face of these attacks on their education and freedom of expression, Tucson students continued to fight back and organized to form UNIDOS, or United Non-Discriminatory Individuals Demanding Our Studies. This grassroots youth group held vigils, organized press conferences, and, in an act of civil disobedience, took over a school board meeting, chaining themselves to the chairs so that the board could not consider a resolution that would make Mexican American Studies an elective instead of a means to satisfy core requirements. By the end of 2011, however, their voices would be suppressed even further by an Administrative Law Judge named Lewis D. Kowal, who sided with Huppenthal and affirmed his decision to withhold state aid until the district came into compliance with the law. Under such a dire financial and legal threat, members of the TUSD governing board and Superintendent John Pedicone felt that they were left with little choice but to comply.

The teachers who had worked for years to build the MAS program found themselves in a state of uncertainty and with no guidance about how to proceed mid-year without a curriculum. At the time this decision came down, Tucson High Magnet School literature teacher and MAS program co-founder Curtis Acosta was not actually scheduled to teach any works by Mexican American authors in his senior-level

Chicano literature class that week. He was about to introduce *The Tempest*, a text he had originally included in the course to give students the opportunity to "experience that writers and artists from other ethnicities are conscious of the issues and themes in their lives, their history."[36] Inspired by the work of multicultural studies scholar Ronald Takaki, who wondered whether *The Tempest* might be read as "a prologue for America," Acosta saw in Shakespeare's text the potential for counternarratives that could be used to reframe the colonial power dynamics that shaped the U.S. Southwest in particular.[37] Although Acosta's students in previous years expressed some initial skepticism about reading a Shakespeare play in this context, he recalled that "they immediately made connections to immigration, Mexican culture, and the legacy of Chican@ civil rights with Caliban's language."[38] Like many readers and writers who have experienced the effects of colonization, racism, and oppression, these high school students in Tucson identified with Caliban and his desire to reclaim his sovereignty and right to self-determination. Acosta observed in them a sense of "respect for Shakespeare in his construction of Caliban and his willingness to 'fight' for his island regardless of the drastically inverted power relationship between Caliban and Prospero."[39]

Acosta's lesson plan and his students' responses to Caliban's resistance were aligned more specifically with a rich Chicanx literary tradition that grapples with the tensions of feeling alienated in one's own land and living between two colonial tongues. As Antonio C. Márquez writes in "Voices of Caliban: From Curse to Discourse," "the impulse to find new languages, to create meaningful dialogue, to shape powerful forms of discourse, and 'to write back' with authority and purpose characterizes the most engaging works in contemporary

Chicano literature. The key element is language and it is concomitant with definitions of self and culture."⁴⁰ In other words, Caliban offered an early glimpse of the forms of cultural emancipation that students examined in Acosta's course and throughout the MAS program. Many of the Chicanx, Latinx, Indigenous, and Black writers they studied also used the colonial languages imposed on them to articulate the complexities of their identities and to counteract the dominant narratives in which they were either dehumanized or not represented at all.

Given his particular approach to this canonical anglophone text and his former students' engagement with it, Acosta knew that *The Tempest* could serve as a litmus test for showing just how much HB 2281 would restrict his teaching. In an interview featured in the 2012 documentary *Outlawing Shakespeare*, Acosta recounts his experience of a recorded meeting with school administrators, who told him that he could continue to teach *The Tempest* only if he avoided "delv[ing] into issues ... from a critical race theory perspective"⁴¹:

> I brought up *The Tempest* at the meeting the day after they gaveled our program dead because I knew darn well if I could get an answer about my pedagogy, my curriculum, and the themes that we approach in our academic spaces—if I could get them to define what's legal or not legal, what's in compliance or not in compliance through the Bard, then I knew it was gonna hit the fan. And I also knew that nothing that I have constructed before was going to be safe for consumption moving forward. In essence, I knew that if they were going to tell me you can't teach *The Tempest* in that way, that everything I taught was gone, and I wanted to know that because I wanted to know how I was supposed to go forward as a teacher in midstream of a year with no curriculum.⁴²

In Acosta's view, Shakespeare's play about "a European man from Italy, the Duke of Milan, taking power over an island in the New World and enslaving two of the natives" presciently forecasted the very issues at the core of this targeted attack on a curriculum centered on Mexican American and Indigenous histories, cultures, and worldviews.[43] It would be difficult, if not impossible, for him to teach The Tempest in this context without addressing its "strong themes of race, colonization, oppression, class and power."[44] And even if Acosta himself somehow managed to avoid such topics, past experience suggested that students would likely make the connections on their own in their essays or in discussion. Would the class therefore be in violation of the law? Would Acosta risk losing his job? The only path forward through this climate of confusion and fear, he wisely concluded, was to stop teaching the play altogether. "In my hands," Acosta later explained, "it was far too dangerous. It's almost like it becomes weaponized in the hands of a teacher of color."[45]

The de facto banning of Shakespeare's play that resulted from this conversation between Acosta and school administrators was soon followed by an actual prohibition on seven books, which the district ordered to be boxed up and taken to a storage facility.[46] The Tempest was not on this list, but for many, especially Acosta, it may as well have been. If it wasn't advisable to teach Shakespeare under this law, then none of the books on the list of texts included in the MAS curriculum were safe. When news outlets began reporting on the ban, with Shakespeare often front and center, a spokesperson for TUSD attempted to regain control of the narrative, explaining in a news release that "'The Tempest' and other books approved for curriculum [were] still viable options for instructors," but MAS teachers, students, and supporters recognized a ban when they saw and felt one.[47] For Rodolfo Acuña, whose foundational textbook *Occupied America: A History of Chicanos* was one of the seven books expressly prohibited by the district, the colonial racism he saw in *The Tempest* encapsulated the situation quite well:

> Prospero is the colonizer; Caliban, the colonized. Prospero looks at Caliban as being genetically inferior. The story betrays Prospero's colonial mentality; he has little respect for the natives or the environment. His demeanor resembles that of [TUSD] Superintendent [John] Pedicone and leaders of the white establishment of Tucson who regard Mexicans, whether born on this side or the other side of the border, as aliens.[48]

As "the father of Chicano Studies," Acuña had seen this story play out before. The banning of the MAS program is part of a larger pattern of dispossession and alienation that has affected the lived experiences of Mexicans and Mexican Americans for centuries. The fact that this series of events mapped so easily onto *The Tempest* says less about the enduring relevance of Shakespeare than it does about the enduring realities of colonialism. It confirms Edward Said's assertion in *Culture and Imperialism* that "each new American reinscription of *The Tempest* is…a local version of the old grand story, invigorated and inflected by the pressures of an unfolding political and cultural history."[49] Attempts to suppress a curriculum designed to engage students in a truthful understanding of this unfolding history only affirmed its importance. To invoke a line from *The Tempest*, HB 2881 and its proponents proved that "what's past is prologue" (2.1.253).

After years of long, drawn-out, and expensive court battles, HB 2281 was officially ruled unconstitutional and permanently blocked in 2017 by Judge A. Wallace Tashima of the

United States District Court for the District of Arizona. In his opinion for *González v. Douglas*, the lawsuit brought by Tucson high school students and their parents against the State Superintendent of Instruction, Tashima concluded that the "enactment and enforcement" of the law "were motivated by racial animus" and that the legislation had a "disproportionate impact on Latino students."[50] Because there was no reasonable pedagogical motivation but demonstrable political and racial motivations for the passing and implementation of HB 2281, Tashima determined that students' First Amendment rights to receive information and their Fourteenth Amendment rights to equal protection under the law had been violated.

Some of the most conclusive evidence of the racial animus that Tashima identified was a series of comments that then-state senator John Huppenthal had been posting on political blogs under two pseudonyms shortly after he was elected to be the next State Superintendent of Instruction in late 2010. On one occasion, he wrote the following about Spanish-speaking immigrants:

> Caucasians aren't reproducing themselves, so all population growth has to be immigration.
>
> We are condemning ourselves to a second rate future if we don't reestablish the melting pot with a strong flow of immigrants engaging in economic activity, not crime.
>
> We all need to stomp out balkanization. No spanish radio stations, no spanish billboards, no spanish tv stations, no spanish newspapers. This is America, speak English.[51]

Playing into right-wing demographic paranoia about reproduction, racial replacement, and the labor force, Huppenthal apparently accepted the reality that the U.S. economy depends on immigrants but chose to demonize them by associating them with crime and a refusal to assimilate. With no acknowledgment of the fact that Spanish predates English in Arizona, this elected official leaned into linguistic racism as he called for the elimination of Spanish media of any kind, repeating a familiar refrain about the identification of "America" with "English." Huppenthal went on to reiterate his desire to consume Mexican labor only under certain assimilatory conditions as he continued: "I don't mind them selling Mexican food as long as the menus are mostly in English."[52] Some of his comments were more directly targeted toward the TUSD MAS program: "The rejection of American values and embracement of the values of Mexico in La Raza classrooms is the rejection of success and embracement of failure."[53] This assessment of what was happening in "La Raza classrooms" was not only reductive and based on a false binary that aligned the United States with success and Mexico with failure, but it also willfully ignored just how successful the MAS program had been in increasing graduation rates and sustaining student engagement.

Tashima's ruling was cause for celebration among MAS teachers, students, and supporters, who felt a sense of relief and validation after so many years of fighting. For Curtis Acosta, the decision was a deeply affirming "punctuation to a long journey."[54] It was also an occasion for mourning the loss of a program that could have supported the growth of even more students. In the aftermath of the 2012 dismantling of the MAS curriculum, many of the teachers responsible for building it either were forced out of Tucson schools or resigned to protect themselves and their families. In 2013, a federal judge reinstated the 1978 desegregation order I mentioned at the outset of this chapter and ruled that the district must offer "culturally relevant courses," but the community trust and investment that the MAS teachers had cultivated would prove difficult to restore in a climate of fear and intimidation.[55] While the future of MAS in Tucson remained uncertain in the years after HB 2281 was passed, the movement for ethnic studies grew even stronger in cities and states around the country, in large part because of what had unfolded in Arizona. Since 2012, nineteen states plus the District of Columbia have passed legislation or created policies that require ethnic studies to be incorporated into K-12 curricula or state standards.[56] In 2021, California made ethnic studies a high school graduation requirement that will take effect with the class of 2030. The growth of this movement is both a testament to the transformative template set forth by the Tucson MAS program and a painful reminder of what could have been in Arizona.

THE PRESENT-FUTURE

As promising as the recent progress in support of ethnic studies may be, it has been increasingly overshadowed by an alarming rise in white conservative backlash against the movement for racial and social justice. Following the uprisings in response to the murder of George Floyd in the summer of 2020, a dizzying number of laws and policies intended to restrict education on topics related to race, racism, or the history of non-white people have been passed or proposed in at least thirty-six states.[57] This coordinated effort has coalesced around attempts to ban "critical race theory" (CRT), an academic and legal framework for studying systemic racism that Republican lawmakers have eagerly co-opted as a catch-all term for any efforts to promote anti-racism or to teach the history of race. Arguing that CRT teaches white children to feel guilty and children of color that they are oppressed, many conservative politicians and parents latched onto the idea that truthful engagement with the long legacies of racism in this country is divisive and anti-American.

Confirming that the anti-CRT movement is a repackaging and amplification of the ideas behind HB 2281, Tom Horne rode this new wave of conservatism right back into the office of Arizona State Superintendent for Public Instruction in 2022. "Liberals are trying to indoctrinate our school children to hate America," he claimed on his campaign website. "They want our children to believe that America is a racist country."[58] Horne also reinforced his outdated and bigoted beliefs about language as he promised to resume his campaign against bilingual education, arguing that "instead of Spanish-speaking students being forced to learn English, they want to return to bilingual education which leaves most students unable to be fluent in English, which means they cannot succeed in this country."[59] Fortunately, his efforts to dismantle successful evidence-based dual language programs have thus far failed.[60]

Echoes of HB 2281 have resounded elsewhere in this new era of epistemic control. In 2021, the Tennessee legislature passed a bill that threatened to withhold state funding from schools whose teachers engaged in discussions of race and sex. Under this new law, which outlined fourteen "prohibited concepts," teachers would be in violation for conveying the idea that "this state or the United States is fundamentally or irredeemably racist or sexist," or for "promoting or advocating the violent overthrow of the U.S. government."[61] This and many other laws like it have had a chilling effect on educators, who are offered little guidance about how to stay in compliance. Left to interpret the deliberately vague language themselves, teachers often report that they feel forced to self-censor, much as Curtis Acosta did with *The Tempest* in 2012, or to leave their jobs altogether.[62]

In Texas, where I live and teach, it was not long after Governor Greg Abbott signed an "anti-CRT" bill known as HB 3979 in 2021 that Republican lawmakers returned to another familiar target: books. As chair of the House Committee on General Investigating, Republican state representative Matt Krause issued a letter to the Texas Education Agency and selected district superintendents, informing them that he would be "initiating an inquiry into Texas school district content."[63] In addition to questioning the presence of 850 books on school library shelves, Krause directed them to identify any other books containing content related to human sexuality or "material that might make students feel discomfort, guilt, anguish, or any other form of psychological distress because of their race or sex or convey that a student, by virtue of their race or sex, is inherently racist, sexist, or oppressive, whether consciously or unconsciously."[64] Governor Abbott himself soon followed with a letter that directed the Texas Education Agency, the Texas State Library and Archives Commission, and the State Board of Education "to immediately develop statewide standards to prevent the presence of pornography and other obscene content in Texas public schools, including in school libraries."[65] Just as it did in Tucson, the weaponization of book lists and content audits has created a culture of fear and confusion but on a much larger scale. Writing from within her community in El Paso, Jazmine Janay Cuevas observes that "for humanities educators whose subject matter delves into the complexities and controversies of the human condition, the situation is becoming increasingly untenable."[66]

As the Librotraficantes prepared to celebrate the tenth anniversary of their first caravan from Houston to Tucson in the early months of 2022, the uptick in restrictive legislation and book banning confirmed their fears that Arizona had been a testing ground for broader attacks on intellectual freedom. For a group of activists who mobilized in response to efforts to take books out of the hands of young people, the renewed call to action was loud and clear, but this time the call was coming from within their own state. As then-Texas poet laureate and founding member of the Librotraficantes Lupe Mendez wrote in an essay for *Texas Observer* magazine, "The Republican Party intends to deny children access to books, authors and an education that would spur their intellectual growth. And in an effort to satisfy their base, Republicans in Texas are pushing away the one population that needs their attention the most: youth—and more pointedly—youth of color."[67]

While such attempts to curb discussions of race or histories of oppression felt familiar to those who had been paying attention in 2012, the regulations around the teaching of gender identity and sexuality reflected a ratcheting up of censorship. This new layer of backlash has been especially evident in Florida, where state lawmakers passed two highly restrictive laws on the teaching of race and the teaching of gender identity and sexual orientation during the same legislative session in 2022. Under the Stop the Wrongs to Our Kids and Employees—or Stop WOKE—Act, for instance, Governor Ron DeSantis declared the Advanced Placement African American History course to be in violation of state law, and Florida schools were required to change the standards for teaching U.S. history so that "instruction includes how slaves developed skills which, in some instances, could be applied for their personal benefit."[68] According to the Parental Rights in Education Act, colloquially known among critics as the "Don't Say Gay" law, school personnel or third parties in Florida are also not allowed to engage in classroom instruction on sexual orientation or gender identity for children in kindergarten through third grade "or in a manner that is not age-appropriate or developmentally appropriate for students in accordance with state standards."[69] The law also encourages parents to sue their school districts if they believe them to be in violation of these terms.

As schools set out to make adjustments to their curricula, lesson plans, and reading lists in light of these new laws, Shakespeare made international news once again in 2023, when his plays were caught up in the controversy over how to determine which books "contain pornography or obscene depictions of sexual conduct."[70] In an attempt to avoid potentially sexual content while still preparing students for standardized texts, school officials in Hillsborough County, which includes the city of Tampa, decided to include only excerpts from plays such as *Romeo and Juliet*, *Macbeth*, and *Hamlet*.[71] While state officials clarified that these and five other Shakespearean works remain on the list of acceptable texts to teach, the uncertainty introduced by the law has resulted in mixed messages for teachers and their students.[72] Speaking to a reporter from the *Tampa Bay Times*, Gaither High School reading teacher Joseph Cool lamented, "the rest of the nation – no, the world – is laughing at us. Taking Shakespeare in its entirety out because the relationship between Romeo and Juliet is somehow exploiting minors is just absurd."[73] It *is* absurd, just as it was absurd to remove *The Tempest* from the Tucson curriculum. But the problem in both cases is that the law—much like Prospero's approach to governing the island—was deliberately designed to silence the voices of the marginalized and to exert control through education rather than to liberate through learning. The media attention on Shakespeare is a well-intentioned effort to demonstrate the extent of the harm caused by such bans, but it also detracts from the even more troubling reality that knowledge created by and about queer people, trans people, and people of color is the true target.

Lawmakers have not stopped with K-12 education. Similarly restrictive legislation that applies to public colleges and universities has been adopted in several states. Of particular concern in higher education are the bills that aim to defund diversity, equity, and inclusion programs and initiatives created to support historically underrepresented students and to educate campus communities more broadly about issues related to race, gender, sexuality, religion, disability, and class. Although these laws have not yet affected classroom instruction, they have nevertheless produced a culture of fear that is at odds with the belief that diverse and inclusive campus environments allow students of all backgrounds to thrive in college. Moreover, the restrictions on what students can learn while they are in elementary, middle, and high school will undoubtedly affect their ability to access higher education as well as their preparedness to engage in the types of transformative critical thinking that such learning opportunities should foster. In short, if these laws are allowed to stay in place, they will have ripple effects for generations to come.

When the news about the dismantling of the Tucson MAS program was fresh and the media was still buzzing about the de facto banning of *The Tempest*, Shakespeare scholar Peter Holland used his platform as a plenary speaker during the 2012 meeting of the Shakespeare Association of America to sound the alarm about what he perceived to be an indicator of inhumanity on the part of the state of Arizona.[74]

Our humanity, Holland argued, is what "allows us to learn and to enjoy our learning."[75] Anything intended to stifle that ability for others can only be described as an inhumane act, one that denies their humanity. As I complete this book at the end of 2024, such inhumanity threatens to become the defining quality of public education in this country if we allow conservative legislators to act out of fear and a desire to control the narrative. It is up to us to stay presente—to engage in "act[s] of solidarity as in responding, showing up, and standing with"—not just when Shakespeare is on the line but when learning itself is under attack.[76] We must actively resist the types of forgetting on which domination so often depends, and we must advocate for policies that humanize education and proceed from the premise that schools should not be sites of oppression but rather spaces of liberation, validation, and empowerment. Now is the time to build coalitions, to combat erasure, and to commit to protecting opportunities for all students to engage meaningfully with truthful narratives about the past, not only because it is the prologue to our present, but also because, in the words of Curtis Acosta, "students are the present-future."[77]

NOTES

1 Arizona House of Representatives, House Bill 2281. 49th Legislature, 2nd Regular Session, 2010. https://www.azleg.gov/legtext/49leg/2r/bills/hb2281s.pdf. Governor Jan Brewer signed this bill into law just one month after she approved SB 1070, the anti-immigrant legislation I discussed in the previous chapter.

2 Cambium Learning, Inc., "Curriculum Audit of the Mexican American Studies Department Tucson Unified School District" (National Academic Educational Partnership, 2011). For the University of Arizona study, see Nolan L. Cabrera, Jeffrey F. Milem, and Ronald W. Marx, "An Empirical Analysis of the Effects of Mexican American

Studies Participation on Student Achievement within Tucson Unified School District," Report to Special Master Dr. Willis D. Hawley on the Tucson Unified School District Desegregation Case (University of Arizona College of Education, 2012). See also Nolan Cabrera, Jeffrey F. Milem, Ozan Jaquette, and Ronald W. Marx, "Missing the (Student Achievement) Forest for All the (Political) Trees: Empiricism and the Mexican American Studies Controversy in Tucson," *American Educational Research Journal* 51, no. 6 (2014): 1084–118.

3 Tony Diaz, *The Tip of the Pyramid: Cultivating Community Cultural Capital* (University of New Orleans Press, 2022), 215.

4 Lorna Dee Cervantes, "A Chicano Poem," *Huizache: The Magazine of Latino Literature* 2 (Fall 2012), 8–9. "A Chicano Poem" was later republished in Cervantes's collection *Sueño* (Wings Press, 2013), 92–3. This poem is reproduced with permission from Lorna Dee Cervantes.

5 Thomas Jefferson, et al., "The Declaration of Independence: A Transcription," National Archives and Records Administration, accessed November 28, 2024, https://www.archives.gov/founding-docs/declaration-transcript.

6 Diana Taylor, *¡Presente! The Politics of Presence* (Duke University Press, 2020), 4.

7 Ruben Espinosa, "Beyond The Tempest: Language, Legitimacy, and La Frontera," in *The Shakespeare User: Critical and Creative Appropriations in a Networked Culture*, ed. Valerie M. Fazel and Louise Geddes (Palgrave, 2017), 42.

8 Luis Alberto Urrea, "Luis Alberto Urrea," *The Progressive Magazine*, January 27, 2012, https://progressive.org/latest/luis-alberto-urrea/.

9 All citations of *The Tempest* are from William Shakespeare, *The Tempest*, ed. Virginia Mason Vaughan and Alden T. Vaughan, The Arden Shakespeare Third Series (Bloomsbury, 2011).

10 On the play's Mediterranean contexts, see Ambereen Dadabhoy, *Shakespeare through Islamic Worlds* (Routledge, 2024), 39–78. See also Barbara Fuchs, "Conquering Islands: Contextualizing The Tempest," *Shakespeare Quarterly* 48, no. 1 (1997): 45–62. For an overview of the Caribbean and American contexts of *The Tempest* and its afterlives, see Peter Hulme and William H. Sherman, eds., *The Tempest and Its Travels* (Reaktion Books, 2000).

11 For more on the word "profit" and language learning, see Kathryn Vomero Santos, "Profit," in *Logomotives: Words that Change the World, 1400–1700*, ed. Marjorie Rubright and Stephen Spiess (Edinburgh University Press, 2025).

12 On the play's treatment of service, slavery, and liberty, see Urvashi Chakravarty, *Fictions of Consent: Slavery, Servitude, and Free Service in Early Modern England* (University of Pennsylvania Press, 2022), 171–97.
13 Tom Lindsay, "'Which First Was Mine Own King': Caliban and the Politics of Service and Education in *The Tempest*," *Studies in Philology* 113, no. 2 (2016): 422.
14 Julia Reinhard Lupton, "Creature Caliban," *Shakespeare Quarterly* 51, no. 1 (2000): 17.
15 Debapriya Sarkar, "*The Tempest*'s Other Plots," *Shakespeare Studies* 45 (2017): 222.
16 Virginia Mason Vaughan and Alden T. Vaughan, "*The Tempest* and Early Modern Conceptions of Race," in *The Cambridge Companion to Shakespeare and Race*, ed. Ayanna Thompson (Cambridge University Press, 2021), 141. On the play's construction of Caliban as monstrous, see Katherine Schaap Williams, *Unfixable Forms: Disability, Performance, and the Early Modern English Theater* (Cornell University Press, 2021), 186–218.
17 Patricia Akhimie, *Shakespeare and the Cultivation of Difference: Race and Conduct in the Early Modern World* (Routledge, 2018), 152.
18 Jonathan Goldberg, "The Print of Goodness," in *The Culture of Capital: Property, Cities, and Knowledge in Early Modern England*, ed. Henry S. Turner (Routledge, 2002), 236.
19 Nedda Mehdizadeh, "Drowning the First Folio: Co-laboring and the Value of Knowledge in *The Tempest*," *Shakespeare Quarterly* 74, no. 3 (2023): 236. On textuality in *The Tempest*, see James Kearney, *The Incarnate Text: Imagining the Book in Reformation England* (University of Pennsylvania Press, 2009).
20 Mehdizadeh, "Drowning the First Folio," 237.
21 For an analysis of several such afterlives, see Alden T. Vaughan and Virginia Mason Vaughan, *Shakespeare's Caliban: A Cultural History* (Cambridge University Press, 1991) and Chantal Zabus, *Tempests after Shakespeare* (Palgrave, 2002). Other and more recent examples are addressed in this book's introduction and third chapter.
22 Roberto Fernández Retamar, "Caliban: Notes Toward a Discussion of Culture in Our America," trans. Lynn Garafola, David Arthur McMurray, and Roberto Márquez, *The Massachusetts Review* 15, no. 1/2 (1974), 24. The quotation reads as follows in Spanish: "No conozco otra metáfora más acertada de nuestra situación cultural, de nuestra realidad […] ¿qué es nuestra historia, qué es nuestra cultura, sino la historia, sino la

cultura de Calibán?" Roberto Fernández Retamar, *Calibán. Apuntes sobre la cultura en nuestra América* (Editorial Diógenes, 1971), 30. In making this analogy, Fernández Retamar is responding, in part, to Uruguayan writer José Enrique Rodó, who argued in a 1900 essay that Ariel was a positive symbol for the intellectual relationship that Latin America should have to Europe. See Rodó, *Ariel*, trans. Margaret Sayers Peden (University of Texas Press, 1988).

23 Mexican American Liberation Committee, "THS Issues," *Coraje*, No. 1 (March 1969): 2.

24 Mexican American Liberation Committee, "THS Issues," 2.

25 Eduardo Rios, "Challenge to Teachers, Students," *Coraje*, no. 3 (July 1969): 6.

26 For more on this period of educational activism in Arizona, see Darius V. Echevarría, *Aztlán Arizona: Mexican American Educational Empowerment, 1968–1978* (University of Arizona Press, 2014).

27 On the mass mobilization of Latinxs across the United States during the early decades of the twenty-first century, see Chris Zepeda-Millán, *Latino Mass Mobilization: Immigration, Racialization, and Activism* (Cambridge University Press, 2017). For more on student activism, see Margarita Berta-Ávila, Anita Tijerina Revilla, and Julie López Figueroa, eds., *Marching Students: Chicana and Chicano Activism in Education, 1968 to the Present* (University of Nevada Press, 2011).

28 For an interview with Dolores Huerta about this incident, see *Outlawing Dolores Huerta: The Tucson Diaries*, dir. Gabriel Buelna, October 17, 2013, The Nonprofit Network, YouTube video, 56:24, https://www.youtube.com/watch?v=oIDY9gsspuE.

29 Press release from Horne quoted in Daniel Scarpinato, "Tucson High Will Get GOP Speaker," *Arizona Daily Star*, April 26, 2006. For a transcript of Margaret Garcia Dugan's remarks, see "Full Text of Dugan's Speech," *Arizona Daily Star*, May 12, 2006.

30 On the politics and implications of Proposition 203, see Wayne E. Wright, "The Political Spectacle of Arizona's Proposition 203," *Educational Policy* 19, no. 5 (2005): 662–700. See also Eric J. Johnson, "Arbitrating Repression: Language Policy and Education in Arizona," *Language and Education* 26, no. 1 (2012): 53–76.

31 Eric Sagara, "'Equal-Time' Talk Fuels Protest," *Tucson Citizen*, May 13, 2006.

32 Tom Horne, "An Open Letter to the Citizens of Tucson," June 11, 2007.
33 Ruben Espinosa, "Chicano Shakespeare: The Bard, the Border, and the Peripheries of Performance," in *Teaching Social Justice through Shakespeare: Why Renaissance Literature Matters Now*, ed. Hillary Eklund and Wendy Beth Hyman (Edinburgh University Press, 2019), 76.
34 Henry A. Giroux, *Youth in Revolt: Reclaiming a Democratic Future* (Routledge, 2013), 82.
35 See Cambium Learning, Inc., "Curriculum Audit," 69.
36 Quoted in Elias Serna, "Tempest, Arizona: Criminal Epistemologies and the Rhetorical Possibilities of Raza Studies," *The Urban Review* 45, no. 1 (2013): 50.
37 Ronald Takaki, *A Different Mirror: A History of Multicultural America*, rev. ed. (Back Bay Books, 2008), 28.
38 Quoted in Elias Serna, "Tempest, Arizona," 51.
39 Quoted in Elias Serna, "Tempest, Arizona," 51.
40 Antonio C. Márquez, "Voices of Caliban: From Curse to Discourse," *Confluencia* 13, no. 1 (1997): 167.
41 ThreeSonorans, "TUSD vs The Tempest - To Teach or Not To Teach," January 17, 2012, YouTube video, 6:19, https://www.youtube.com/watch?v=KlWpYz1KyjE&t.
42 *Outlawing Shakespeare: The Battle for the Tucson Mind*, dir. Fernando James Orozco and Gabriel Buelna, The Nonprofit Network, YouTube video, 41:52, October 31, 2012, https://www.youtube.com/watch?v=anChx_9TF-Q.
43 ThreeSonorans, "TUSD vs The Tempest."
44 Quoted in Jeff Biggers, "Tucson Says Banished Books May Return to Classrooms," *Salon*, January 18, 2012, https://www.salon.com/2012/01/18/tucson_says_banished_books_may_return_to_classrooms/.
45 Tim Wise (host), "Dangerous Knowledge: Dr. Curtis Acosta Discusses the Assault on Mexican American Studies in Tucson," *Speak Out with Tim Wise*, October 31, 2017, podcast, 56:31.
46 The seven prohibited books included the following: *Critical Race Theory: An Introduction* by Richard Delgado and Jean Stefancic; *500 Years of Chicano History in Pictures*, ed. Elizabeth Martinez; *Message to Aztlán* by Rodolfo "Corky" Gonzales; *Chicano! The History of the Mexican American Civil Rights*

Movement by F. Arturo Rosales; *Occupied America: A History of Chicanos* by Rodolfo Acuña; *Pedagogy of the Oppressed* by Paulo Freire; and *Rethinking Columbus: The Next 500 Years* by Bill Bigelow.

47 Tucson Unified School District, "Reports of TUSD Book Ban Completely False and Misleading," news release, January 17, 2012. This release is dated January 17, 2011, but it is clear from context and news coverage that it was actually published in 2012.

48 Rodolfo F. Acuña, "When Do You Start Counting?" *The Progressive Magazine*, January 30, 2012, https://progressive.org/latest/start-counting/.

49 Edward W. Said, *Culture and Imperialism* (Vintage Books, 1994), 213.

50 *González v. Douglas*, United States District Court, District of Arizona, 269 F. Supp. 3d 948 (2017), 966.

51 Quoted in Laurie Roberts, "John Huppenthal: All Spanish Media Should Be Silenced," *The Arizona Republic*, June 24, 2014, https://www.azcentral.com/story/laurie-roberts/2014/06/24/john-huppenthal-anonymous-blog-posts-latino-comments/11312133/.

52 Quoted in *González v. Douglas*, 958.

53 Quoted in *González v. Douglas*, 958.

54 Quoted in Ari Bloomekatz, "Victory for Mexican American Studies in Arizona: An Interview with Curtis Acosta," August 31, 2017, https://rethinkingschools.org/2017/08/31/acosta/.

55 Gabriel Matthew Schivone and StudentNation, "US District Judge Orders TUSD to Reinstate 'Culturally Relevant Courses,'" *The Nation*, February 12, 2013, https://www.thenation.com/article/archive/us-district-judge-orders-tusd-reinstate-culturally-relevant-courses/.

56 Sylvia Kwon, "Ethnic Studies Legislation: State Scan." Comprehensive Center Network, 2021.

57 For a summary and map of these efforts as of February 1, 2022, see Cathryn Stout and Thomas Wilburn, "CRT Map: Efforts to Restrict Teaching Racism and Bias Have Multiplied across the U.S.," *Chalkbeat*, June 9, 2021, updated February 1, 2022, https://www.chalkbeat.org/22525983/map-critical-race-theory-legislation-teaching-racism.

58 "Tom Horne's Plan to Make Arizona's Public Schools the Best in the Nation," Tom Horne for Superintendent, accessed June 17, 2024, https://www.electtomhorne.com/toms-plan.

59 "Tom Horne's Plan."

60 When Horne declared the state's dual language programs to be in violation of Proposition 203, Arizona Attorney General Kris Mayes opined that Horne has no statutory authority to punish schools that adopted a model approved by the State Board of Education in 2019. Horne attempted to take legal action against the attorney general and the governor, but a trial judge dismissed his lawsuit in early 2024, declaring that he also has no authority to sue in his capacity as State Superintendent of Instruction.

61 This language was repeated in similar bills introduced in Kentucky, Mississippi, North Dakota, and South Dakota.

62 See Juliet Dee, "Do Bans on Teaching 'Divisive Concepts' Interfere with Students' Right to Know?" *Journal of Academic Freedom* 13 (2022): 1–15.

63 Matt Krause to Texas Education Agency and Selected Superintendents, October 25, 2021, https://static.texastribune.org/media/files/965725d7f01b8a25ca44b6fde2f5519b/krauseletter.pdf.

64 Matt Krause to Texas Education Agency and Selected Superintendents.

65 Greg Abbott to Mike H. Morath, Martha J. Wong, and Keven Ellis, November 8, 2021, https://gov.texas.gov/uploads/files/press/O-Morath_Wong_Ellis202111081428.pdf.

66 Jazmine Janay Cuevas, "Texas: The Censored, the Obscene, the Pornographic, and the Humanities," The Humanities Collaborative, February 2022, https://humanitiescollaborative.utep.edu/project-blog/texas-humanities.

67 Lupe Mendez, "The Texas GOP Has Declared War on Books. I've Seen This Before," *Texas Observer*, January 14, 2022, https://www.texasobserver.org/the-texas-gop-has-declared-war-on-books-ive-seen-this-before/.

68 Florida Department of Education and Florida State Board of Education, "Florida's State Academic Standards – Social Studies, 2023," https://www.fldoe.org/core/fileparse.php/20653/urlt/6-4.pdf.

69 Florida House of Representatives, House Bill 1557, 2022 Legislative Session, https://www.flsenate.gov/Session/Bill/2022/1557.

70 Quoted in Mike Schneider, "Shakespeare and Penguin Book Get Caught in Florida's 'Don't Say Gay Laws,'" *Associated Press News*, August 8, 2023, https://apnews.com/article/lgbtq-florida-book-ban-tango-b5e985c99c189f406baa0f1cee8ad7fb.

71 Marlene Sokol, "Hillsborough Schools Cut Back on Shakespeare, Citing New Florida Rules," *Tampa Bay Times*, August 7, 2023, https://www.tampabay.com/news/education/2023/08/07/hillsborough-schools-cut-back-shakespeare-citing-new-florida-rules/.

72 Jeffrey S. Solochek, "Shakespeare Belongs in Classrooms, Florida Says, Knocking Hillsborough," *Tampa Bay Times*, August 8, 2023, https://www.tampabay.com/news/education/2023/08/08/shakespeare-belongs-classrooms-florida-says-knocking-hillsborough/.

73 Quoted in Sokol, "Hillsborough Schools."

74 Holland published a lightly revised and expanded version of this talk soon after the conference. See Peter Holland, "Shakespeare, Humanity Indicators, and the Seven Deadly Sins," *Borrowers and Lenders: The Journal of Shakespeare and Appropriation* 7, no. 1 (2012), https://borrowers-ojs-azsu.tdl.org/borrowers/article/view/90/178.

75 Holland, "Shakespeare, Humanity Indicators, and the Seven Deadly Sins."

76 Taylor, ¡Presente!, 4.

77 Quoted in Jing Fong, "When This Teacher's Ethnic Studies Classes Were Banned, His Students Took the District to Court—and Won," *YES!*, April 26, 2014, https://www.yesmagazine.org/issue/education-uprising/2014/04/26/interview-with-curtis-acosta.

REFERENCES

Abbott, Greg. Greg Abbott to Mike H. Morath, Martha J. Wont, and Kevin Ellis. November 8, 2021. https://gov.texas.gov/uploads/files/press/O-Morath_Wong_Ellis202111081428.pdf.

Acuña, Rodolfo F. "When Do You Start Counting?" *The Progressive Magazine*, January 30, 2012. https://progressive.org/latest/start-counting/.

Akhimie, Patricia. *Shakespeare and the Cultivation of Difference: Race and Conduct in the Early Modern World*. Routledge, 2018.

Arizona House of Representatives. House Bill 2281. 49th Legislature. 2nd Regular Session. 2010. https://www.azleg.gov/legtext/49leg/2r/bills/hb2281s.pdf.

Berta-Ávila, Margarita, Anita Tijerina Revilla, and Julie López Figueroa, eds. *Marching Students: Chicana and Chicano Activism in Education, 1968 to the Present*. University of Nevada Press, 2011.

Biggers, Jeff. "Tucson Says Banished Books May Return to Classrooms." *Salon*, January 18, 2012. https://www.salon.com/2012/01/18/tucson_says_banished_books_may_return_to_classrooms/.

Bloomekatz, Ari. "Victory for Mexican American Studies in Arizona: An Interview with Curtis Acosta." *Rethinking Schools*, August 31, 2017. https://rethinkingschools.org/2017/08/31/acosta/.

Buelna, Gabriel, dir. *Outlawing Dolores Huerta: The Tucson Diaries*. The Nonprofit Network. October 17, 2013. YouTube video, 56:23. https://www.youtube.com/watch?v=oIDY9gsspuE.

Cabrera, Nolan L., Jeffrey F. Milem, and Ronald W. Marx. "An Empirical Analysis of the Effects of Mexican American Studies Participation on Student Achievement within Tucson Unified School District." Report to Special Master Dr. Willis D. Hawley on the Tucson Unified School District Desegregation Case. University of Arizona College of Education, June 20, 2012.

Cabrera, Nolan, Jeffrey F. Milem, Ozan Jaquette, and Ronald W. Marx. "Missing the (Student Achievement) Forest for All the (Political) Trees: Empiricism and the Mexican American Studies Controversy in Tucson." *American Educational Research Journal* 51, no. 6 (2014): 1084–118.

Cambium Learning, Inc. "Curriculum Audit of the Mexican American Studies Department Tucson Unified School District." National Academic Educational Partnership, May 2, 2011.

Cervantes, Lorna Dee. "A Chicano Poem." *Huizache: The Magazine of Latino Literature* 2 (2012): 8–9.

Cervantes, Lorna Dee. *Sueño*. Wings Press, 2013.

Chakravarty, Urvashi. *Fictions of Consent: Slavery, Servitude, and Free Service in Early Modern England*. University of Pennsylvania Press, 2022.

Cuevas, Jazmine Janay. "Texas: The Censored, the Obscene, the Pornographic, and the Humanities." The Humanities Collaborative, February 2022. https://humanitiescollaborative.utep.edu/project-blog/texas-humanities.

Dadabhoy, Ambereen. *Shakespeare through Islamic Worlds*. Routledge, 2024.

Dee, Juliet. "Do Bans on Teaching 'Divisive Concepts' Interfere with Students' Right to Know?" *Journal of Academic Freedom* 13 (2022): 1–15.

Diaz, Tony. *The Tip of the Pyramid: Cultivating Community Cultural Capital*. University of New Orleans Press, 2022.

Dugan, Margaret Garcia. "Full Text of Dugan's Speech." *Arizona Daily Star*, May 12, 2006.

Echevarría, Darius V. *Aztlán Arizona: Mexican American Educational Empowerment, 1968–1978*. University of Arizona Press, 2014.

Espinosa, Ruben. "Beyond *The Tempest*: Language, Legitimacy, and *La Frontera*." In *The Shakespeare User: Critical and Creative Appropriations in a Networked Culture*, edited by Valerie M. Fazel and Louise Geddes. Palgrave, 2017.

Espinosa, Ruben. "Chicano Shakespeare: The Bard, the Border, and the Peripheries of Performance." In *Teaching Social Justice through Shakespeare: Why Renaissance Literature Matters Now*, edited by Hillary Eklund and Wendy Beth Hyman. Edinburgh University Press, 2019.

Fernández Retamar, Roberto. *Calibán. Apuntes sobre la cultura en nuestra América*. Editorial Diógenes, 1971.

Fernández Retamar, Roberto. "Caliban: Notes Toward a Discussion of Culture in Our America." Translated by Lynn Garafola, David Arthur McMurray, and Roberto Márquez. *Massachusetts Review* 15, no. 1/2 (1974): 7–72.

Florida Department of Education and Florida State Board of Education. "Florida's State Academic Standards – Social Studies, 2023." https://www.fldoe.org/core/fileparse.php/20653/urlt/6-4.pdf.

Florida House of Representatives. House Bill 1557. 2022 Legislative Session. https://www.flsenate.gov/Session/Bill/2022/1557.

Fong, Jing. "When This Teacher's Ethnic Studies Classes Were Banned, His Students Took the District to Court—and Won." *YES!* April 26, 2014. https://www.yesmagazine.org/issue/education-uprising/2014/04/26/interview-with-curtis-acosta.

Fuchs, Barbara. "Conquering Islands: Contextualizing *The Tempest*." *Shakespeare Quarterly* 48, no. 1 (1997): 45–62.

Giroux, Henry A. *Youth in Revolt: Reclaiming a Democratic Future*. Routledge, 2013.

Goldberg, Jonathan. "The Print of Goodness." In *The Culture of Capital: Property, Cities, and Knowledge in Early Modern England*, edited by Henry S. Turner. Routledge, 2002.

Holland, Peter. "Shakespeare, Humanity Indicators, and the Seven Deadly Sins." *Borrowers and Lenders: The Journal of Shakespeare and Appropriation* 7, no.1 (2012). https://borrowers-ojs-azsu.tdl.org/borrowers/article/view/90/178.

Horne, Tom. "An Open Letter to the Citizens of Tucson," June 11, 2007. https://www.scribd.com/document/32001977/An-Open-Letter-to-the-Citizens-of-Tucson.

Horne, Tom. "Tom Horne's Plan to Make Arizona's Public Schools the Best in the Nation." Tom Horne for Superintendent. Accessed June 17, 2024. https://www.electtomhorne.com/toms-plan.

Hulme, Peter, and William H. Sherman, eds. *The Tempest and Its Travels*. Reaktion Books, 2000.

Johnson, Eric J. "Arbitrating Repression: Language Policy and Education in Arizona." *Language and Education* 26, no. 1 (2012): 53–76.

Kearney, James. *The Incarnate Text: Imagining the Book in Reformation England*. University of Pennsylvania Press, 2009.

Krause, Matt. Matt Krause to Texas Education Agency and Selected Superintendents. October 25, 2021. https://static.texastribune.org/media/files/965725d7f01b8a25ca44b6fde2f5519b/krauseletter.pdf.

Kwon, Sylvia. "Ethnic Studies Legislation: State Scan." Comprehensive Center Network, 2021.

Lindsay, Tom. "'Which First Was Mine Own King': Caliban and the Politics of Service and Education in *The Tempest*." *Studies in Philology* 113, no. 2 (2016): 397–423.

Lupton, Julia Reinhard. "Creature Caliban." *Shakespeare Quarterly* 51, no. 1 (2000): 1–23.

Márquez, Antonio C. "Voices of Caliban: From Curse to Discourse." *Confluencia* 13, no. 1 (1997): 158–69.

Mehdizadeh, Nedda. "Drowning the First Folio: Co-laboring and the Value of Knowledge in *The Tempest*." *Shakespeare Quarterly* 74, no. 3 (2023): 233–46.

Mendez, Lupe. "The Texas GOP Has Declared War on Books. I've Seen This Before." *Texas Observer*, January 14, 2022. https://www.texasobserver.org/the-texas-gop-has-declared-war-on-books-ive-seen-this-before/.

Mexican American Liberation Committee. "THS Issues." *Coraje*, no. 1. March 1969.

Orozco, Fernando James, and Gabriel Buelna, dir. *Outlawing Shakespeare: The Battle for the Tucson Mind*. The Nonprofit Network. October 31, 2012. YouTube video, 41:52. https://www.youtube.com/watch?v=anChx_9TF-Q.

Rios, Eduardo. "Challenge to Teachers, Students." *Coraje*, no. 3. July 1969.

Roberts, Laurie. "John Huppenthal: All Spanish Media Should Be Silenced." *The Arizona Republic*, June 24, 2014. https://www.azcentral.com/story/laurie-roberts/2014/06/24/john-huppenthal-anonymous-blog-posts-latino-comments/11312133/.

Rodó, José Enrique. *Ariel*. Translated by Margaret Sayers Peden. University of Texas Press, 1988.

Said, Edward W. *Culture and Imperialism*. Vintage Books, 1994.

Sagara, Eric. "'Equal-Time' Talk Fuels Protest." *Tucson Citizen*, May 13, 2006.

Santos, Kathryn Vomero. "Profit." In *Logomotives: Words that Change the World, 1400–1700*, edited by Marjorie Rubright and Stephen Spiess. Edinburgh University Press, 2025.

Sarkar, Debapriya. "The Tempest's Other Plots." *Shakespeare Studies* 45 (2017): 203–30.

Scarpinato, Daniel. "Tucson High Will Get GOP Speaker." *Arizona Daily Star*, April 26, 2006.

Schivone, Gabriel Matthew, and StudentNation. "US District Judge Orders TUSD to Reinstate 'Culturally Relevant Courses.'" *The Nation*, February 12, 2013. https://www.thenation.com/article/archive/us-district-judge-orders-tusd-reinstate-culturally-relevant-courses/.

Schneider, Mike. "Shakespeare and Penguin Book Get Caught in Florida's 'Don't Say Gay Laws.'" *Associated Press News*, August 8, 2023. https://apnews.com/article/lgbtq-florida-book-ban-tango-b5e985c99c189f406baa0f1cee8ad7fb.

Serna, Elias. "Tempest, Arizona: Criminal Epistemologies and the Rhetorical Possibilities of Raza Studies." *The Urban Review* 45, no. 1 (2013): 41–57.

Shakespeare, William. *The Tempest*. Edited by Virginia Mason Vaughan and Alden T. Vaughan. The Arden Shakespeare Third Series. Bloomsbury, 2011.

Sokol, Marlene. "Hillsborough Schools Cut Back on Shakespeare, Citing New Florida Rules." *Tampa Bay Times*, August 7, 2023. https://www.tampabay.com/news/education/2023/08/07/hillsborough-schools-cut-back-shakespeare-citing-new-florida-rules/.

Solochek, Jeffrey S. "Shakespeare Belongs in Classrooms, Florida Says, Knocking Hillsborough." *Tampa Bay Times*, August 8, 2023. https://www.tampabay.com/news/education/2023/08/08/shakespeare-belongs-classrooms-florida-says-knocking-hillsborough/.

Stout, Cathryn, and Thomas Wilburn. "CRT Map: Efforts to Restrict Teaching Racism and Bias Have Multiplied Across the U.S." *Chalkbeat*, June 9, 2021. Updated February 1, 2022. https://www.chalkbeat.org/22525983/map-critical-race-theory-legislation-teaching-racism.

Takaki, Ronald. *A Different Mirror: A History of Multicultural America*. Rev. ed. Back Bay Books, 2008.

Taylor, Diana. ¡*Presente! The Politics of Presence*. Duke University Press, 2020.

ThreeSonorans. "TUSD vs The Tempest - To Teach or Not To Teach." January 17, 2012. YouTube video, 6:19. https://www.youtube.com/watch?v=KlWpYz1KyjE.

Tucson Unified School District. "Reports of TUSD Book Ban Completely False and Misleading." News release. January 17, 2012.

Urrea, Luis Alberto. "Luis Alberto Urrea." *The Progressive Magazine*, January 27, 2012. https://progressive.org/latest/luis-alberto-urrea/.

Vaughan, Alden T., and Virginia Mason Vaughan, *Shakespeare's Caliban: A Cultural History*. Cambridge University Press, 1991.

Vaughan, Virginia Mason, and Alden T. Vaughan. "*The Tempest* and Early Modern Conceptions of Race." In *The Cambridge Companion to Shakespeare and Race*, edited by Ayanna Thompson. Cambridge University Press, 2021.

Williams, Katherine Schaap. *Unfixable Forms: Disability, Performance, and the Early Modern English Theater*. Cornell University Press, 2021.

Wise, Tim. "Dangerous Knowledge: Dr. Curtis Acosta Discusses the Assault on Mexican American Studies in Tucson." *Speak Out with Tim Wise*. October 31, 2017. Podcast, 56:31.

Wright, Wayne E. "The Political Spectacle of Arizona's Proposition 203." *Educational Policy* 19, no. 5 (2005): 662–700.

Zabus, Chantal. *Tempests after Shakespeare*. Palgrave, 2002.

Zepeda-Millán, Chris. *Latino Mass Mobilization: Immigration, Racialization, and Activism*. Cambridge University Press, 2017.

Further Reading and Resources

Shakespeare in Tongues is the product of my own learning from scholars and knowledge holders in many different traditions. In the spirit of the interdisciplinary, cross-cultural, and transhistorical curiosity that animated this book, I have compiled the following list of readings and resources. While some of the materials detailed below are referenced throughout the chapters, I highlight them here as well to encourage further engagement beyond these pages.

One of the most comprehensive lists of publications and resources about the Indian boarding school system in the United States has been maintained by the National Native American Boarding School Healing Coalition (NABS) and made available through their database at boardingschoolhealing.org. Primary documents, secondary scholarship, and bibliographies are also available on the Genoa Indian School Digital Reconciliation Project website (genoaindianschool.org) and the Carlisle Indian School Digital Resource Center (carlisleindian.dickinson.edu). The two-volume report produced by the U.S. Department of the Interior's Federal Indian Boarding School Initiative is currently available online at interior.gov along with several detailed appendices and references.

Among the many works gathered in the above locations, David Wallace Adams's *Education for Extinction: American Indians* and the Boarding School Experience, 1875–1928 (University Press of Kansas, 1995 and 2020) remains one of the most thorough overviews of the U.S. boarding school system. Ojibwe scholar Brenda J. Child's Boarding School Seasons: American Indian Families, 1900–1940 (University of Nebraska Press, 1998) and K. Tsianina Lomawaima's They Called It Prairie Light: The Story of Chilocco Indian School (University of Nebraska Press, 1994) are two early studies that center the voices of Native students and their families. Along with art curator Margaret L. Archuleta, Lomawaima and Child served as the editors of Away from Home: American Indian Boarding School Experiences, a guide for an exhibit that has been open to visitors at the Heard Museum in Phoenix, Arizona, since 2000. Boarding School Blues: Revisiting American Indian Educational Experiences (edited by Clifford E. Trafzer and Jean A. Keller with an introduction by Lorene Sisquoc of the Fort Sill Apache and Mountain Cahuilla Tribes; University of Nebraska Press, 2006) offers an array of scholarly essays on the complexities of the boarding school system.

Readers' knowledge of this difficult history and its legacies will be deepened by engagement with primary sources and accounts featured in books such as Boarding School Voices: Carlisle Indian Students Speak (edited by Arnold Krupat; University of Nebraska Press, 2021); From the Boarding Schools: Apache Indian Students Speak (edited by Arnold Krupat; University of Nebraska Press, 2023); and Recovering Native American Writings in the Boarding School Press (edited by Jaqueline Emery; University of Nebraska Press, 2017). Ruth Spack's America's Second Tongue: American Indian Education and the Ownership of English, 1860–1900 (University of Nebraska Press, 2002) and Amelia V. Katanski's Learning to Write "Indian": The Boarding School Experience and American Indian Literature (University of Oklahoma Press, 2005) both draw on first-person narratives to study the linguistic and literary impacts of boarding school education. Written by NABS co-founder Denise K. Lajimodiere (Turtle Mountain Band of Chippewa), *Stringing Rosaries: The History, the Unforgivable, and the Healing of Northern Plains American Indian Boarding School Survivors* (North Dakota State University Press, 2019) features interviews with sixteen survivors.

A substantial body of work has been published on analogous assimilatory institutions in the settler nations of Canada, Australia, and New Zealand. *A Knock at the Door: The Essential History of Residential Schools from the Truth and Reconciliation Commission of Canada* (University of Manitoba Press, 2015) is one place to begin learning about the Canadian residential school system and its impacts. J. R. Miller's *Shingwauk's Vision: A History of Native Residential Schools* (University of Toronto Press, 1996) offers another historical overview, and Theodore Niizhotay Fontaine's *Broken Circle: The Dark Legacy of Indian Residential Schools* (Heritage House Publishing, 2010) is just one among several survivor memoirs and other works of literature by First Nations writers that address the lasting effects of the residential school system. Along with *Bringing them Home*, the 1997 report of the National Inquiry into the Separation of Aboriginal and Torres Strait Islander Children from their Families conducted by Australia's Human Rights and Equal Opportunity Commission, Anna Haebich's *Broken Circles: Fragmenting Indigenous Families, 1800–2000* (Fremantle Arts Centre Press, 2000) provides deep insight into the histories of the Stolen Generations of Indigenous children in Australia. *A Civilising Mission? Perceptions and Representations of the Native Schools System* (edited by Judith Simon and Linda Tuhiwai Smith; Aukland University Press, 2001) draws on oral histories and testimonies to study the many facets of the state schooling system designed to assimilate Māori children in Aotearoa New Zealand.

As survivors and their descendants continue to grapple with the lasting legacies of the U.S. federal Indian boarding school system, Native American scholars and artists have drawn our attention to the impossibility of disentangling Indigenous engagements with Shakespeare from the histories of attempted cultural eradication in which his works were implicated. As Mohegan playwright, director, and scholar Madeline Sayet notes in her play *Where We Belong*, many Indigenous Shakespeare productions and adaptations have emerged from language and cultural revitalization movements. Sayet discusses examples of such works and her own collaborations with the Native Shakespeare ensemble at Amerinda (American Indian Artsts, Inc.) in "Indigenizing Shakespeare Movement," a video created for the Throughlines project at the Arizona Center for Medieval and Renaissance Studies. This video, along with a transcript and other resources, is available at throughlines.org.

Looking beyond the works I discuss in this book, I want to use this occasion to highlight several Indigenous reimaginings of and engagements with Shakespeare. Taos Pueblo playwright James Lujan's play *Kino and Teresa*, which was commissioned by the South Broadway Cultural Center in Albuquerque, New Mexico, in 1999 and produced by Native Voices at the Autry in 2005, is an adaptation of *Romeo and Juliet* set in the aftermath of the Pueblo Revolt of 1680 and the Spanish Reconquista of 1692. Seminole/Mvskoke playwright Tara Moses's play *Hamlet, El Príncipe de Denmark* is a bilingual Spanish and English adaptation of *Hamlet* set in colonial Mexico that was produced by telatúlsa as part of the 2018 Día de los Muertos festival in Tulsa, Oklahoma. Both of these plays are available in Volume 1 of *The Bard in the Borderlands: An Anthology of Shakespeare Appropriations en La Frontera*, edited by Katherine Gillen, Adrianna M. Santos, and Kathryn Vomero Santos (ACMRS Press, 2023).

In 2022, Moses also directed a production of *Othello* with an Indigenous Futurism and Black liberation framework for the South Dakota Shakespeare Festival. A 2024 film created by the Sealaska Heritage Institute documents the 2007 Perseverance Theatre performance of the Tlingit *Macbeth* at the National Museum of the American Indian in Washington, DC. Conceived and directed by non-Native director Anita Maynard-Losh, translated into Tlingit by Johnny Marks, and performed by an all-Alaska Native cast, this bilingual production of *Macbeth* was first staged in Juneau, Alaska, in 2004. Maynard-Losh discusses the community-based creative process for this project in an essay published in *Weyward Macbeth: Intersections of Race and Performance* (edited by Scott L. Newstok and Ayanna Thompson; Palgrave, 2010).

While we certainly have much to learn from the various publications and presentations by Akwesasne Mohawk scholar Scott Manning Stevens and Kānaka Maoli scholar L. Lehua Yim that I cite throughout this book, their "tri-interview" with Kim F. Hall in *Seeing Race Before Race: Visual Culture and the Racial Matrix in the Premodern World* (edited by Noémie Ndiaye and Lia Markey; ACMRS Press, 2023) is essential for reexamining the epistemologies and worldviews that have dominated the study of the period that we refer to today as early modernity. I likewise recommend spending time with the dialogue among Bethany Hughes (Choctaw), Tara Moses (Seminole/Mvskoke), Mary Kathryn Nagle (Cherokee), and Madeline Sayet (Mohegan) that was recently published in *Shakespeare/Skin: Contemporary Readings in Skin Studies and Theoretical Discourse* (edited by Ruben Espinosa; Arden Shakespeare, 2024).

There are many studies and resources related to the multifaceted topic of Indigenous language revitalization. Two recent handbooks offer useful overviews of the field and will point readers to specific histories, contexts, and practices: *Indigenous Language Revitalization in the Americas* (edited by Serafín M. Coronel-Molina and Teresa L. McCarty; Routledge, 2016) and *The Routledge Handbook of Language Revitalization* (edited by Leanne Hinton, Leena Huss, and Gerald Roche; Routledge, 2018). Hosted by Tlingit and Haida scholar X̱'unei Lance Twitchell, *The Tongue Unbroken* (*Tlél Wudak'óodzi K̲aa L'óot'*) podcast features interviews and conversations with scholars, activists, artists, and families actively engaged in revitalization movements. (It is worth noting here that when Twitchell was a university student studying Tlingit, he played the role of Ross in the 2007 performance of the Tlingit *Macbeth* and served as a language coach for the cast.) Important insights into current language revitalization efforts can also be found in two recent PBS programs. The second season of the *Native America* series features a 2023 episode titled "Language is Life," which focuses on the revitalization of the Navajo, Passamaquoddy, and Cherokee languages. The 2021 PBS documentary *Chasing Voices: The Story of John Peabody Harrington*, directed by Daniel Golding (Quechan), details the work of linguist John P. Harrington and the language revitalization efforts that have emerged from his notes and recordings, including that of Samala (Ineseño) and Šmuwič (Barbareño). For those interested in learning more about the Santa Ynez Band of Chumash Indians and the Samala language in particular, the website for the newly opened Santa Ynez Chumash Museum and Cultural Center (sychumashmuseum.org) offers a robust set of resources.

Without a doubt, Gloria E. Anzaldúa's semi-autobiographical *Borderlands/La Frontera: The New Mestiza* (Aunt Lute Books, 1987) is the most influential theoretical text on the experience of living in the U.S.–Mexico Borderlands. For decades, it has provided readers with frameworks and vocabularies for understanding the complex linguistic, racial, and gendered legacies of the region's multilayered colonial histories. Historian Emma Pérez's *The Decolonial Imaginary: Writing Chicanas into History* (Indiana University Press, 1999) has similarly galvanized both scholars and artists to disrupt dominant narratives about the Borderlands and to push back against colonial methodologies. Several studies (including this one) have used the theories of both Anzaldúa and Pérez, among others, to analyze Borderlands art, performance, and cultural production. The essays in Arturo J. Aldama, Chela Sandoval, and Peter J. García's *Performing the US Latina and Latino Borderlands* (Indiana University Press, 2012), for instance, illustrate the necessity of using interdisciplinary, multilingual, and decolonial approaches to examine the region's culturally hybrid performance practices and the expression of Borderlands identities and experiences. Ila Nicole Sheren's *Portable Borders: Performance Art and Politics on the US Frontera Since 1984* (University of Texas Press, 2015) and Amy Sara Carroll's *REMEX: Toward an Art History of the NAFTA Era* (University of Texas Press, 2017) both provide accounts of the political and cultural history of border art generated in the final decades of the twentieth century and the early decades of the twenty-first. Roberto D. Hernández's *Coloniality of the US/Mexico Border: Power, Violence, and the Decolonial Imperative* (University of Arizona Press, 2018) illuminates the ways in which the racialized and gendered violence that has grown up around the border is part of a long and ongoing colonial history.

The imperative to examine the intersecting histories and structures of colonialism, racism, sexism, epistemic violence, and economic oppression has fueled the development of critical ethnic studies and social justice pedagogies. Christine E.

Sleeter and Miguel Zavala's *Transformative Ethnic Studies in Schools: Curriculum, Pedagogy, and Research* (Teachers College Press, 2020) presents a helpful overview of the theories and practices animating such work in U.S. classrooms. *Rethinking Ethnic Studies* (edited by R. Tolteka Cuauhtin, Miguel Zavala, Christine E. Sleeter, and Wayne Au; Rethinking Schools, 2019) brings together writings and reflections by many of the leading teachers and activists working within critical ethnic studies frameworks. *Knowledge for Justice: An Ethnic Studies Reader* (edited by David K. Yoo, Pamela Grieman, Charlene Villaseñor Black, Danielle Dupuy, and Arnold Ling-Chuang Pan; University of Washington Press, 2021) is a joint publication of UCLA's four ethnic studies research centers that brings together essays on the intellectual, social, and political struggles that have shaped ethnic studies research and teaching in higher education spaces. Paulo Freire's *Pedagogy of the Oppressed* (1968) and bell hooks's *Teaching to Transgress: Education as the Practice of Freedom* (Routledge, 1994) remain touchstones for these growing fields of pedagogical theory and practice.

The frameworks that inform critical ethnic studies and social justice pedagogies have also been influential among scholars and teachers of Shakespeare. For educators who wish to use Shakespeare to help students develop racial literacy and engage in thoughtful conversations about how race continues to be constructed within systems of power and domination, Ambereen Dadabhoy and Nedda Mehdizadeh's *Anti-Racist Shakespeare* (Cambridge University Press, 2023) is an excellent open access resource. *Teaching Social Justice through Shakespeare: Why Renaissance Literature Matters Now* (edited by Hillary Eklund and Wendy Beth Hyman; Edinburgh University Press, 2019) is another open access book that outlines a series of thoughtful approaches to cultivating classroom environments that foster ethical thinking, collaborative learning, and meaningful action.

Many of the pedagogical approaches outlined in these two books are indebted to several field-defining studies of Shakespeare and race that remain required reading. Kim F. Hall's *Things of Darkness: Economies of Race and Gender* (Cornell University Press, 1996) and Margo Hendricks and Patricia Parker's collection *Women, "Race" and Writing in the Early Modern Period* (Routledge, 1994) are two groundbreaking books that brought race and racism to the fore in a field that often refused to engage with such topics. Ayanna Thompson's *Passing Strange: Shakespeare, Race, and Contemporary America* (Oxford University Press, 2011)—along with her edited collection *Colorblind Shakespeare: New Perspectives on Race and Performance* (Routledge, 2006)—equips readers with the necessary tools and vocabularies for grappling with complex issues of race in contemporary performance, film, and media. Peter Erickson's *Citing Shakespeare: The Reinterpretation of Race in Contemporary Literature and Art* (Palgrave, 2007) is a model for how to understand the ways that race shapes contemporary artists' invocations and revisions of Shakespeare.

It is a testament to these foundational studies that the list of books and articles on Shakespeare and race continues to grow. In the *Spotlight on Shakespeare* series, Ruben Espinosa's *Shakespeare on the Shades of Racism* (Routledge, 2021) and Ambereen Dadabhoy's *Shakespeare through Islamic Worlds* (Routledge, 2024) both demonstrate the value of bold and dynamic cross-historical thinking about the construction of race and the functions of racism in early modern texts and their contemporary echoes. Vanessa I. Corredera's *Reanimating Shakespeare's Othello in Post-Racial America* (Edinburgh University Press, 2022) and Joyce Green MacDonald's *Shakespearean Adaptation, Race and Memory in the New World*

(Palgrave, 2020) are essential for understanding the complexities of race in North American adaptations, appropriations, and performances of Shakespeare. Jesus Montaño's *Young Latinx Shakespeares: Race, Justice, and Literary Appropriation* (Palgrave, 2024) offers a robust interdisciplinary examination of how Latinx writers have reimagined Shakespeare to create space for young readers to explore issues of race, language, gender, and sexuality. Miles Grier's *Inkface: Othello and White Authority in the Era of Atlantic Slavery* (University of Virginia Press, 2023) traces the histories and technologies of race-making in transatlantic and early American performances of Shakespeare's *Othello*. Ian Smith's *Black Shakespeare: Reading and Misreading Race* (Cambridge University Press, 2022) draws on the Black American intellectual tradition to show how systemic whiteness has shaped interpretations of Shakespeare's plays and often obscured their treatment of race. Written in an accessible manner for a wide audience, Farah Karim-Cooper's *The Great White Bard* (Viking, 2023) offers readers a set of entry points into discussions about the intersections of race, gender, and otherness in Shakespeare's works and their legacies.

Several special issues and edited collections published in the last decade will give readers an excellent sense of just how lively, multifaceted, and urgently needed such discussions are. They include the 2016 special issue of *Shakespeare Quarterly* on Shakespeare and race (edited by Kim F. Hall and Peter Erickson); the 2020 forum on Shakespeare and Black America in *The Journal of American Studies* (edited by Kim F. Hall and Patricia A. Cahill); *The Cambridge Companion to Shakespeare and Race* (edited by Ayanna Thompson; Cambridge University Press, 2021); *White People in Shakespeare: Essays on Race, Culture and the Elite* (edited by Arthur Little, Jr.; Arden Shakespeare, 2023); *The Oxford Handbook of Shakespeare and Race* (edited by Patricia

Akhimie; Oxford University Press, 2024); and *Shakespeare/Skin: Contemporary Readings in Skin Studies and Theoretical Discourse* (edited by Ruben Espinosa; Arden Shakespeare, 2024).

It is my ardent hope for the field of Shakespeare studies and the humanities more broadly that we continue to engage in boldly interdisciplinary, multilingual, cross-cultural, and transhistorical thinking as we ask bigger and deeper questions, thereby expanding what we know, who we know, and how we know.

Index

Note: *Italic* page numbers refer to figures and page numbers followed by "n" denote endnotes.

Abbott, Greg 189
Acosta, Curtis 180–3, 186, 189, 193
Acuña, Rodolfo 184; *Occupied America: A History of Chicanos* 184
Adams, Joseph Quincy 5–8, 12, 23
Akhimie, Patricia 172
Alarcón, Francisco X., "Para Los Nueve del Capitolio/For the Capitol Nine" 143; *Poetry of Resistance: Voices for Social Justice* 143, 144
Albanese, Denise 12
Alcaraz, Lalo 122
Aldama, Arturo J. 112
alienation 17, 121, 174, 184
American Sign Language 1
American Southwest 9, 24, 106, 120, 163, 165, 181
American West 8, 24, 55
Anaya, Rudolfo, *Bless Me, Ultima* 166
Anglo-American identity 23, 50
Anglo-American supremacy 31
anti-CRT movement 188
anti-racism 187
Anzaldúa, Gloria E. 20, 25, 28, 123, 129, 133, 148; *Borderlands/La Frontera* 10, 25, 28, 121, 123, 127, 129, 151n9, 153n23; "How to Tame a Wild Tongue" 121
Applegate, Richard B. 92–5
Arapaho 47

Arce, Julissa 17
Arizona House Bill 2281 (HB 2281) 161, 162, 166, 167, 179, 182, 184, 185, 187, 188
Arizona Senate Bill 1070 (SB 1070) 142–4
Army Theatre (Corpus Christi, Texas) 9
Asian Americans 16, 33n39
Asian immigrants 7
assimilation 3–6, 10, 16, 28, 31, 43, 51, 54–6, 77; agenda of Carlisle 48, 50; cultural 75; definition of 14; education 40–4, 147; forced 26, 57, 92; immigrants 3, 6, 15; institutional pressures 3, 147; linguistic 6, 10–12, 16, 26, 40–4, 66, 72, 92, 111, 147; policies 85n70; rites/riots of 13–24

Baldwin, James, "Why I Stopped Hating Shakespeare" 13–14
Banned Book Bashes 162
BAW/TAF *see* Border Art Workshop/Taller de Arte Fronterizo (BAW/TAF)
"Betrayal at Wounded Knee Creek, The" (Byrd) 44
Between Two Knees (the 1491s) 73
BIA *see* Bureau of Indian Affairs (BIA)

Biden, Joe 77
bilingual education 2, 175, 178, 179, 188
Bill Emerson English Language Empowerment Act (1996) 2
Black Americans 7, 14
Bless Me, Ultima (Anaya) 166
Blumenbach, Johann Friedrich 140
Booher, Mark 95, 101, 108
Border Art Workshop/Taller de Arte Fronterizo (BAW/TAF) 133, 134
Border Field State Park 123–4, 127, 134, 135
Borderlands/La Frontera (Anzaldúa) 10, 25, 28, 121, 123, 127, 129, 133, 147, 151n9, 153n23
Border Protection, Antiterrorism, and Illegal Immigration Control Act of 2005 (H.R. 4437) 177
Border Tableau 133
Border Wedding, The (Gómez-Peña and Hicks) 133, 134
Brewer, Jan 142, 143
Bright Eyes (Inshata-Theumba, Susette La Flesche) 68, 84n63
Bristol, Michael 13
Buffalo Bill 56, 67
Bureau of Indian Affairs (BIA) 42, 84–5n70
Byrd, Sidney H. 40, 43–5, 54, 78n10; "The Betrayal at Wounded Knee Creek" 44

California Assembly Bill 544 95
Cannibal (Sinclair) 19
cannibalism 18
Canning, Charlotte M. 9
Cantos de adolescencia (Songs of Youth) (Paredes) 120–1
Cantú, Norma Elia 143
Carlisle Arrow, The 48, 49
Carlisle Indian Industrial School 10, 11, 42, 47–51, 80n20
Carlisle Press 48

Carmona, Christopher 143–4
Carter administration 128
Castillo, Ana, *So Far from God* 166
Castro, Eugenio 141
Cervantes, Lorna Dee, "A Chicano Poem" 162–4
Chase, Horace R. 67, 84n62
"Chicano Poem, A" (Cervantes) 162–4
Chicana/o/x literature 143–4, 162, 181–2
Chicana/o/xs 150, 175; *see also* Mexican Americans
Chicano Studies 184
Child, Brenda J. 57, 77, 80n25
Chinese Exclusion Act (1882) 7
Chumash Revolt (1824) 93
Cisneros, Sandra, *The House on Mango Street* 166
citizenship 10, 43, 106, 120
Civilization Fund Act (1819) 10, 41
Code of Indian Offenses 42
Codeswitch: Fires from Mi Corazon (De Anda) 144
colonial/colonialism 20, 21, 26, 58, 101, 140, 167, 184; cruelties of 46, 59; cultural 30; discourses 19; dominance of English 2, 41; education system 46, 63; enslavement 22; oppression 22, 60, 63, 174; power 43, 181; racism 26, 184; settler *see* settler colonialism; survival under 42, 58–59; violence *see* violence
Common Core State Standards for English Language Arts 13
conformity 13, 31, 179
Cool, Joseph 191
Coraje 175
Corredera, Vanessa I. 24, 30
counternarratives 24, 174, 176, 181
COVID-19 pandemic 125

critical ethnic studies 176; *see also* ethnic studies
critical race theory (CRT) 176, 182, 187, 188
Cuevas, Jazmine Janay 189
cultural capital 30, 46, 51, 85n71, 162, 172
cultural colonialism 30
cultural genocide 43, 46, 51
cultural imperialism 122

Dawes Act (1887) 42, 84n66
De Anda, Iris 119, 142, 144; *Codeswitch: Fires from Mi Corazon* 144; "This is not Just Poetry" 150; "To be a Pocha or not to be" 28, 142, 144–9
decolonial imaginary 24, 96, 98, 106, 112
Demeter, Jason M. 7
de-Mexicanization 133
DeSantis, Ron 190
Diaz, Tony 162, 166
displacement 20, 41
dispossession 26, 41, 52
diversity 2
diversity, equity, and inclusion 192
"Don't Say Gay" law (Florida) 191; *see also* Parental Rights in Education Act
Dugan, Margaret Garcia 178
Dundy, Elmer S. 68, 69

East Los High 144
educational inequality 175
End of the Line 133
English-only policies, Official English 1–3
enslavement 2, 3, 8, 10, 22, 23, 164, 168; *see also* slavery
Erickson, Peter 29
Espinosa, Ruben 25, 29–30, 166, 179
ethnic chauvinism 179
ethnic studies 162, 176, 179, 187

Fanestil, John 131
Federal Indian Boarding School Initiative 74–5, 77
federal Indian boarding school system 10, 12, 41, 45, 46, 48, 51, 52, 56–7, 62, 70, 72, 74–7
Fernández Retamar, Roberto 139, 174
First Amendment 185
Floyd, George 187
Folger Shakespeare Library 5, 12, 23
Foster, Emma H. 48
1491s, the, *Between Two Knees* 73
Fourteenth Amendment 185
free speech 2
Friendship Park 124, 125, 125–7, 131, 132, 153n22
Friends of Friendship Park 132
Friends of the Indian 43

"Gabble Like a Thing Most Brutish" (Sinclair) 19
Galván Rodríguez, Odilia, *Poetry of Resistance: Voices for Social Justice* 143, 144
García, Peter J. 112
García Echeverría, Olga 119
Geddes, Louise 24
gendered violence 60
Genoa U.S. Indian Industrial School 26, 40–5, 52–4, 53, 56, 57, 63, 66, 67, 72, 80n23, 85n70; Genoa Indian School Digital Reconciliation Project 54; Genoa Indian School Foundation 52–3
Gillen, Katherine 24, 64
Giroux, Henry A. 179
Goin, Peter 125, 128
Goldberg, Jonathan 172
Gomez, Richard 95
Gómez-Peña, Guillermo 28, 133–4, 137–41, 149; *The Border Wedding* 133, 134; "El Hamlet

Fronterizo" 28, 129–31, 135, 141–2, 144, 153n27; Hamlet fronterizo/border Hamlet persona 123, 134, 135, 138, 139, 142
González, José Cruz 95; *Invierno* 27, 95–112, 101, 108
González v. Douglas (2017) 185
Goodburn, Amy 54
Grant, Ulysses S. 8, 41
Great Plains Indians 41

Haaland, Deb 74–7, 83n57
Haas, Mary 93
Hajratwala, Minal, "On Shakespeare and the Quest for Belonging" 14
Hall, Kim F. 29
Hamlet (Shakespeare) 28, 49, 119, 122–3, 131, 135, 137, 139–41, 147–9, 152n15, 191
"Hamlet Fronterizo, El" (Gómez-Peña) 28, 129–31, 135, 144
Harrington, John Peabody 92–4, 111, 113n7
Hendricks, Margo 30–1
Henry IV, Part 1 (Shakespeare) 15–16
Henry IV, Part 2 (Shakespeare) 16–17
Henry V (Shakespeare) 16
Herrera, Spencer 119
Hicks, Emily, *The Border Wedding* 133, 134
Ho-Chunk 54–5; *see also* Winnebago
Holland, Peter 192–3
Hong, Cathy Park 17–18
Horne, Tom 178, 179, 188, 199n60
House on Mango Street, The (Cisneros) 166
"How to Tame a Wild Tongue" (Anzaldúa) 121
Huerta, Dolores 177, 178, 196n28
Hughes, Bethany 72
Huppenthal, John 179–80, 185–6

immigrants 3, 6, 7, 15–21, 52, 104, 105, 142, 177, 185
immigration 3, 6, 7, 128, 132, 142, 177, 181, 185
imperialism: American 3, 21; cultural 122; linguistic 5
Indian Appropriations Act (1871) 42
Indian Peace Commission 41
Indian Reorganization Act 85n70
Indian Self-Determination and Education Assistance Act 12, 85n70
Indian Territory 58, 68
Indigenous Peoples 2, 8, 23, 41–3, 46, 50, 52, 62, 70, 77, 93, 162, 172, 176
Indolent Boys, The (Momaday) 63
intellectual freedom 190
intellectual superiority 172
interracial marriage 9, 101
Invierno (González) 27, 95–112, 101, 108

Jacobs, Margaret 51, 78n6
Jamaican Patois 19–20
Johnson–O'Malley Act (1934) 85n70
Johnson–Reed Act (1924) 7
justice 27, 55–71, 74, 150; legal 45; political 25; racial 187; retributive 67; social 24–5, 176, 187

K-12 education 187, 192
Kamloops Indian Residential School 75
Kang, Jay Caspian 3
Keesick, Thomas Moore 57, 83n52
Kinsley, Elisabeth H. 7
Kiowa Boarding School 63
Korean Americans 18
Kowal, Lewis D. 180
Krause, Matt 189

Lakota 44, 65
language revitalization 4, 12, 24, 27, 55, 76, 94–5
Leal, Luis 119
Lee, Chang-rae, *Native Speaker* 15–18
legal justice 45
Librotraficantes 161, 162, 165, 190
linguistic imperialism 5
linguistic oppression: and assimilation 10–12, 23, 26, 40–4, 66, 72, 92, 111; resistance 4, 139, 173–4; revitalization *see* language revitalization; settler colonialism 3, 4
linguistic racism 186
linguistic superiority 172
linguistic terrorism 20, 123
Lipps, Oscar 48
Littlebear, Minnie Greywolf 55
Little Priest Tribal College 55
Lomawaima, K. Tsianina 44
Longfellow, Henry Wadsworth, *The Song of Hiawatha* 50, 81n34
Lozano, Rosina 32n19, 106, 115n26, 151n6
Lupton, Julia Reinhard 170

MacDonald, Joyce Green 30
Madison, Lyman 48
MALC *see* Mexican American Liberation Committee (MALC), University of Arizona
Manahatta (Nagle) 73
Manifest Destiny 2, 9, 27, 56
Marieval Indian Residential School 75
Márquez, Antonio C. 181–2
Marr, Jack 92
Marshall, Kathleen 111
MAS *see* Mexican American Studies (MAS)
Matlin, Marlee 1
Mayes, Kris 199n60

McCoy, Tim 47
McDonald, James 56
Measure for Measure (Shakespeare) 26, 45, 52, 55, 59–61, 64, 65, 69–70, 96
MEChA *see* Movimiento Estudiantil Chicano de Aztlán (MEChA)
Medina, Cruz 122
Mehdizadeh, Nedda 173
Mendez, Lupe 190
Mendieta, Eduardo 138–9
Merchant of Venice, The (Shakespeare) 68
mestiza consciousness 123
Mexican American Legal Defense and Educational Fund 175
Mexican American Liberation Committee (MALC), University of Arizona 175
Mexican Americans 121, 122, 162, 175, 176, 179, 180, 183, 184; *see also* Chicana/o/xs
Mexican American Studies (MAS) 28, 29, 161, 162, 164, 167, 174–8, 180, 182–4, 186, 187, 192
Mexican Revolution 120
Mexterminator Project, El 140, 141
migration 4, 26, 29, 31, 131, 132
missions 9; missionaries 10, 41, 93; Mission Santa Ynez 113n4
Mohegan 22–3
Momaday, N. Scott, *The Indolent Boys* 63
Morton, Samuel George 140
Movimiento Estudiantil Chicano de Aztlán (MEChA) 178

Nagle, Mary Kathryn, *Manahatta* 73; *Waaxe's Law* 84n63
National Association for the Advancement of Colored People 175–6
National Native American Boarding School Healing Coalition 74, 76

Native activism 12, 85n70
Native American Languages Act (1990) 12
Native Americans 12, 26, 43, 45, 51, 68, 164
Native languages 12, 52, 72, 95
Native Speaker (Lee) 15–18
Native survivance 55
Native Voices at the Autry 45, 52, 83n51
nepantla 123, 148
Newland, Bryan 74–5
Nguyen, Viet Thanh 20–1, 34n52
Nixon, Pat 124, 127

Occupied America: A History of Chicanos (Acuña) 184
Off the Rails (Reinholz) 26, 27, 45, 46, 52, 55–75, 58, 71, 77
"On Shakespeare and the Quest for Belonging" (Hajratwala) 14
Operation Gatekeeper program 131–2
oppression 13, 51, 121, 123, 181, 183, 190; and enslavement 22; colonial 22, 60, 63, 174; linguistic *see* linguistic oppression; racial *see* racial oppression
Oregon Shakespeare Festival (OSF) 23, 45, 72, 73, 83n51
O'Reilly, Bill, *The O'Reilly Factor* 177–8
Othello (Shakespeare) 8, 9
Outlawing Shakespeare 182

Page Act (1875) 7
Pallone, Frank 2–3
"Para Los Nueve del Capitolio/ For the Capitol Nine" (Alarcón) 143
Paredes, Américo, *Cantos de adolescencia* (Songs of Youth) 120–1
Parental Rights in Education Act (Florida) 190–1; *see also* "Don't Say Gay" law

Pawnee 54, 58, 59, 63, 66
Peace Policy (1869) 41
Pedicone, John 180, 184
Pérez, Emma 24, 96, 98, 106
Pocha Nostra, La 134; *El Mexterminator Project* 140, 141
pocho, definition of 120, 151–2n9
Pocho-ization 133, 137
Pocho Magazine 122
Poetry of Resistance: Voices for Social Justice (Alarcón and Galván Rodríguez) 143, 144
Poets Responding to SB 1070 143–4
Ponca 68
Pratt, Richard Henry 10, 42, 56
premodern critical race studies 30–1
Proposition 203 (Prop 203) 178, 196n30, 199n60
Public Theater, The (New York) 23, 73

race 10, 12, 29, 30, 62, 140, 172, 187–90, 192
racial justice 187
racial oppression 51, 60, 64, 68, 99, 140, 142, 162, 172, 179, 185–187
racial violence 26, 32n12, 60, 62, 140, 185, 188
racism 26, 140, 172, 181; anti-immigrant 19; colonial 184; linguistic 186; systemic 187
Rauch, Bill 45
Raza Studies, La 176, 180, 186
Real ID Act (2005) 132
Red Man and Helper, The 48
Reinholz, Randy 26–7, 45, 46, 52–5, 96; *Off the Rails* 26, 27, 45, 46, 52, 55–75, 58, 71, 77
Reservation Dogs 73
retributive justice 67
reverse anthropology 139
Richmond, Charles 48

right to self-determination 173, 181
Rios, Eduardo 175
Rios, Pedro 132
rites/riots of assimilation 13–24
Romeo and Juliet (Shakespeare) 109, 191
Rutherford Falls 73

Said, Edward 184
Samala (Ineseño) 27, 93–8, 107, 109–111
Samala–English Dictionary 94–5, 111
Sand Creek Massacre 62
San Diego Border Patrol 125
Sandoval, Chela 112
San Patricios 115n20
Santa Ynez Band of Chumash Indians 27, 93–5, 97
Santa Ynez Chumash Culture Day 97
Santos, Adrianna M. 24
Sayet, Madeline 4, 47, 51, 73–4, 84n63, 85n71; *Where We Belong* 11, 22–3, 47, 73, 85n71
school desegregation 176, 186
school segregation 9, 12, 175
Scott, Jean Bruce 45
Secure Fence Act (2006) 132
settler colonialism 9, 11, 22, 42; assimilation 43; British 2, 5, 7–8; Euro-American 104; laws 59, 63; linguistic oppression and resistance 4; and Native Americans 41; racial hierarchy 64; violence 60, 62, 64, 105
settler violence 60, 62, 64, 105
sexual abuse 40, 66, 109, 164
Shakespeare, William (works): *Hamlet* 28, 49, 119, 122–3, 131, 135, 137, 139–41, 147–9, 152n15, 191; *Henry IV, Part 1* 15–16; *Henry IV, Part 2* 16–17; *Henry V* 16; *Measure for Measure* 26, 45, 52, 55, 55, 60, 70, 96; *The Merchant of Venice* 11, 49, 68; *Othello* 8, 9; *Romeo and Juliet* 49, 109, 191; *The Tempest* 17–20, 22, 28, 29, 139, 166–77, 181–4, 189, 191–2; *Twelfth Night* 152n20; *The Winter's Tale* 27, 95, 96, 99, 101, 103–5, 108, 111, 112
Shakespeare Association of America 192
Shakespeare Quarterly 29
Sifuentes, Roberto 140, 141
Sinclair, Safiya 19–20; *Cannibal* 19; "Gabble Like a Thing Most Brutish" 19
slavery 2–4, 7, 8, 10, 20, 22, 23, 65, 164, 167, 168, 170, 171, 190; *see also* enslavement
Smialkowska, Monika 51
Smith, Ian 122
Smithsonian's Bureau of American Ethnology 92
Šmuwič (Barbareño) 94, 113n7
social justice 24–5, 176, 187
social justice pedagogy 176
So Far from God (Castillo) 166
Solares, María Ysidora del Refugio 93, 94, 97, 111
Song of Hiawatha, The (Longfellow) 50
Sonoran Desert 132
Sorkin, Aaron 1
Standing Bear 67–9; *see also United States, ex rel. Standing Bear v. George Crook*
Stevens, Scott Manning 11, 26, 46, 52
Stop the Wrongs to Our Kids and Employees (Stop WOKE) Act 190
systemic racism 187

Takaki, Ronald 181
Tashima, A. Wallace 184–5
Taylor, Diana 25–6; "¡presente!" 165
Tempest, The (Shakespeare) 17–20, 22, 28, 29, 139, 166–77, 181–4, 189, 191–2

Texas Education Agency 189
Texas House Bill 3979 (HB 3979) 189
Texas State Library and Archives Commission 189
"This is not Just Poetry" (De Anda) 150
Thompson, Ayanna 30
Tibbles, Thomas Henry 68
"To be a Pocha or not to be" (De Anda) 28, 119, 142, 144–9, 151n2
Tortilla Curtain 128, 153n24
Treaty of Guadalupe Hidalgo (1848) 9, 105, 120, 124, 152–3n21
Tucson Unified School District (TUSD) 28, 161, 175–6, 178, 180, 183, 184, 186
Twelfth Night (Shakespeare) 152n20

Union Pacific Railroad 56
United Non-Discriminatory Individuals Demanding Our Studies (UNIDOS) 180
United States (U.S.): U.S. Army 8; U.S. Army Corps of Engineers 131; U.S. Congress 41, 42, 77; U.S. Customs and Border Protection 132; U.S. Department of Homeland Security 123; U.S. Department of the Interior 42, 74–6; U.S. House of Representatives 1, 177; U.S. House of Representatives Committee on Indian Affairs 81n29; U.S. Immigration and Naturalization Service 128; U.S. invasion of Mexico (1846) 8, 104–7; U.S. Truth and Healing Commission on Indian Boarding Schools 76
United States, ex rel. Standing Bear v. George Crook 68
Urrea, Luis Alberto 167

U.S.–Mexico border 8, 9, 28, 105, 120, 122–4, 124, 125, 127, 128, 131–3, 135–7, 139, 142, 150, 164, 177
U.S.–Mexico Borderlands (La Frontera) 24, 25, 28, 121, 123, 129, 141, 148, 150

Vasconcelos, José 120
Vaughan, Alden T. 172, 195n21
Vaughan, Virginia Mason 172, 195n21
violence 66, 67, 105, 129; colonial *see* settler violence; epistemic 25; gendered 60; linguistic 25; sexual 60, 62; racial *see* racial violence
Visual Sovereignty Project 73
Vizenor, Gerald 55

Walsh, Catherine E. 112
Waaxe's Law (Nagle) 84n63
Weld, Theodore D. 6
West Wing, The 1–3
Where We Belong (Sayet) 11, 22, 23, 47, 73
Whitewater, Stanford 54
Winnebago 54, 55; *see also* Ho-Chunk
"Why I Stopped Hating Shakespeare" (Baldwin) 13–14
Williams, Nora J. 60
Winter's Tale, The (Shakespeare) 27, 95, 96, 99, 101, 103–5, 108, 111, 112
Wolfe, Patrick 43
Wounded Knee Massacre (1890) 44

Yee, Mary 94
Yim, L. Lehua 30

Zavalla, Nakia 95, 97, 110–11
Zepeda, Ofelia 167
Zul, Esteban 122
Zuroski, Eugenia 46

For Product Safety Concerns and Information please contact our EU representative GPSR@taylorandfrancis.com
Taylor & Francis Verlag GmbH, Kaufingerstraße 24, 80331 München, Germany

www.ingramcontent.com/pod-product-compliance
Lightning Source LLC
Chambersburg PA
CBHW050532300426
44113CB00012B/2059